Holding Bishops Accountable

Holding Bishops Accountable

 HOW LAWSUITS HELPED
THE CATHOLIC CHURCH
CONFRONT CLERGY SEXUAL ABUSE

TIMOTHY D. LYTTON

HARVARD UNIVERSITY PRESS
Cambridge, Massachusetts, and London, England   2008

Library of Congress Cataloging-in-Publication Data

Lytton, Timothy D., 1965–
  Holding bishops accountable : how lawsuits helped the Catholic Church confront clergy
sexual abuse / Timothy D. Lytton.
     p. cm.
  Includes bibliographical references and index.
  ISBN-13: 978-0-674-02810-4 (alk. paper)
  1. Liability for child sexual abuse—United States.   2. Child sexual abuse by clergy—
United States.   3. Catholic Church—Trials, litigation, etc.   4. Trials (Child sexual abuse)—
United States.   I. Title.
  KF1328.5.C45 L98 2008
  345.73'0253—dc22
                 2007043597

To
Peter Schuck, Guido Calabresi,
Martha Minow, and Tony Kronman
for your steady encouragement
and wise counsel

And to Rachel Anisfeld

"A woman of valor is a rare find; her worth is far beyond that of rubies. Her husband trusts in her with all his heart, and lacks no good thing."

PROVERBS 31:10–11

Contents

Timeline of Events

First Wave

1984–1985	Gauthe case in Lafayette, Louisiana
June 1985	National Conference of Catholic Bishops meeting in Collegeville, Minnesota
1989	Mrozka case in Minneapolis and St. Paul

Second Wave

1991–1993	Porter case in Fall River, Massachusetts
1992	Five Principles adopted by the National Conference of Catholic Bishops
1993	Ad Hoc Committee on Sexual Abuse established by the National Conference of Catholic Bishops
1993–1994	Bernardin case in Chicago
1994–1996	Restoring Trust, vols. 1–3, published by Ad Hoc Committee on Sexual Abuse
1997–1998	Kos case in Dallas
1998	O'Grady case in Stockton, California

Third Wave

2002	Geoghan case file unsealed in Boston
June 2002	Dallas Charter adopted by U.S. Conference of Catholic Bishops
2003	California suspends statute of limitations for one year
2004	John Jay Report issued by the U.S. Conference of Catholic Bishops

Holding Bishops Accountable

Introduction

Father Gilbert Gauthe was a popular parish priest in the farming community of Henry, Louisiana.[1] In the five and a half years since his arrival, many parishioners had come to treat him as a family member. He dined regularly in their homes and was often invited along on vacations. He provided help in times of personal crisis. He monitored police messages on a CB radio in his car and sped to the scene of accidents to offer assistance. Father Gauthe organized activities for the boys of the community, who were naturally attracted to the hip, energetic priest who rode a dirt bike, drove a black Camaro Z28, and shot ducks from the roof of the rectory. He trained the boys to assist him at Mass, and he took them boating, camping, fishing, and hunting.

He also sexually abused them.

During his years as the parish priest in Henry, Father Gauthe fondled and sodomized dozens of prepubescent boys. He did it in the rectory, on trips, and in the church after Mass. His victims suffered both psychological and physical damage. One nine-year-old victim was hospitalized for rectal bleeding. When Father Gauthe visited him in the hospital, the boy's parents did not understand why the boy hid when he heard the priest's voice outside his room in the hallway.

Father Gauthe's predations eventually came to light in the summer of 1983. One evening at bedtime, nine-year-old Craig Sagrera tearfully told his parents that "God doesn't love me." When they questioned him, the boy described how he had been molested by Father Gauthe. The Sagreras discussed the matter with other parents, many of whom questioned their own sons and discovered that Gauthe had molested them too. With the help of a local attorney, Paul Hebert, several parents complained to the local bishop in Lafayette. The bishop removed Gauthe, sent him off for treatment, and offered to pay the boys' therapy bills. The diocese refused, however, to announce publicly the reason for Father Gauthe's departure or to notify the parents of other possible victims. Frustrated by this response, six families asked Hebert to file a civil lawsuit. Hebert enlisted the help of Raul Bencomo, a well-known plaintiffs' attorney from New Orleans. They filed suits against not only Gauthe but also against several diocesan officials, the bishop, and the archbishop of New Orleans. Shortly thereafter, the suits were settled. Both sides wished to keep the terms of settlement confidential out of concern for the victims' privacy and perhaps also to protect the Church from scandal. The presiding judge agreed to seal the case files.

A court clerk leaked information about the suits to a local television reporter, Dee Stanley, who reported that an unnamed local priest had molested children. No further details were available. When Hebert and Bencomo filed new lawsuits on behalf of four additional victims and their families in June 1984, both sides again requested that the case files be sealed. Reporting on these new suits, Stanley disclosed Gauthe's name but was unable to identify any of the victims. Frustrated with Hebert's and Bencomo's insistence on keeping the suits out of the press, one plaintiff family, the Gastals, retained a new attorney, J. Minos Simon, who agreed to help them confront the Church publicly. Simon immediately filed a motion to remove the seal of secrecy, which the judge granted.

Making the case file publicly accessible had a predictable and dramatic effect on press coverage. Print coverage of the Gauthe affair began in local newspapers shortly thereafter in November 1984. Six months later, stories appeared in regional papers such as the *Dallas Morning News* and the *Houston Post*. By the summer of 1985, the case was national news, with articles appearing in the *New York Times*, the *Washington Post*, and *Time* magazine.

Depositions and church files obtained through discovery revealed that Gauthe had a history of sexually molesting young boys dating back to 1971. These documents also showed that church officials knew of the problem and repeatedly reassigned him without disclosing this knowledge to unsuspecting parishioners. Plaintiffs' attorney Simon built his case around this theme of church officials' reassignment of Gauthe from parish to parish despite their awareness of the danger he posed to children. Journalists covering the affair relied heavily on litigation documents and interviews with Simon, and news coverage increasingly focused less on Gauthe than on the failure of church officials to adequately address the problem.

As the litigation unfolded, Simon and investigative journalist Jason Berry uncovered other priests known by church officials to have sexually molested children within the diocese, as well as other similar cases in dioceses around the country. In June 1985, the *National Catholic Reporter* published a story detailing abuse allegations against priests in California, Oregon, Wisconsin, New York, Pennsylvania, New Jersey, and Rhode Island.[2] Within a year of Simon's successful effort to remove the seal of secrecy from the Gastal file and to litigate the case more aggressively, the issue of clergy sexual abuse had become a national story about a nationwide scandal.

A mixture of moral outrage, fear of liability, and growing concern among Catholics led bishops around the country to begin discussing the need for a more adequate response to the problem. The National Conference of Catholic Bishops (NCCB) took up the issue of clergy sexual abuse at its June 1985 meeting in Collegeville, Minnesota. The bishops heard from psychological and legal experts about the causes and effects of child sexual abuse by clergy, and they considered recommendations for handling incidents in the future. These recommendations, developed over the next few years, included responding promptly to credible allegations, removing accused priests for evaluation and treatment, reporting allegations to law enforcement, reaching out to victims, and dealing openly with the issue in affected communities.

The Gastals won their lawsuit against the diocese. In order to stem the flow of damaging disclosures arising out of the discovery process, the Church stipulated liability. In a trial solely dedicated to the issue of damages, a jury awarded the Gastals $1.25 million. The Church appealed and the Gastals eventually settled for $1 million. Two dozen lawsuits by other Gauthe victims followed, for which the diocese and its insurers eventually paid out a total of $22 million. Gauthe himself was criminally prosecuted, pled guilty, and received a twenty-year prison sentence.

The Impact of Clergy Sexual Abuse Litigation on Policymaking

Since the Gauthe case, sexual abuse victims and their attorneys have filed thousands of lawsuits around the country. This book tells the story of how these lawsuits have played a central role in shaping policy responses to clergy sexual abuse. The book demonstrates that litigation was essential in bringing the scandal to light in the first place, focusing attention on the need for institutional reform, and spurring church leaders and public officials into action. It reveals how pleadings, discovery documents, and depositions provided most of the information underlying media coverage of the scandal. It shows how the litigation strategy of plaintiffs' lawyers gave rise to a widespread belief that the real problem was not the actions of individual priests but rather the Church's institutional failure. And it documents how policymakers responded to the problem of clergy sexual abuse under pressure created by private lawsuits.

The Gauthe case nicely illustrates these themes. Prior to Simon's public and aggressive litigation of the Gastals' claim in 1984, local media reporting of sexual abuse by clergy was scant and infrequent, with no national media coverage of the issue. Prosecutions were rare, public discussion and policy debate nonexistent. The ongoing litigation drama—pleadings that named high church officials as defendants, shocking revelations during the discovery process, and tearful trial testimony by an eleven-year-old sexual abuse victim—generated sustained local coverage in Lafayette and attracted regional and national media attention. The Gauthe case began the process of raising awareness about clergy sexual abuse.

Simon built his case primarily against church officials. He framed the problem not in terms of Gauthe's individual crimes but in terms of the Church's institutional failure. Throughout the clergy sexual abuse scandal, church officials and commentators have offered alternative frames for the scandal. They have suggested that clergy sexual abuse is better understood as a relatively small problem blown out of proportion by an anti-Catholic press, or the inevitable result of greater tolerance of homosexuality within the Church, or the product of an oversexed popular culture. Some have argued that parents are partly to blame for entrusting their children to the unsupervised care of priests. Notwithstanding these alternatives, the view that has most shaped public perceptions and policy responses remains the one promoted by plaintiffs' lawyers: that church officials should be held accountable for failing to do what was in their power to stop the abuse.

The Gauthe case was instrumental in placing the issue of clergy sexual abuse on the agendas of church policymakers and government officials. The bishops' discussion of clergy sexual abuse at the 1985 NCCB meeting in Collegeville was a direct result of concern over further liability and scandal following the Gauthe case. The policy alternatives that they discussed were shaped by the Gauthe litigation's focus on institutional failure. The post-Collegeville recommendations—prompt response to allegations, removal of accused priests, increased reporting to law enforcement, victim outreach, and greater openness—are all institutional reforms. The Gauthe case also put pressure on the local district attorney to prosecute Gauthe, and it provided information essential to his conviction. Later cases have placed the problem of clergy sexual abuse on state legislative agendas and, like the Gauthe case, have shaped policy discussions and created pressure to enact reforms.

Tort Litigation as a Policy Venue

This book examines tort litigation from a new perspective. Tort litigation has traditionally been viewed as a means of dispute resolution and risk regulation. As a means of dispute resolution, tort litigation provides a neutral forum in which to resolve claims for redress by injury victims. It resolves these claims on the basis of liability rules that specify when individuals may be held responsible for injuries that they cause to others. As a means of risk regulation, tort litigation encourages potential injurers and potential injury victims to reduce risk and to insure against it. For potential injurers, the prospect of liability creates incentives to exercise care and to purchase insurance to cover the cost of liability in the event of an accident. For potential victims, the limitations on recovery in tort provide incentives to exercise care to protect oneself from injury and to purchase insurance to cover the cost of injury in the event of an accident.[3]

My analysis of clergy sexual abuse litigation differs from these traditional views in three ways. First, whereas traditional views focus on how tort litigation resolves disputes and regulates risk, my analysis of clergy sexual abuse litigation looks at how tort litigation uncovers hidden information, frames problems, and influences policy agendas. Second, traditional views focus on litigation *outcomes*. Dispute resolution occurs only at the end of litigation, with a settlement or a final judgment, and risk regulation is an aftereffect of litigation, resulting from liability rules promulgated in judicial opinions. By contrast, my analysis highlights the policy impact of the litigation *process*. I explore ways in which pleading, discovery, and trial influence policymaking. Third, the traditional risk regulation view sees tort litigation as an alternative to other forms of regulation. Tort litigation, on this account, *competes* with self-regulation, legislative regulation, or agency regulation. According to the traditional view, regulation by tort law only makes sense where these other forms of regulation do not exist or where they fail to operate effectively; otherwise, they either render regulation by tort litigation redundant or preempt it altogether. In my analysis, however, tort litigation *complements* these other forms of regulation. Producing relevant information, framing issues, and attracting attention to them are all ways in which tort litigation makes these other forms of regulation more effective.

This book presents tort litigation as one of several institutional venues in which policy responses to clergy sexual abuse were forged. My analysis builds on recent case studies of tobacco and gun litigation in which scholars have shown how the tort litigation process shaped policy responses to tobacco-related illness and gun violence.[4] Compared to tobacco and gun litigation, however, clergy sexual abuse litigation offers a more attractive example of tort litigation's impact on policymaking. Whereas tobacco and gun litigation have produced, at best, only modest advances in tobacco control and violence reduction, clergy sexual abuse litigation made it possible for child sexual abuse victims to hold publicly accountable one of the largest, richest, and most powerful institutions in America, and it forced reluctant church and government officials to adopt sensible policies to address a widespread problem.

The successes of clergy sexual abuse litigation, however, have not been without cost. Fear of litigation has led some church officials to conceal information that they might otherwise have disclosed. Heightened suspicion of priests has impaired their ability to perform many pastoral duties, and mistrust of the hierarchy has damaged the credibility of the Church. Judgments, settlements, and litigation costs have forced some dioceses to scale back their educational, healthcare, and antipoverty programs, and, in some cases, to file for bankruptcy. Any fair assessment of clergy sexual abuse litigation's success must take stock of these costs. While I argue that clergy sexual abuse litigation has played a beneficial role in the creation of effective policy responses to clergy sexual abuse, I do not wish to downplay its significant financial and human costs. This requires a hard look at the very real damage wrought by the litigation. In my view, which I shall develop throughout the book, clergy sexual abuse litigation has been, on balance, good for victims, the Church, and the larger society.

Any defense of tort litigation as a policy venue must confront three powerful objections. First, litigation skeptics question the *effectiveness* of lawsuits in promoting policy change. Gerald Rosenberg argues forcefully in his careful study of constitutional litigation, *The Hollow Hope,* that "U.S. courts can *almost never* be effective producers of significant social reform," and that litigation is a drain on the scarce resources of reform advocates who could achieve more through the political process.[5] Second, tort-reform advocates question the *efficiency* of tort litigation as a means of compensation, risk regulation, and policy change. Peter Huber and Walter Olson contend that whatever benefits tort litigation might have are insignificant when compared to the costs of frivolous claims and inflated jury awards, which have caused widespread fear of liability, the withdrawal of essential products and services, and the stifling of safety innovation.[6] Third, tort-reform advocates also challenge the *legitimacy* of using tort litigation as a means of promoting policy change. They argue that the job of courts is to resolve disputes and to enforce legislative mandates, not to make public policy. Using courts to make public policy will, in the end, they assert, politicize the judiciary, undermine the integrity of the litigation process, and erode public confidence in the courts.[7]

Clergy sexual abuse litigation offers a powerful counterexample to these claims of litigation skeptics and tort-reform advocates. The litigation has been an effective means of achieving significant policy reform. It has played an essential role in uncovering the problem of clergy sexual abuse, framing it in terms of institutional failure and the need for institutional reform, attracting attention to it, and creating pressure for reform. Moreover, the litigation's benefits in terms of promoting policy responses to clergy sexual abuse outweigh its costs. And finally, clergy sexual abuse litigation shows that courts have a legitimate role to play in policymaking. The litigation enhanced the efforts of church officials, law enforcement, and state governments to develop and enforce policies aimed at reducing clergy sexual abuse, and its success is likely to strengthen public respect for and confidence in the civil justice system.

This case study of clergy sexual abuse litigation does not establish that the influence of tort litigation on policymaking is always beneficial. There is ongoing debate about the value of litigation for regulation—for example, in the regulation of consumer products and pharmaceuticals. One should be careful about making general claims about the policymaking benefits of tort litigation solely on the basis of clergy sexual abuse litigation. Determining the effectiveness, efficiency, and legiti-

macy of tort litigation as a policy venue in other cases requires individ-
ualized analysis. At the very least, however, the lessons of clergy sexual
abuse litigation give us reason to revisit the case for tort reform and to
reconsider skepticism regarding the usefulness of litigation in addressing social problems.

It bears emphasis at the outset that my primary claims in this book
focus on tort litigation's impact on policymaking. I argue that clergy
sexual abuse litigation enhanced the efforts of policymaking institutions
such as the U.S. Conference of Catholic Bishops (USCCB), law enforcement agencies, and state legislatures. I do not attempt to argue that litigation reduced the rate of clergy sexual abuse. While there is evidence
that it has—and I shall refer to that evidence in chapter 2—this claim is
significantly harder to substantiate. My aim is to show that tort litigation has improved efforts to address clergy sexual abuse by generating
information, focusing on the institutional dimensions of the problem,
and making it a priority among policymakers. I will have little to say
about whether the resulting policies were ultimately successful in reducing abuse. But even if we assume, for the sake of argument, that they
were not, I would still maintain that it is better to have addressed the
problem and failed than to have remained ignorant about it, disre-
garded its institutional dimensions, or given it less priority. Even failed
policies provide useful experience that can inform subsequent attempts
to solve a problem.

Plan of the Book

The book begins in Part I with an overview of clergy sexual abuse litigation. Chapter 1 presents a short history of clergy sexual abuse litigation from 1984 to 2007. It introduces landmark cases involving Gilbert
Gauthe, James Porter, Cardinal Joseph Bernardin, Rudolph Kos, Oliver
O'Grady, and John Geoghan, as well as consolidated claims against the
archdioceses of Boston and Los Angeles. The chapter examines reactions to these cases among church officials, victims, and lawyers on
both sides, and it highlights a growing difference in perspective that has
fueled the litigation for more than twenty years. Chapter 2 offers a statistical portrait of clergy sexual abuse litigation. It reviews existing data
on the nature and scope of clergy sexual abuse in the Catholic Church
from 1950 to 2006, and it presents new data on the rate of legal claims
between 1984 and 2006. Chapter 3 surveys the legal issues at the heart of

clergy sexual abuse litigation. It examines theories of liability, defenses, settlement practices, insurance coverage, and bankruptcy.

The chapters in Part II analyze distinct mechanisms by which clergy sexual abuse litigation influenced policymaking. Chapter 4 examines how litigation framed the problem of clergy sexual abuse as one of institutional failure and how this frame dominated media coverage of the issue. Chapter 5 explores how lawsuits raised concern about clergy sexual abuse among the general public and the Catholic laity, and placed clergy sexual abuse on the policy agendas of church officials, law enforcement, and state legislatures. Chapter 6 looks at how litigation generated new information about clergy sexual abuse by compelling disclosure of church records and encouraging further investigation of the problem by church and government officials.

Part III defends the value of the litigation. Chapter 7 presents an assessment of the costs and benefits of clergy sexual abuse litigation. It considers a variety of quantitative and qualitative data and finds that the benefits of the litigation outweigh its costs. Chapter 8 concludes the book by arguing that clergy sexual abuse litigation offers a compelling example of how, under certain conditions, tort litigation can play a vital role in the policymaking process. It also addresses the objections of litigation skeptics and tort-reform advocates who assert that lawsuits are an ineffective, inefficient, and illegitimate way to promote social change.

Why Focus on the Catholic Church?

This book deals exclusively with lawsuits against the Catholic Church. Consequently, it may raise concerns about anti-Catholic bias. For this reason, it bears emphasis at the outset that clergy sexual abuse within the Catholic Church is part of a larger phenomenon of child sexual abuse that occurs in other religious denominations and in secular institutions throughout society. Moreover, there has been a great deal of clergy sexual abuse litigation against other religious denominations. I do not wish to suggest that child sexual abuse is more prevalent in the Catholic Church than in other institutions, that Catholic doctrine or practice makes Catholic clergy more prone to child sexual abuse, or that the Catholic Church deserves to be sued more than other institutions. On a personal level, while I am not a Catholic, I have worked for several Catholic organizations in the United States and abroad, and I have high regard for the Church's many contributions to social welfare and political debate throughout the world. I also believe that strong religious institutions are vital to a liberal society. So let me explain why this book focuses on the Catholic Church.

I am interested in clergy sexual abuse lawsuits for what they reveal about the impact of tort litigation on policymaking in private and governmental institutions. Press coverage, published reports by the USCCB, and investigations by state attorneys general and grand juries have made publicly available extensive information about the nature and scope of child sexual abuse by priests, institutional responses to it by diocesan officials, efforts at policy reform, and the costs of litigation. There is simply no comparable information base on which to build a study like this of any other religious denomination or social institution. Moreover, the leadership of the Catholic Church claims that policy reforms instituted since 1985 have made the Church a leader in addressing child sexual abuse. If it is true that the Church is now at the forefront of efforts to reduce child sexual abuse, and if it is true—as I argue throughout this book—that tort litigation was essential to those efforts, then lawsuits against the Catholic Church provide an especially powerful example of how tort litigation can enhance policymaking.

There is a great deal of finger pointing and scapegoating in discussions of clergy sexual abuse. Depending upon whom one talks to, blame is directed at bishops, priests, victim advocates, church reformers, church traditionalists, plaintiffs' attorneys, diocesan counsel, insurance lawyers, therapists, journalists, parents, and gay-rights groups. Rather than focusing on blame, this book attempts to understand the dynamics of conflict that have fueled litigation over clergy sexual abuse, and how this litigation contributed to a better understanding of the problem and to new policies designed to address it.

PART ONE

An Overview of Clergy
Sexual Abuse Litigation

Clergy sexual abuse litigation is an enormously complex phenomenon. It includes thousands of lawsuits across the country, spanning more than twenty years from the mid-1980s to the present. Most of the legal claims in these lawsuits are based on incidents dating back to the 1960s, '70s, and '80s, with some dating as far back as the 1950s. The litigation has raised a host of thorny legal issues such as the legal duties of religious organizations to supervise clergy, the role of statutes of limitation in child sexual abuse cases, and the scope of protection against civil litigation provided by the free exercise clause of the First Amendment.

This part of the book examines the broad outlines of clergy sexual abuse litigation from three perspectives. Chapter 1 sketches the history of the litigation, from the Gauthe case in 1984 to the present. Chapter 2 presents a statistical portrait of the litigation, examining available data on clergy sexual abuse within the Catholic Church and litigation against the Church. Chapter 3 analyzes legal issues, including claims and defenses, litigation strategies, settlement practices, insurance coverage, and bankruptcy.

CHAPTER ONE

A Short History

The idea that there was going to be widespread
litigation involving clergy sexual abuse was not on
anyone's radar in 1984.

— MARK CHOPKO, FORMER GENERAL COUNSEL, U.S.
CONFERENCE OF CATHOLIC BISHOPS

Litigation against the Catholic Church for clergy sexual abuse predates the Gauthe case. One can find reports of criminal prosecutions of priests dating back to the nineteenth century, and in the decades before the Gauthe case, dioceses around the country quietly settled civil claims.[1] At the time the Gastals filed their lawsuit against Gauthe and the Diocese of Lafayette, dioceses in California, Oregon, Idaho, Wisconsin, Minnesota, New York, Pennsylvania, New Jersey, and Rhode Island were facing criminal and civil litigation for clergy sexual abuse.[2] Prior to the Gauthe case, however, incidents of clergy sexual abuse were viewed as rare and isolated occurrences, and they attracted limited local press coverage or, more often, no press coverage at all.

The Gastals' lawsuit against Gauthe and the Diocese of Lafayette was the first case of clergy sexual abuse to attract national attention. In conjunction with concurrent cases around the country, it created the impression of a pervasive, nationwide problem. The case inspired other victims to come forward and, in increasing numbers, to file lawsuits. It also sparked a sustained effort among bishops to address clergy sexual abuse within the Church. For these reasons, the Gauthe case provides a good place to begin a short history of the litigation.

I have divided this history into three periods, or waves, of litigation, each inaugurated by a significant case. The first wave of litigation, from 1984–1991, begins with the Gauthe case. The second wave, from 1992–2001, starts with the case of Father James Porter in Fall River, Massachusetts. The third wave, from 2002 to the present, was sparked by the case of Father John Geoghan in Boston. I highlight these and several other landmark cases for two reasons. First, these cases themselves wrought significant changes on the course of clergy sexual abuse litigation, and they influenced policymaking. In this chapter I introduce the cases, and in later chapters I offer evidence of their influence on policymaking. Second, these cases provide salient points of reference to structure what would otherwise be a large, unwieldy mass of information. In addition to surveying landmark cases, I discuss important legal and policy trends that characterize each of the three waves of litigation.

The First Wave: 1984–1991

By all accounts, the Gauthe case was a wake-up call for the Church. News coverage in the *New York Times,* the *Washington Post, Time* magazine, and the *National Catholic Reporter* raised public awareness of clergy sexual abuse. News coverage also prompted concern among Catholics. As Mark Chopko, former general counsel for the U.S. Conference of Catholic Bishops (USCCB), explains, the key to understanding the Gauthe case's impact was "the energy that it gave to the people in the pews . . . [I]t's not a problem for bishops if the *New York Times* gets excited about it. It's a real problem for bishops to know that their people are outraged by it, and both of these things were happening at the same time."[3]

This is not to say, however, that the bishops were unaware of clergy sexual abuse prior to the Gauthe litigation. To the contrary, personnel files in dioceses around the country document complaints dating back to the 1930s. Nor was awareness of clergy sexual abuse prior to the Gauthe case restricted to individual bishops in their dioceses. As early as the 1970s, the National Conference of Catholic Bishops (NCCB), precursor to the USCCB, supported the development of programs within the Church designed specifically to treat priests who sexually abused minors. According to psychotherapist and former priest Richard Sipe,

> In 1976 the Servants of the Paraclete [a Catholic religious order] opened what was perhaps the first program in the world with a treatment regime designed to treat psychosexual disorders including disorders involving the sexual abuse of minors. The ability of the Catholic community to design and implement such a program is both a reflection of the need for such a program and the degree of knowledge of the scope of the problem of sexual misconduct with children by Catholic priests and religious. The fact that preparations for the opening of this program were years in the making demonstrates widespread knowledge of existing sexual misconduct with minors by Catholic clergy by the late 1960s and early 1970s.

It should be noted that the Paraclete program treats only Catholic priests and religious on recommendation from their bishops or religious superiors. The bishop or religious superior is responsible for all treatment costs and is provided with periodic progress reports on the Catholic priest or brother patient . . . The Bishops Conference contributed money in the 1970s to the Paracletes to support the development of their program. Since the goals and purposes of the treatment program were well known within the Catholic hierarchy, the goals and purposes would have been known to the Bishops Conference as well. The Bishops Conference also issued directives regarding the retention or destruction of the treatment reports provided to the Bishops—and the Paracletes and their staff followed these directives.

I conclude that the bishops of the United States, individually and collectively, were by the 1970s, well aware of certain psychological problems of priests, including sexual involvement with minors.[4]

Thus the Gauthe case did not mark the bishops' first awareness of clergy sexual abuse. They had known about it for decades. Rather the litigation—by publicly exposing the bishops' role in facilitating abuse—roused them to reassess their understanding of the problem and to confront the inadequacy of their responses to it.

The impact of the Gauthe case was greatly magnified by concurrent events. Similar cases in other states made it possible for the editors of the *National Catholic Reporter* to characterize the Gauthe case as part of a "broader scandal," a "national . . . crisis facing the bishops."[5] In addition, the mid-1980s were a time of widespread public concern over child sexual abuse. Criminal prosecutions and civil trials against daycare centers and youth programs such as the Boy Scouts and the Fresh Air Fund generated intense press coverage. In response, states ratcheted up their reporting requirements and relaxed their statutes of limitation for child sexual abuse. Childcare and youth programs fingerprinted volunteers, conducted background checks, and required references. The drama of the Gauthe case, the simultaneous outbreak of similar cases in other dioceses, and widespread public concern over child sexual abuse converged to create what Chopko calls "the perfect storm."[6]

This perfect storm was also a wake-up call for abuse victims, who began to come forward in increasing numbers. The volume of complaints brought to local chanceries rose sharply. Based on data from a study commissioned by the USCCB, chanceries received 328 abuse reports in the five years prior to the commencement of the Gauthe litigation (1980–1984). That number rose to 817 in the five years following (1985–1989).[7] Victims and their families also contacted lawyers. Jeff Anderson, a plaintiffs' attorney, recalls that following news coverage of a lawsuit that he filed in 1984 against the Archdiocese of St. Paul and Minneapolis based on the sexual misconduct of Father Thomas Adamson, "other survivors began to stream, literally, into my office . . . [They were] outraged by the [Church's] denial and [had] now come to realize that they weren't alone . . . And that led me to just start to file suits pretty vigorously on behalf of them."[8] Steve Rubino, another plaintiffs' attorney, reports that in the years following the Gauthe case, "hundreds of cases around the country were being quietly settled."[9]

One notable lawsuit during this early period was *Mrozka v. Archdiocese of St. Paul and Minneapolis and Diocese of Winona,* a 1989 case litigated by Jeff Anderson on behalf of an Adamson victim. The jury found the church defendants liable for willful indifference and awarded the plaintiff $855,000 in compensatory damages and $2.7 million in punitive damages—the first punitive damages award against the Church in a clergy sexual abuse case. (The punitive damage award was reduced by the trial judge to $187,000.)

The years following the Gauthe case, from 1985–1991, were a time of learning for both sides in the litigation. Bishops were developing a better understanding of the problem of clergy sexual abuse, its legal implications, and how to address it more effectively. At the same time, victims and their attorneys were uncovering the role of church officials in facilitating child sexual abuse by clergy.

In response to the Gauthe case and the growing revelation of a nationwide problem, the bishops sought a better understanding of clergy sexual abuse, and they began to formulate new policies to deal with it. The NCCB staff began to research the problem of clergy sexual abuse and to offer advice to bishops facing allegations within their dioceses. Concurrently, Gauthe attorney Ray Mouton, canon lawyer Father Thomas Doyle, and psychiatrist Father Michael Peterson, the director of a treatment program for priest sex abusers, wrote a report entitled *The Problem of Sexual Molestation by Roman Catholic Clergy: Meeting the Problem in a Comprehensive and Responsible Manner,* which they distributed to bishops. At a June 1985 NCCB meeting in Collegeville, Minnesota, the bishops dedicated an entire day of executive session to examining the psychological, legal, and moral aspects of clergy sexual abuse within the Church. They also considered nonbinding recommendations for how individual dioceses could best respond to the problem, and they charged the Committee on Priestly Life & Ministry to undertake further consideration of the matter. Following the Collegeville meeting, the NCCB staff helped dioceses develop training programs to prevent child abuse, policies for reporting it, and protocols for assisting victims and their families. The NCCB staff also provided ongoing support to diocesan attorneys. The advice offered by the NCCB staff during these years was the basis for policies later adopted by the bishops.[10]

While the Gauthe case was the primary catalyst fueling the bishops' reconsideration of their approach to clergy sexual abuse, it was not the only one. As early as 1982, two years before the Gauthe case, the NCCB staff began offering legal advice to diocesan officials dealing with allegations of clergy sexual abuse. In response to allegations against other priests and changes in state laws regarding mandatory reporting of child sexual abuse, individual dioceses and state Catholic conferences in Florida and New Jersey began formulating new personnel policies in the spring of 1985, before the Collegeville meeting.

Prior to the Gauthe case, bishops had ignored complaints, denied allegations, blamed victims, reassigned offenders, failed to report crimes to police, and concealed information. In the aftermath of the Gauthe case, the bishops resolved to change all of this. Bishop Howard Hubbard of Albany, New York, describes this period as follows:

> I think the bishops really felt that we were dealing with the issue constructively and that we were taking the appropriate steps to make sure that the behavior didn't continue—that it was addressed aggressively . . . A major factor . . . was a deeper appreciation of the harm experienced by victims in terms of the trauma that this abuse created for them. I think prior to that, we were aware that it was morally wrong. We were aware that it was inappropriate. But I don't think we had any insight into the depth of the effect of this abuse on individuals and their families. And that, I think, is the greatest learning that took place between '85 and '92.
>
> [In addition,] I think that the Gauthe case made bishops and church leaders aware of the liability to which they were exposed once sexual abuse occurred, especially if they didn't address it immediately, and of the potential consequences if there was a reoffense following such behavior. In other words, you were effectively on notice if you had someone who was a danger to the community, and if you didn't take serious steps to protect the community, you were opening yourself to major liability. And that, I think, put that whole dimension of the issue before the bishops and the Church in a way it hadn't been present before.[11]

Thus the bishops understood this period as a time of reform, focused on developing greater empathy for victims and more effective strategies for dealing with offenders. Failure to do so, they began to realize, could subject them not only to public scandal but also to significant financial loss.

The years from 1984 to 1991 were also a period of learning for victims and their attorneys, learning that fueled litigation against the Church. Press coverage of the Gauthe litigation led victims to reevaluate their own experiences. Victims who had blamed themselves now blamed their abusers and unresponsive church officials. Victims who had thought that their abuse was a one-time, isolated event now suspected that they were not alone. Victims who had feared that no one would believe them now had reason to hope that their accusations might be taken seriously. Victims who had assumed that it would be impossible to confront the Church and win now contacted lawyers, who filed lawsuits on their behalf.

As the number of lawsuits filed increased, so, in turn, did the number of victims willing to come forward. "What was occurring during this time," recalls plaintiffs' attorney Sylvia Demarest,

> is that people were beginning to . . . believe that something like this was possible . . . [B]ecause of the power of the Church—the power of the theology and the power of the priests—the victims were silent. You may have been abused, but you may have believed that you were the only one or that you did something that caused you to be abused by father, because obviously father was, you know, someone who wouldn't do this, et cetera, et cetera.
>
> So you see a pattern that occurs, and word reaches different places that this is occurring and that it occurred in this way. Then victims hear it and they go, "well, you know, I'm not alone." This pattern was repeated even in individual dioceses against individual priests. You would see a victim come forward and it would be reported in the media and then people in the parish would go, "well this is the only mistake father ever made," and then two days later ten more people would come forward.
>
> It was the acquisition of the ability to believe that it wasn't your fault, that maybe there was something wrong with father, that the bishop wasn't perfect, that when the bishop told you that this was the first time father ever did that, he was lying through his friggin' teeth. It was the acquisition of this knowledge and the increase in the level of anger among ordinary Catholics that, I think, fueled this pebble [i.e., the Gauthe case] growing into a landslide as it went down the mountain.
>
> And that was what was going on [during] that period of time. It may not have looked like anything was going on on the surface, but around the country more and more cases were being filed. More and more people were acquiring the knowledge. More and more victims were coming forward. More and more lies were being exposed.[12]

Thus while the bishops were beginning to appreciate the depth of the victims' pain, the victims were growing increasingly aware of the bishops' role in facilitating abuse.

For the lawyers too, this was a time of learning. It was plaintiffs' lawyers, for the most part, who exposed the bishops' role in clergy sexual abuse. At first, discovery yielded little proof of any knowledge on the part of bishops that abuse was occurring. Bishops denied knowingly reassigning priests with a history of abuse, and diocesan personnel files offered little or no evidence. Jeff Anderson recounts how, with the help of Father Thomas Doyle, he learned that bishops kept damaging information concerning a priest not in the priest's personnel file but in a "secret archive" mandated by canon law, to which only the bishop is to have a key.[13] "I began to realize," recalls Anderson, "that these [secret] files contained excruciatingly clear evidence of [the bishops'] knowledge and complicity and their protection of multiple offenders . . . I then began to subpoena the files in every case."[14]

Steve Rubino recounts how he learned of *The Official Catholic Directory,* an annual publication that includes information about the clerical assignments of U.S. priests. This allowed him to trace the assignment history of any particular priest, which might include periods of sick leave, assignment to treatment facilities, or unaccounted-for periods without any assignment. The subsequent assignment of the priest to a new parish offered clues to the practice of reassigning known offenders.[15]

The combination of documents from secret archives and information from the directory provided a "road map for depositions," explains Rubino. "We learned exactly what to ask." Anderson and Rubino collaborated with church insiders Doyle and Sipe, meeting to talk informally about cases, discuss strategy, and share information.[16] Thus in the aftermath of the Gauthe case, plaintiffs' lawyers waged a long-term campaign of building a little more discovery information in each case they litigated—what Anderson describes as "a base of knowledge that is cumulatively obtained."[17]

The Second Wave: 1992–2001

In the fall of 1989, thirty-nine-year-old Frank Fitzpatrick began to have flashbacks of sexual abuse that he had suffered at the hands of Father James Porter almost thirty years earlier as a twelve-year-old boy in North Attleboro, Massachusetts.[18] Under pretext of taking Fitzpatrick to a game at the Boston Garden, Porter had instead driven him to a secluded house, where he fed the boy mince pie laced with sedatives and forcibly sodomized him. When the thirty-nine-year-old Fitzpatrick wrote a letter to the local bishop in Fall River requesting information about Porter's whereabouts and explaining why he wanted it, he received a personal call from Chancellor Monsignor John Oliveira, who said he knew only that Porter had gone elsewhere and had left the priesthood. When Fitzpatrick pressed for information—such as Porter's current address, social security number, or even a middle initial—Oliveira told him that the diocesan records "didn't have any of that." "Maybe it's a sign," added Oliveira. "Maybe it would be best to leave it in the hands of the Lord."

Undeterred, Fitzpatrick, a private detective, located Porter in Oakdale, Minnesota. Porter was by then married with children. Fitzpatrick contacted the Oakdale police and told them about Porter, but they replied that there was little they could do about an incident thirty years ago in another state. A call to the local district attorney in Massachusetts received a similar response. As a result of the call to the Oakdale police, however, the FBI interviewed Porter in connection with the recent disappearance of an eleven-year-old boy. While Porter denied any knowledge of the boy, he did admit to molesting thirty to forty children while he was a Catholic priest. The FBI did nothing.

Seeking to verify his own recently recovered memories, Fitzpatrick called Porter several times, and he recorded the telephone conversations. "How many boys were there altogether?" asked Fitzpatrick in one call. "I don't know . . . it could have been quite a few," answered Porter. "Do you remember me in particular?" asked Fitzpatrick. "No," Porter replied, "I don't even recognize the name." Later in the conversation, Porter mused, "It's funny how everything's worked out . . . it's been marvelous, I mean, especially me, mentally . . . I got to look back at how fortunate I was that I didn't get creamed." "See, the thing that bothered me," responded Fitzpatrick, "was that it was covered up in North Attleboro." "Oh, they did that in a lot of places," explained Porter. "I guess their attitude then was to try to stop a lot of people from getting . . . figuring they could cover it up, and . . . hope to help the ones that had been . . . you know what I mean?"[19]

In December 1990, Fitzpatrick made an official criminal complaint to the North Attleboro police and the Bristol County district attorney. He gave them copies of the tapes of his telephone conversations with Porter. The district attorney again declined to prosecute, explaining that the charges were too dated.

Hoping to find other Porter victims, Fitzpatrick called fellow classmates from St. Mary's Grammar School, where Porter had served as priest. He also placed ads in local newspapers. He spoke publicly of his abuse in Providence, Rhode Island, to an audience of 200 people, and his denunciation of Porter appeared on the nightly news of three Providence TV stations. Victims from St. Mary's, as well as the other parishes to which Porter had been assigned, began to contact Fitzpatrick.

In the summer of 1991, Fitzpatrick and several other victims—now calling themselves "survivors" of Father Porter—contacted plaintiffs' attorney Eric MacLeish. While a civil suit would normally have been prevented by the statute of limitations—ten years from the victim's reaching the age of majority—the statute tolled if the defendant left the state. But MacLeish had another problem: Massachusetts law capped the liability of charitable institutions at $20,000. MacLeish suggested that instead of filing a lawsuit, they should pursue a media strategy. If they could get nine to fifteen survivors willing to go public and appear in the newspapers and on television, he predicted, the Church, eager to avoid scandal, would settle their claims for more than the $20,000 each that they could get by litigating. Fitzpatrick and his small band of survivors set about convincing others to go public.

In the spring of 1992, a local Boston television station broadcast an interview with Fitzpatrick and seven other Porter survivors who told their stories of abuse. The reporter interviewing them, Joe Bergantino, had also interviewed Porter by telephone and taped the conversation, which was also broadcast. "How many children did you molest?" asked Bergantino. "Oh, jeez, I don't know," responded Porter, "well, let's put it anywhere, you know, from fifty to a hundred, I guess." Within three months of the broadcast, sixty-eight additional survivors in Massachusetts came forward, contacting Fitzpatrick and Bergantino and making reports to police and the district attorney's office. Survivors of other priests also began contacting Fitzpatrick.

In July 1992, *Prime Time Live with Diane Sawyer* aired a thirty-minute story on ABC about the Porter case, featuring twenty-five survivors. Following the broadcast, more survivors came forward, including individuals molested by Porter in Minnesota and in New Mexico, where he had been sent for treatment in the late 1960s. That summer, articles appeared in national print media such as the *New York Times, USA Today, Newsweek,* and *People* magazine. Fitzpatrick was also interviewed on National Public Radio and CNN.

By September, Porter was finally indicted in Massachusetts on forty-six counts of sodomy and indecent assault involving thirty victims whose cases had not exceeded the statute of limitations. On the same day, he was also indicted in Minnesota for molesting the babysitter of his children.

MacLeish's strategy was working perfectly, and by October he settled claims by sixty-eight Porter survivors against the Diocese of Fall River for an undisclosed sum, reported in the *Boston Globe* as "at least $5 million."[20] This was, to date, the largest group settlement of sexual abuse claims against the Church. MacLeish negotiated the settlement with newly appointed Bishop Sean O'Malley, who, a decade later, would replace Cardinal Bernard Law in Boston at the height of the next wave of clergy sex abuse litigation. MacLeish subsequently secured similar settlements with the diocese on behalf of a group of thirty-one Porter survivors, and then, once again, on behalf of two more. While Porter's criminal conviction in Minnesota was overturned on appeal, he was finally convicted and sentenced in December 1993 in Massachusetts and is currently serving an eighteen- to twenty-year prison sentence.

The details of Porter's crimes are chilling. In his first assignment, as a priest in North Attleboro at St. Mary's Church and Elementary School from 1960 to 1963, Porter allegedly molested over 100 known victims, ages six to fourteen. He groped children in the hallways and on the playground. He called them into his office and fondled them, and he took them into his private living quarters where he engaged in oral sex and sodomized them. He even molested children in their own beds when, as a dinner guest, he went up to tuck them in while their parents sat downstairs in the kitchen. He took them to his parents' beach house in Rhode Island, as he did with Frank Fitzpatrick, where he wrestled and had sex with them.

No less chilling is the evidence of church officials' complicity. Nuns teaching in the school knew of but failed to complain about Porter's predations. When parents and relatives of several victims complained to St. Mary's pastor Ed Booth and Father Armando Annunziato that Porter had sexually assaulted their children, Booth informed them that Porter was receiving treatment, and he scolded them, "What are you trying to do, crucify him?!" On one occasion, Annunziato walked in on Porter raping a young boy in the rectory, made eye contact with the boy, turned around, and left. On another occasion, Annunziato knocked at the office door while Porter was locked in the office with another young boy. When Porter refused to let him in, Annunziato told him, "It's getting late, time for everyone to go home." Bishop James Connolly sent

Porter to Boston for psychiatric treatment, including electroshock therapy. He then transferred Porter to another parish.

In his next assignment, from 1963–1965, in Sacred Heart Church in Fall River, twenty-five miles away, Porter molested more children. Following more complaints, Bishop Connolly reassigned Porter to St. James Church in New Bedford, fifteen miles from Fall River, where he worked from 1965–1967. A diocesan official warned the other priests at St. James to watch Porter because "he has a problem with little boys." Porter molested children at St. James too.

Finally, in 1967, Connolly sent Porter to a New Mexico treatment facility run by the Servants of the Paraclete. While in treatment, Porter was allowed to say Mass at churches in New Mexico and Texas, where, according to the Paraclete's records, he practiced "his old failings." In 1969, the Paracletes transferred Porter to their center in Minnesota. They recommended him for a parish assignment to a bishop in Minnesota, informing him that Father Porter had suffered a breakdown: "During the throes of his illness, he did have some moral problems which were, from all appearances, the result of his illness, something for which he was not really responsible . . . Now, having recovered, he gives every sign of having the former problems under control."[21] Porter was assigned to St. Phillip's parish in Bemidji, Minnesota, where he molested more children. In 1974, Porter applied for and was granted permission to leave the priesthood.

At no point throughout the Porter saga did church officials ever warn parishioners at any of Porter's assignments, nor did they ever report anything to the police. Diocesan personnel records in Fall River indicate that church officials there were aware in the 1960s of over thirty complaints of child sexual abuse lodged against Porter. By all accounts, Porter's victims number well over 100—some put the total closer to 200—molested during his fourteen years in ministry in Massachusetts, Minnesota, New Mexico, and Texas.

Within the history of clergy sexual abuse litigation, the Porter case is a significant moment. The shocking number of Porter's victims—that one individual could do so much damage—made a deep impression. "The Porter case," explains Albany bishop Hubbard, "probably more than the Gauthe case, captured the fact that there could be serial victims . . . The major lesson learned was that if there was one victim . . . there was the potential for multiple victims, which was, I think, an awareness that maybe had not sunk in up until that point in time."[22]

The geographical range of Porter's offenses—from Massachusetts to Texas to Minnesota—left little doubt in anyone's mind that clergy sexual abuse was a national problem. The large number of victims and broad geographic sweep of the Porter case attracted national television coverage, which greatly magnified the impact of the case.

The age of Porter's victims—now middle-aged adults—also gave the case special significance. "Personally," recalls former USCCB general counsel Chopko, "it was significant because all the Porter victims are my age. And so when this was happening, you're watching people on ABC . . . talk about what happened to them when they were in grade school. And I started getting calls from my contemporaries saying 'What's the matter? What's going on? You know, why doesn't the Church understand?'" Chopko points out that, as was the case with the Gauthe affair, the impact of the Porter case was further magnified by concurrent events: "There was the situation in Canada with the collapse of the Christian Brothers Boarding School [an orphanage in Newfoundland run by a Catholic order where widespread sexual abuse of boys was uncovered]. We began to be aware of abuse claims in other countries, besides Canada, you know, Ireland and continental Europe, and places like that. So Porter was a piece of that puzzle, and it was a fairly big piece of that puzzle."[23]

The Porter case exposed the inadequacy of the Church's response to clergy sexual abuse to an even wider audience than had the Gauthe case. "It was clear that people knew what Porter was about," recalls Chopko. "There was some attempt at therapeutic intervention, but there'd been really no good follow up for him." The bishops responded by redoubling their reform efforts. "It led to yet another wholesale look at the policy," explains Chopko. At the June 1992 NCCB meeting, the bishops held a day-long executive session on clergy sexual abuse, at the end of which the group formally affirmed a nonbinding set of "Five Principles" to guide bishops' responses to clergy sexual abuse. The principles were: prompt response to allegations, removal of accused priests, increased reporting to law enforcement, victim outreach, and greater official transparency. At the November 1992 NCCB meeting, the bishops created a subcommittee to study the problem of clergy sexual abuse, and in February 1993, the subcommittee convened a two-day think tank in St. Louis, including a broad variety of experts, to discuss the issue. At the June 1993 NCCB meeting, the bishops appointed an Ad Hoc Committee on Sexual Abuse with a six-point mandate to assist bishops in dealing more effectively with offending priests: responding to victims and their families, addressing the damage to clergy morale, screening candidates for ministry and assessing possible reassignment of offenders, training church employees and volunteers to prevent abuse, and combating the larger societal problem of child sexual abuse. From its formation in 1993 to 2001, the Ad Hoc Committee on Sexual Abuse led the bishops' reform efforts, regularly reporting back to the bishops and publishing a three-volume report, *Restoring Trust,* which documented its reviews of diocesan policies and recommendations.[24]

For victims and their attorneys, the Porter case revealed what many characterized as an organized conspiracy among the bishops to protect child molesters and to conceal the widespread problem of clergy sexual abuse within the Church. "The Porter case hit the news," recalls plaintiffs' attorney Demarest, "and there we found that bishops between states had cooperated with each other . . . [There was] documentation that not only had they known about him where he came from in Massachusetts but that the bishops cooperated to send him somewhere else. In fact, several bishops in several states cooperated even though they knew his history and that he was still an abuser when he was finally contacted [by Fitzpatrick] and found [in Minnesota]. That was critically important."[25] In the wake of the Porter case, some plaintiffs' attorneys began filing lawsuits against the Church under the Racketeer Influenced and Corrupt Organizations (RICO) Act, a federal law designed to fight organized crime. Plaintiffs' attorney Rubino called the scandal "Organized Religion's Watergate."[26]

Like the Gauthe case, the Porter case led many victims to come forward for the first time. Recalls David Clohessy, national director of the Survivors Network of those Abused by Priests (SNAP), a victim support and advocacy group formed in 1989, "any time the issue's in the press, some survivors get the courage and the strength to come forward and report to police or prosecutors or [to seek out] civil attorneys or support groups . . . We began in 1989, but we certainly got a lot more calls after the Porter case."[27]

The Porter case generated enormous momentum in terms of press coverage favorable to victims, but the momentum was short lived. In November 1993, Rubino filed a lawsuit on behalf of Steven Cook who alleged that he had been sexually abused by Chicago archbishop Cardinal Joseph Bernardin in the mid-1970s while Cook was a student in a Cincinnati seminary and Bernardin was archbishop of Cincinnati.[28]

Cook's lawsuit also alleged sexual abuse by an instructor at the seminary, Father Ellis Harsham.

Prior to filing the suit, Rubino had been contacted by a CNN reporter, who taped an interview with Cook to be played as part of "Fall from Grace," a special report on clergy sexual abuse within the Catholic Church. CNN planned to air the program right after the filing of the lawsuit on the eve of the November NCCB meeting in Washington, D.C. The day before the lawsuit was to be filed, Bernardin was informed of it. He immediately called a preemptive press conference, where he vehemently denied the accusations, stating firmly: "While I have not seen the suit and I do not know the details of the allegation, there is one thing I do know, and I state this categorically: I have never abused anyone in all my life anywhere, anytime, anyplace." Within minutes of his denial, Bernardin was headline news on CNN, his denial juxtaposed to taped portions of Cook's accusations.

The next day, NCCB president, Baltimore Archbishop William Keeler, publicly defended Bernardin, stating that "Cardinal Joseph Bernardin's distinguished career of service to the church provides a firm foundation for confidence in his categorical denial of the allegations made against him in recent days . . . We express our complete confidence in his ultimate vindication." While defending Bernardin, Keeler attacked CNN and the rest of the media by suggesting that "being first with the story is, for some, a value that outweighs providing the best and most accurate reporting."

As details of Cook's lawsuit unfolded—that his memories of abuse were recovered as a result of hypnosis conducted by an unlicensed therapist treating him for dysentery pain associated with AIDS, from which he was suffering—the credibility of the charges against Bernardin began to fall apart. Journalists, commentators, and even victim advocates became increasingly reluctant to express support for Cook's charges. Three and a half months after filing the suit, Cook recanted, stating at a press conference, "I now realize that the memories which arose during and after hypnosis are unreliable. I can no longer proceed in good conscience." Doyle and other sources insist that Cook was paid in exchange for his recantation, although church officials deny it, and Rubino refuses to discuss the case.[29] The claims against Harsham were quietly settled with the Cincinnati archdiocese. Cook subsequently died of AIDS, Bernardin from cancer. Prior to their deaths, the two met in Bernardin's private residence and were reconciled.

"The Bernardin case," explains Clohessy, "was an extraordinary set-back for our movement." The case raised questions about the reliability of victims' memories in subsequent cases. Recalls plaintiffs' attorney Anderson, "We had been making solid progress in awareness, in public opinion, and in litigation, and then, when Bernardin hit, the roof fell in . . . Because of the Bernardin case, all of a sudden, people stopped believing survivors who reported abuse that happened a decade or more ago. There was this false memory/false allegation kind of view that permeated public opinion . . . And so after that, every time there was an old case where there was a delayed reporting—as there is in most of these cases—the first specter raised is false memory, false allegation, implantation, unethical therapist, blah, blah, blah. And so, it hurt the movement. It really set us back."[30] Moreover, the widespread perception that CNN had overreached chilled reporting on the issue. But while the Bernardin case led to a dramatic reduction in media coverage of clergy sexual abuse, it did not stop victims and their attorneys from pursuing claims.

In the years following the Porter case, according to Rubino, lawyers on both sides remained in "settlement mode." On one hand, the Church was still very concerned about avoiding the public scandal that would attend trials. On the other hand, plaintiffs' attorneys were rarely successful in obtaining the evidence buried in personnel and secret diocesan files necessary to clearly establish official complicity.[31]

The case against Father Rudy Kos and the Diocese of Dallas in 1997 reenergized victims and plaintiffs' attorneys, and it marked the beginning of the end of quiet settlements.[32] Eleven victims and family members sued Kos, diocesan officials, the bishop, and the NCCB alleging that Kos had sexually molested the victims between 1981 and 1992 during his assignments to three Dallas-area parishes and that church officials had failed to protect them by ignoring complaints by parishioners and warnings by fellow priests and therapists. The plaintiffs included the parents of one boy who had committed suicide as a result of the abuse.

Uncharacteristically, the Church refused to settle the case, and the plaintiffs' attorneys—Windle Turley and Sylvia Demarest—took it to trial. Discovery and trial testimony revealed that in annulling Kos's unsuccessful marriage as a precursor to admitting him to seminary, church officials had failed to investigate a suggestion by his ex-wife that he had a problem with boys. At seminary, Kos frequently slept with a young boy whom he had unofficially adopted as his "son." At his first parish assignment, he used video games, gifts, and beer to attract boys into having sex with him. A fellow priest wrote of Kos to diocesan officials that "There is an overnight guest in his room four nights out of every week on average." Kos received instructions from Monsignor Robert Rehkemper, the vicar general of the diocese, to stop having boys visit. At his second assignment, Kos continued to molest boys. In 1988, the bishop promoted him to pastor at a third church, St. John's Nepomucene Catholic Church. Two parishioners who ran the youth program wrote a letter directly to Bishop Thomas Tschoepe in 1989, complaining about Kos's relationships with boys. "Another thing that is concerning us," they wrote, "is that on several occasions, Fr. Kos has boys over to spend the entire night." When the assistant pastor at St. John's met with Monsignor Rehkemper and described Kos to a therapist in 1991, the therapist informed them that Kos sounded like a "classic, textbook pedophile." The following year, the assistant pastor sent a twelve-page letter to the new bishop, Charles Grahmann, complaining again about the presence of boys in Kos's room and describing how Kos would hold the boys tightly and rub against them. Finally, in 1992, Kos was sent to the Paraclete treatment center in New Mexico.

That same year, twenty-one-year-old Jay Lemberger fatally shot himself as a result of ten years of sexual abuse by Kos. His parents had no idea that he had been abused. Kos read a homily at the funeral.

When they realized what had happened to their son, the Lembergers joined seven Kos victims in a lawsuit against Kos and church officials, seeking $146.5 million in damages. The fifty-two-year-old Kos was, by that time, living in San Diego under an assumed name and working as a paralegal. He never responded to the suit, and a default judgment was entered against him. The NCCB was eventually dismissed from the suit. Diocesan officials took a beating at trial and in the press, and the jury awarded the plaintiffs a record $119.6 million verdict, $101 million in compensation and $18.6 million in punitive damages. The jury was so appalled by diocesan officials' denials that it took the extraordinary measure of including a message with the verdict admonishing them to "Please admit your guilt and allow these young men to get on with their lives." When the Church threatened to file for bankruptcy, the plaintiffs settled for $31 million. Kos was eventually charged criminally and convicted. He is currently serving a life sentence in Texas prison.

The Kos case, explains Anderson, "was another watershed because of the size of the verdict and the number of plaintiffs. It really put the spotlight on again, in a new and more vivid way, [revealing] the scope of the cover-up in the crucible of the courtroom."[33] The case, according to Rubino, provided two key legal advances for plaintiffs in subsequent cases. First, it framed the Church's wrongdoing in terms of simple, traditional principles of negligence that were less susceptible to dismissal than novel theories like clergy malpractice. Second, the court denied the Church's First Amendment challenges to the claim. Judges in cases prior to the Kos case, especially state trial judges, explains Rubino, "were easily intimidated by First Amendment arguments raised by church defendants. After the Kos case, courts around the country were better equipped to address them . . . The First Amendment was no longer an automatic roadblock" to plaintiffs' claims.[34]

Former USCCB general counsel Chopko has a very different impression of the Kos case's significance. "Kos was," he recalls, "the high water mark for what I call exotic legal claims . . . [The plaintiffs] sued the Conference of Bishops on an allegation that we had not acted as a—and I'm not making this up—reasonably prudent religion . . . There was also a very broad-based conspiracy claim, a fiduciary duty claim, and they had a complaint [with a RICO count in it that was] completely unfounded, but they dropped that out. It was one of these very novel, broad-reaching liability claims directed at us and through us at the entire Church."[35] During the course of the litigation, explains Chopko, the NCCB was dismissed from the case without prejudice. Thus, while for plaintiffs' attorneys the legal significance of the case was that it finally set tort claims against the institutional church on a solid, traditional doctrinal footing, from Chopko's perspective it revealed the failure of "exotic" legal theories to extend liability beyond individual local wrongdoers.

Perceptions differ also as to the impact of the case on public opinion. For plaintiffs' attorneys, the pendulum of public opinion began to swing back in their favor for the first time since the Bernardin affair. In the wake of the Kos verdict, "the public," suggests Anderson, "really came to believe this is an enormously grave problem that has not gone away."[36] "It was front-page, above-the-fold news around the world," recalls Demarest.[37] By contrast, church officials believed that the public reaction to the Kos verdict reflected positive progress in their ability to deal with clergy sexual abuse. Recalls Chopko,

Kos, when it happened, was a national story for about two days. We had a completely different reaction to it than we had in other cases. We did not have a bishops' spokesperson when Porter happened, but in Kos we had a chairman of the bishops' committee on camera—on *Nightline,* on *60 Minutes,* and on all these other talk shows to talk about what the Church was doing. We were able to show leadership. We were able to show that we were proactive and that we were not afraid of the story and that we were trying to deal with it the best we could. It was a regional story for a long time, but it was not illustrative of the bad things that the Church was doing like Porter was. Porter just ran for weeks.[38]

Thus for plaintiffs' attorneys, the Kos case signified a successful attempt to expose publicly an ongoing conspiracy in the Church to cover up clergy sexual abuse, while for the bishops it offered an opportunity to show the public just how much they had already done to address the problem. This gap in perceptions became a chasm during the third and final wave of litigation that began with the Geoghan case in Boston in 2002.

The Third Wave: 2002–Present

In the wake of Gauthe, Porter, and Kos, the central elements of the Geoghan case were sadly familiar to those following the clergy sexual abuse scandal.[39] The Geoghan case exposed—once again—the story of a priest who molested multiple victims in several parish assignments over the course of many years. His crimes were covered up by diocesan officials who repeatedly reassigned him to new parishes without alerting parishioners or public authorities. And in each new assignment, he abused more children.

What distinguished the Geoghan case from its predecessors was the astounding scope of the abuse and the cover up. Two hundred Geoghan victims, molested over a thirty-three-year period, filed claims, and experts estimate that the total number of Geoghan's victims could be as high as 800. Geoghan himself became a symbol of the clergy sexual abuse scandal. The cover-up implicated no fewer than six bishops and ultimately forced Cardinal Bernard Law, the highly influential archbishop of Boston, to step down and seek refuge in Rome. The wave of litigation initiated by the Geoghan affair turned out to be a tidal wave that wreaked financial destruction on the Boston archdiocese. The Geoghan case, in the words of Albany bishop Hubbard, was the Church's "worst-case nightmare."[40]

Father John Geoghan was ordained in 1962 and assigned as a priest to Blessed Sacrament Parish in Saugus, Massachusetts, where he later admitted to molesting four boys. Father Anthony Benzevich reportedly informed church officials at the time that Geoghan brought boys into his bedroom, but Benzevich subsequently denied this during a pretrial deposition in 2000. Geoghan was briefly reassigned to St. Bernard's Church in Concord in 1966, and then subsequently assigned to St. Paul's Parish in Hingham in 1967. When several parents complained to church officials that they had found Geoghan molesting their sons, he was sent for psychiatric treatment in 1968 to the Seton Institute in Baltimore, and then restored to his post at St. Paul's, where he continued to molest young boys. In 1973, Joanne Mueller, a single mother, discovered that Geoghan had molested all four of her sons over the course of several years during which he helped her by taking the boys on outings and minding them in her home. She alleges that she informed Father Paul Miceli, a priest in a neighboring parish, and that Miceli assured her that he would take care of the problem. She further alleges that Miceli made her promise to keep the abuse a secret in order to protect the boys and avoid scandal to the Church. While Miceli did confront Geoghan and warn him to stay away from the Mueller boys, he never reported the abuse to church officials. In later legal proceedings, Miceli admitted confronting Geoghan in response to an anonymous telephone complaint, but he denied Mueller's account of their conversation.

In 1974, Geoghan was assigned to St. Andrew's Parish in Jamaica Plain. In 1980, Maryetta Dussourd discovered that Geoghan, a regular visitor to her home, had molested seven of the eight children in her home—her three sons and her niece's four boys whom she was raising. (Geoghan, whose victims were almost exclusively boys, did not molest her daughter.) Geoghan molested the boys in their bedroom, performing oral sex on them, fondling them, or forcing them to fondle him. Church files disclose that he "would touch them while they were sleeping and waken them by playing with their penises."[41] Sometimes he would pray while molesting them.

Dussourd complained to Father John Thomas, the pastor of a nearby parish, who confronted Geoghan. Geoghan readily admitted to abusing the seven boys as well as several boys in another family, but he suggested that it "was just two families" and that he did not think it would interfere with his ability to serve the parish.[42] Thomas reported the accusations to Bishop Thomas Daily, administrator of the archdiocese, and Geoghan was immediately placed on sick leave. Thomas then went to reassure Dussourd. He also pressed her not to report Geoghan to the police—urging her to think of Geoghan's elderly mother, not to ruin his career as a priest, to forgive him for his sins, and to spare the Church scandal. Geoghan's sick leave consisted of a year living with his mother in Roxbury, and receiving treatment from Dr. Robert Mullins, a family friend and next-door neighbor with a family practice, and Dr. John Brennan, a psychotherapist with no experience in treating sexual disorders who had recently settled a lawsuit against him brought by a former patient who accused him of sexually molesting her.

A year later, Geoghan was assigned to St. Brendan's Church in Dorchester where he continued to molest boys. In 1982, one of the Dussourd boys ran into Geoghan with another boy at a Jamaica Plain ice-cream parlor, and the Dussourds complained in person to Bishop Daily. Margaret Gallant, Maryetta Dussourd's sister, followed up the meeting with a letter to Cardinal Humberto Medeiros demanding that he take action to control Geoghan. Medeiros replied that forgiveness was the most appropriate response and that he would speak to the priest "in order to find the most Christian way to deal with the problem with him and at the same time remove any source of scandal for the sake of the faithful." Gallant wrote a subsequent letter in 1984 to Medeiros's successor, Cardinal Bernard Law, who responded that "The matter of your concern is being investigated and appropriate pastoral decisions will be made both for the priest and God's people." Based on complaints by several families, Geoghan had already been removed from St. Brendan's and sent again to Mullins and Brennan for treatment. Within months, they declared him fully recovered, and he was reassigned to St. Julia's Parish in Weston.[43]

Despite the fact that diocesan officials and the pastor of St. Julia's were well aware of the previous accusations against him and his treatment history, Geoghan was put in charge of three youth groups, including altar boys. By 1989, more complaints had reached diocesan officials, and Geoghan was again sent off for treatment, this time to St. Luke Institute in Silver Spring, Maryland, where he was diagnosed as a pedophile. He subsequently received therapy at The Institute of Living, in Hartford, Connecticut, and was discharged with a report finding him "moderately improved" and recommending that he be allowed to resume his duties as a priest. When Auxiliary Bishop Robert Banks requested further information from Geoghan's doctors at The Institute of Living, they opined that "The probability he would act out again is quite low. However, we could not guarantee that it would not re-occur."[44] Geoghan was returned to St. Julia's by the end of 1989, where, within weeks, he resumed molesting boys. The accusations continued.

In 1993, Cardinal Law finally removed Geoghan from parish duty, and he was assigned to work at a retirement home for priests. The abuse, however, did not stop with his removal from parish work, and there were several complaints in the ensuing years from parents, including one parent who accused Geoghan in 1995 of molesting a boy at the christening ceremony of the boy's younger sister. Geoghan was placed on administrative leave and sent for more treatment, and in 1998, with Vatican approval, he was defrocked.

In 1996, a handful of victims had approached plaintiffs' attorney Mitchell Garabedian, who had filed suit on their behalf against Geoghan and diocesan officials. By 1997, Garabedian had quietly settled over fifty claims for more than $10 million. The Church's lawyer, Wilson Rogers, Jr., had successfully moved to have all of the case files sealed, which prevented the public release of documents and prohibited Garabedian and his clients from sharing any information from the files with the press. As a result, press coverage remained local and limited. The sealing of files was standard practice in clergy sexual abuse litigation against the Catholic Church. All of this changed in 2002, when the veil of secrecy was lifted.

By late 2001, Garabedian had collected a large group of plaintiffs— eventually referred to as the "Geoghan 86"—with whom Rogers refused to settle. The *Boston Globe,* seeking to publish a series on clergy abuse within the Boston archdiocese, sued to have the case files unsealed. Judge Constance Sweeny ruled in favor of the *Globe,* which published an extensive series of stories in January 2002, focusing on the Geoghan case and revealing other cases involving at least seventy other priests in the Boston archdiocese that had been settled by the Church in exchange for confidentiality agreements. The *Globe*'s coverage sparked national media attention and earned its investigative staff a Pulitzer prize.

The unsealing of the Geoghan documents provided stark evidence that diocesan officials—including Cardinal Law—knew about Geoghan's sexual abuse of children as they moved him from parish to parish. Cardinal Law held a press conference, explaining that "However much I regret having assigned him, it is important to recall that

John Geoghan was never assigned by me to a parish without psychiatric or medical assessments indicating that such assignments were appropriate."[45] He was, as the recently unsealed documents revealed, referring to the assessments by Geoghan family friend Dr. Mullins and Dr. Brennan who were untrained in the evaluation or treatment of sexual disorders, the St. Luke Institute diagnosis of pedophilia, and The Institute of Living's report that, following treatment, Geoghan was "moderately improved" and that "[t]he probability he would act out again is quite low" but that "we could not guarantee that it would not reoccur." The *Globe*'s disclosure of these documents as the basis for Law's decisions to reassign Geoghan to parish work undercut the Cardinal's credibility. Shortly after Law's declaration of a new "zero tolerance" policy for child abusers in the diocese, the *Globe* uncovered more cases of priests who had been reassigned after allegations of sexual abuse and who were still in active ministry.

In the wake of the document disclosure and the *Globe*'s series, the archdiocese sought quickly to settle the claims of the Geoghan 86 and put the cases behind them. In March 2002, the archdiocese agreed to settle the cases for between $15 million and $30 million depending on awards granted to the victims by a mutually agreed upon arbitration process that would assess the severity of abuse in each case. The settlement came just in time to spare Cardinal Law the public embarrassment of a scheduled pretrial deposition in April. This settlement sum was in addition to the prior $10 million paid out in 1997 to earlier Garabedian clients and another $5 million reportedly paid out previously to another approximately fifty Geoghan victims. At the time the settlement was announced, the *Globe* estimated that settlements with Geoghan victims and the hundreds of victims of other priests would cost the archdiocese in excess of $100 million.

In May, however, the archdiocese's finance council rejected the agreement as too expensive. Furious, Garabedian proceeded with discovery and deposed Law on May 8. Under oath, Law insisted that he did not recall events surrounding his reassignment of Geoghan and that it had been handled by his subordinates without his involvement.

With the encouragement of Judge Sweeny, the two sides reached a second settlement agreement of $10 million in September, prior to trial. The perception that the archdiocese had reneged on the first settlement further undermined Law's stature both in Boston and in the Church nationally. The *Globe* quoted plaintiffs complaining about the reduced amount to be paid by the archdiocese in the second settlement. "The cardinal and his lawyers should be ashamed of themselves. I'm not sure how a man of the church, a cardinal and a leader can justify this," said one victim. "These spiritual leaders have conducted themselves like the corporation they are . . . They've acted very immorally," denounced another. "It isn't an apology," said a third. "It's just scattering crumbs to the people and telling them to get out of the way."[46]

The settlement put the Geoghan 86 claims to rest. Geoghan himself was indicted in 1999, convicted in 2002, sentenced to nine years in prison, and murdered shortly thereafter by a fellow inmate. The trouble, however, was just beginning.

In the wake of the Geoghan case, hundreds of victims filed suit against the archdiocese. Massachusetts attorney general Thomas Reilly launched an investigation and published a scathing report. Implicated in the mishandling of abusive priests were Law's former deputies, by this time elevated to leadership positions in prominent dioceses throughout the country: Bishop Thomas Daily in Brooklyn; Bishop William Murphy in Rockville Centre, New York; Bishop John McCormack in Manchester, New Hampshire; Bishop Daniel Hart in Norwich, Connecticut; Bishop Robert Banks in Green Bay, Wisconsin; and Bishop Alfred Hughes in New Orleans.[47] Insisting throughout 2002 that he would never step down, Cardinal Law finally resigned as archbishop of Boston in December and sought refuge from the scandal in Rome. Law's replacement was Sean O'Malley, who had been previously appointed to the Diocese of Fall River to negotiate a settlement with the Porter victims and then assigned to West Palm Beach, Florida, to succeed two bishops who had resigned one after the other due to revelations that they themselves had committed sexual abuse. O'Malley immediately set about settling over 554 claims pending against the Boston archdiocese. In September 2003, the archdiocese agreed to pay $85 million to settle the claims.[48] In March 2006, the archdiocese reached a settlement with another eighty-eight victims, agreeing to resolve their claims in arbitration, with awards averaging $75,000 per victim. This settlement left 100 additional claims unresolved.[49]

The Geoghan case was significant for at least three reasons. First, the publication of actual church documents proving that bishops knowingly and repeatedly reassigned a confirmed abuser had a powerful effect on public opinion. As plaintiffs' attorney Demarest explains, "The importance of what was going on in Boston wasn't merely [Geoghan];

it was the fact that for the first time all of these files were released and everybody got to see them."[50] The disclosure of documents intensified press coverage and put pressure on the Church to settle claims in order to stem the rising tide of scandal. As one attorney involved in the litigation points out, "These cases in Boston were settled without regard to the [$20,000 damage] cap [for lawsuits against charitable organizations] and without regard to the fact that the insurance companies were disclaiming liability. They were settled on the basis that we cannot get past this scandal, we cannot get past this crisis, and resume our role as a church ministering to people, until this goes away."[51]

Second, the Geoghan case revealed the failure of the bishops' reforms, dating back to 1985—at least insofar as they had not been implemented in Boston, giving rise to widespread suspicion that they had not been followed in other places as well. This stoked anger against Cardinal Law among not only the general public and the Catholic laity, but among fellow bishops as well. In the words of Albany Bishop Hubbard,

> If the norms that were developed between 1985 and 1993 had been put into place, the Geoghan case should never have happened, and I do think that, by and large, most bishops did not reassign [offenders], at least not without protections put into place to prevent future harm to the community. I understand that there was some further reassignment, but there was treatment and there was some effort to monitor that that behavior wasn't continuing. And yet, in the Geoghan case, there was reassignment and a continued pattern of reprehensible behavior. And I think that most people feel that that was what was happening as a general norm right up until 2002, but I think that it was more the exception than the rule, and that's why there was such anger on the part of the bishops that we had tried to put in some standards and guidelines and criteria for how to deal with this and they seemed to be ignored in this instance.[52]

Church officials and their lawyers tended to view the Geoghan case as a story about incompetence. By contrast, victims and their lawyers attributed church officials' failure to implement earlier reforms to an organized conspiracy to protect abusive priests and to cover up their crimes.

Third, the Geoghan case put clergy sexual abuse back at the top of the USCCB agenda. At their June 2002 meeting in Dallas, the bishops adopted the *Charter for the Protection of Children & Young People,* a binding policy that proclaimed "zero tolerance" for clergy sexual abuse within the Church, along with a set of *Essential Norms for Diocesan/Eparchial Policies Dealing with Allegations of Sexual Abuse of Minors by Priests or Deacons* to guide implementation of the Charter. The Charter created lay review boards in each diocese to assess claims and make recommendations to the bishop, a National Review Board charged with overseeing compliance with the policy and commissioning a comprehensive study of the problem, and an Office of Child and Youth Protection to assist with implementation of the policy.

While the third wave of clergy sexual abuse litigation began in Boston, it did not end there. Beginning in 2002, dioceses throughout the country faced a storm surge of legal claims. Hardest hit was Los Angeles.[53]

There are many parallels between the scandal in L.A. and the scandal in Boston. Roger Mahony was appointed archbishop of L.A., the nation's largest archdiocese, in 1985, one year after Bernard Law was appointed archbishop of Boston, the nation's fourth largest archdiocese. Both men were subsequently named cardinals by the pope, reflecting their preeminence among American Bishops. By 2002, Mahony was arguably second only to Law in terms of his influence among American bishops. Mahony, like Law, inherited and perpetuated clergy sexual abuse problems and became a focal point of controversy. Revelations in 2002 led Mahony, like Law, to admit publicly to reassigning a priest with a history of child sexual abuse and to declare a zero-tolerance policy for clergy sexual abuse. In the wake of these revelations, protesters followed Mahony, as they did Law, calling for him to step down.

Mahony was first named as a defendant in a clergy sexual abuse lawsuit in 1997 brought by two victims of Father Oliver O'Grady who molested them as children over a ten-year period from the late 1970s to the late 1980s.[54] The lawsuit alleged that Mahony, while serving as bishop of Stockton, California, from 1980 to 1985, reassigned O'Grady to a new parish with a promotion from associate pastor to pastor even though Mahony knew at the time that O'Grady's personnel file contained an admission that he had sexually abused an eleven-year-old girl and despite receiving a psychiatric report that O'Grady was sexually immature. The lawsuit further alleged that Mahony discouraged law enforcement authorities from pursuing an investigation of O'Grady sparked by a report from a psychiatric social worker that O'Grady had admitted to sexually molesting a young boy.

At trial in 1998, Mahony denied that he had known when reassigning O'Grady of the priest's admission that he had sexually abused an eleven-year-old girl, and Mahony also insisted that the matter had been largely handled by his subordinates without his knowledge. Mahony explained that in transferring O'Grady despite his past history of pedophilia, "We relied on the judgment of professionals." Mahony's testimony at the O'Grady trial was essentially the same as Law's deposition testimony and public statements in the Geoghan case.

The jury did not believe Mahony, and they handed down a verdict against the archdiocese, awarding the plaintiffs $6 million in compensatory damages and $24 million in punitive damages. (The trial judge reduced the punitive award to $12 million; both sides appealed, and the plaintiffs settled with the diocese for $7.6 million.) Explained plaintiffs' attorney Jeff Anderson, who litigated the case, "In order to bring in that verdict, the jury had to believe that the cardinal was not telling the truth. If they had believed the cardinal, there would not have been punitive damages under the law." As one juror put it, "I found Mahony to be utterly unbelievable." L.A.'s alternative paper, the *New Times*, observed that "O'Grady wasn't on trial in Stockton . . . Mahony was."

In the end, it was revealed that O'Grady abused at least twenty children over his twenty-two-year career as a priest in the Stockton diocese from 1971 to 1993. His victims ranged in age from a nine-month-old infant, whom he digitally penetrated, to adolescents. He even carried on affairs with the mothers of some of his victims while he was molesting their children. In 1993, O'Grady was arrested and eventually served seven years of a fourteen-year sentence, at which point he was deported back to his native Ireland. The Stockton diocese settled additional claims involving O'Grady in exchange for binding promises by victims to keep the matter confidential.

While little attention was paid to the O'Grady case when it was litigated in 1998, it received extensive media attention in 2002 following the eruption of the scandal in Boston. Recalls one O'Grady victim, "We were just flabbergasted that there was so little attention to the story [in 1998] . . . I can remember calling up reporters and trying to get them to cover it and getting nothing but a ho-hum response. Now, since Boston, it's funny. I've got reporters from those same newspapers who refused to write much of anything about Mahony calling up begging me for interviews."

In 2002, the media began to uncover additional cases of abusive priests reassigned by Mahony whose crimes were concealed from law enforcement. The district attorney launched a grand jury investigation. While Mahony publicly declared his intention to provide full disclosure to the grand jury, the diocese asserted claims of privilege in order to resist handing over many church personnel files. (To be fair, some of the resistance came from accused priests who did not want their files turned over.) Mahony's critics derisively referred to him as "Roger the Dodger." Jeff Anderson filed a federal racketeering claim against Mahony in one lawsuit, and former Oklahoma governor Frank Keating, appointed by the USCCB to head the newly established National Review Board, compared bishops who concealed information about the scandal—and he specifically named Mahony—to Mafia bosses.[55]

The flood of litigation began in earnest in 2003, when the California state legislature suspended the statute of limitations on child sexual abuse claims for a one-year period. This suspension of the statute of limitations, combined with the lack of any charitable damage cap like that in Massachusetts, led to the filing of over 850 civil claims in California, more than 560 of them in L.A. alone, involving more than 200 priests. In January 2005, the Diocese of Orange, California, which was part of the L.A. diocese until 1976, settled with eighty-seven victims for $100 million, exceeding the $85 million 2003 settlement in Boston. In December 2006, the L.A. archdiocese paid $60 million to settle forty-six claims involving allegations of abuse prior to 1953 and after 1986, periods for which the archdiocese did not have commercial insurance coverage. In July 2007, the archdiocese settled the remaining claims for $660 million, $227 million of which insurers agreed to pay.[56]

Throughout the scandal in L.A., Mahony sought to cast himself as a leader in church reform efforts. Early in 2002, he distanced himself from Law. Mahony was critical of Law's response to the crisis, stating publicly when the scandal broke in Boston that "[a]pologies are vitally necessary, but themselves are insufficient."[57] (It should be noted that Law himself was viewed as an early proponent of reform among the bishops in 1985 when he encouraged circulation of the Doyle-Peterson-Mouton report in the wake of the Gauthe case.) In February 2004, Mahony issued a *Report to the People of God: Clergy Sexual Abuse in the Archdiocese of Los Angeles, 1930–2003*. Mahony's cover letter to the report offered an apology, and the report revealed the names of 211 priests working in the archdiocese who were accused of child sexual abuse dating back to 1931. Mahony also launched a *Safeguard the Children* program that by the end of 2005 had trained over 26,000 diocesan personnel, volunteers, and parents in how to prevent, identify, and report child sexual abuse.

Views differ sharply as to the larger significance of the L.A. litigation. Critics of the Church see it as evidence of an ongoing criminal conspiracy among bishops to conceal clergy sexual abuse. Plaintiffs' attorney Demarest contends that there was "a well thought out, well organized, and established cover-up that had various characteristics. Otherwise, you wouldn't have seen the same pattern in every diocese, in every state, all over the place. It was an organized, agreed-to cover-up, and it worked. It worked for quite a long time." She suggests that in asserting claims of privilege to prevent the disclosure of personnel files, Mahony "was doing the rope-a-dope. He obviously has a lot to be accounted for, and he's just drawing this thing out as long as he can. Probably in order to avoid being prosecuted criminally, and I think it's going to work."[58]

By contrast, defenders of the Church find it ironic that plaintiffs' lawyers have been persecuting an institution that they consider to be a national leader in the fight against child sexual abuse. Says J. Michael Hennigan, attorney for the archdiocese, "I don't think that anyone or any institution in the country has come close to doing what the Archdiocese of Los Angeles has done in terms of proactively dealing with changing attitudes and the environment for children."[59] Many also find the size of verdicts and settlements, often for incidents dating back decades, exaggerated. Albany bishop Hubbard, generally in favor of settling claims, recalls that "when we were settling cases [in Albany] in the '90s, we were talking pretty much in the $50,000 to $150,000 range, by and large. Now, there are cases in California that are settling for over $1 million per case."[60]

An Ongoing Clash of Perspectives

Clergy sexual abuse litigation has been fueled by differences of perspective that have evolved over time. During the first wave of litigation following the Gauthe affair, the bishops believed that they were achieving a better understanding of clergy sexual abuse within the Church, and they focused on actively pursuing institutional reforms to address the problem. At the same time, victims and their attorneys were for the first time uncovering the bishops' past wrongdoing and were focused on exposing it. Whereas the bishops sought to move forward, victims and their attorneys wanted to force them to face the past.

The bishops and their supporters perceived the second wave of litigation following the Porter case as an unfair attempt to punish the Church for mistakes made prior to the bishops' reform efforts in the late 1980s and early 1990s. By contrast, victims and their attorneys during this period increasingly believed that litigation was gradually exposing a nationwide conspiracy among the bishops to conceal clergy sexual abuse in the Church.

In the third wave, many bishops and their supporters have come to view ongoing litigation as the product of money-hungry victims and their lawyers seeking to exploit the scandal for financial gain. Their opponents see the bishops' failure to convincingly clean house as evidence of recalcitrance and treachery, as the product of an entrenched culture of secrecy within the Church that protects abusers and that can only be reformed using the tools of the secular legal system.

CHAPTER TWO

Statistics

In the previous chapter, we focused on a handful of landmark cases in order to simplify and structure the complex history of clergy sexual abuse litigation. We turn now to what statistics can teach us about clergy sexual abuse litigation in the aggregate. In the first half of the chapter, I review existing data concerning the nature and scope of clergy sexual abuse within the Catholic Church. I then present original, and more limited data concerning clergy sexual abuse litigation. But first a word of caution is in order. The original data presented in the second half of the chapter is based on small samples which do not support firm conclusions about general trends. My conclusions are tentative and rely on speculation. Nevertheless, available data can provide some information that will be useful in analyzing clergy sexual abuse litigation in later chapters. Where possible, I have tried to combine data from diverse sources which, in conjunction, are more reliable than any one source alone.

The Larger Context of Child Sexual Abuse

Clergy sexual abuse within the Catholic Church is part of a larger phenomenon of child sexual abuse that occurs in other religious denominations, in secular institutions throughout society, and within families. Whether child sexual abuse is more prevalent within the Catholic Church than in other institutions is impossible to say based on existing data. There are no reliable estimates of the prevalence of child sexual abusers in the population at large, and estimates of the prevalence of victims vary widely. Studies of the prevalence of sexual abuse in particular institutions are rare, and the few that do exist do not offer a broad basis for comparison.[1]

Estimates of the number of priests accused of child sexual abuse, the number of victims, and the number of incidents of abuse within the Catholic Church are based on allegations recorded in church personnel files, court filings, and media reports. Since many victims never disclose their abuse, these estimates are, by all accounts, low, and there is no way of knowing by just how much. There are also estimates of the number of priests who sexually abuse children based on clinical experience or small survey samples, but these do not support reliable generalizations.

Clergy Sexual Abuse within the Catholic Church

The most comprehensive data on clergy sexual abuse within the Catholic Church is a study commissioned by the USCCB entitled *The Nature and Scope of Sexual Abuse of Minors by Catholic Priests and Deacons in the United States 1950–2002*. This study was produced by a team of scholars at John Jay College of Criminal Justice. (It is often referred to as the John Jay study.) The John Jay team conducted a survey of U.S. dioceses and religious orders, requesting information about allegations of sexual abuse against priests.[2] The team received responses from 195 dioceses (98 percent of the total) and 140 religious orders (60 percent of the total, representing 80 percent of religious priests). Based on these survey responses, the study reported sexual abuse allegations against 4,392 priests between 1950 and 2002, which represents about 4 percent of all priests active during this period. The study also reported that these allegations were made by 10,667 individual victims.[3] Subsequent audits of dioceses and religious orders by the USCCB in 2004, 2005, and 2006 reported additional allegations against 1,736 priests made by 2,570 victims.[4]

It is important to keep in mind that the John Jay study and the USCCB audits count only allegations. Since many victims never report their abuse, the number of allegations is lower than the number of actual incidents. For the same reason, the number of reported abusers and victims is lower than the actual number of abusers and victims. The study, explains the John Jay team's data analyst, Margaret Smith, provides an account "of what was formally reported to the Church—it is not a victimization survey."[5]

Some victim advocates have asserted that the study and the subsequent audits underestimate even allegations. They offer two arguments. First, the study and the audits rely on survey responses filled out by diocesan officials or diocesan attorneys without any independent verification of the veracity or completeness of their responses.[6] Second, the information provided in the survey responses was based on church personnel files, which in some instances may have been incomplete due to poor record keeping, failure to communicate allegations at the parish level to diocesan officials, or the removal of incriminating material from personnel files to secret archives.[7]

Suspicions that dioceses underreported allegations have been fueled by disparities between allegation counts provided by individual dioceses and those of independent investigators. For example, the Boston archdiocese reported 162 accused priests from 1950 through 2003, while a report by the Massachusetts attorney general found 237 accused priests between 1940 and July 2003 based on documents produced by the archdiocese, documents filed in civil suits, and media reports.[8] The Cleveland diocese turned over the names of only twenty-two priests in April 2002 in response to a subpoena by the local prosecutor investigating allegations of clergy sexual abuse. In December of that year, a grand jury reported 145 accused priests. In 2004, the diocese amended its estimate to 118.[9] The Diocese of Orange, California, publicized the data it provided to the John Jay study, reporting that "16 priests were accused by 47 people." Plaintiffs' attorney John Manly provided the local newspaper with a list of "26 priests, four members of religious orders, and eight lay people credibly accused of having sexually abused children in the diocese."[10]

The importance of these doubts regarding the John Jay study for our purposes is that they reflect a deep mistrust of the Church among victim advocates and plaintiffs' lawyers. Former doctoral student Jennifer Balboni found that among a group of Boston victims, nearly all cited a desire to establish truth as motivation for suing.[11] Victims' lack of confidence in the veracity of church officials and the reliability of church records helps to explain why—even after extensive church disclosures in the John Jay study and annual audits—many continue to view litigation as the most effective means of establishing what they believe to be the truth about clergy sexual abuse.

The John Jay study reveals significant patterns in clergy sexual abuse that have implications for litigation. First, most of the abuse reported by survey respondents was of a very serious nature: 22.4 percent of the allegations reported penile penetration or attempted penile penetration, 26 percent reported the cleric performing oral sex, and 44.9 percent reported touching under the victim's clothes. Less than 2 percent of allegations reported only minor acts such as verbal abuse or the use of pornography. Moreover, two-thirds of victims (71 percent) reported being abused more than once, and over half (52.7 percent) numerous times.[12] The seriousness of most abuse translates into high demands for compensation in litigation and settlement negotiations. The significant monetary value of most victims' injuries also makes it easier to obtain a lawyer since plaintiffs' attorneys typically work on a contingent fee basis. Reported damage awards and settlement payments to individual victims range from thousands of dollars to $5.2 million.[13]

Second, roughly half of accused priests were known or suspected to have had more than one victim.[14] This is significant because knowledge of previous allegations on the part of church officials is often offered by plaintiffs as evidence that the abuse they suffered was foreseeable. Showing that the abuse suffered by a plaintiff was foreseeable is an essential element of establishing liability under a number of legal theories. We will examine these theories in detail in chapter 3.

Third, 80 percent of reported victims were male and over two-thirds (77 percent) were eleven years of age or older when the abuse began. Based on these statistics, some defenders of the Church have attempted to downplay the scandal as primarily a problem of consensual homosexual relationships between sexually immature priests and adolescent boys.[15] As the analysis in chapter 4 will demonstrate, this attempt has largely failed because litigation has focused attention on the institutional failure of bishops rather than the nature of individual relationships between priests and abuse victims.

Fourth, the distribution of alleged incidents of abuse suggests that actual abuse increased steadily in the 1950s and '60s, peaked in the 1970s and 1980, and declined starting in the early 1980s until 2002. Figure 1 depicts the distribution of alleged incidents of abuse by date of the first instance of abuse.[16] A supplementary data analysis published by the John Jay team in 2006 suggests that, while additional victims have come forward since 2002 and will continue to do so in the future, the shape of the curve of alleged incidents during the period between 1950 and 2002 is likely to remain the same. That is, while the study counts only allegations and not actual incidents, it nevertheless provides evidence of what the John Jay team calls "the shape of the crisis."[17] Note in Figure 1 the dramatic declines from 1985 to 1986 and from 1993 to 1994, which coincide with the aftermath of the Gauthe and Porter cases respectively. We shall see in chapter 5 that these landmark cases raised awareness about clergy sexual abuse and spurred church and government officials to implement policies to address the problem. The dramatic declines following the Gauthe and Porter cases further suggest that by raising awareness and promoting policy reforms, litigation may have played a role in reducing the rate of clergy sexual abuse.[18]

Caution is warranted here. As I mentioned in the introduction, my claims in this book concern primarily the impact of litigation on policymaking. Evidence for the litigation's impact on the rate of abuse is considerably less robust. Discerning litigation's impact on the rate of abuse is complicated by the fact that the decline in alleged incidents (and therefore, according to the John Jay supplementary analysis, actual incidents) began prior to the Gauthe litigation, which did not commence until 1984. If litigation did contribute to a decline in clergy sexual abuse, it was only one of a number of factors.

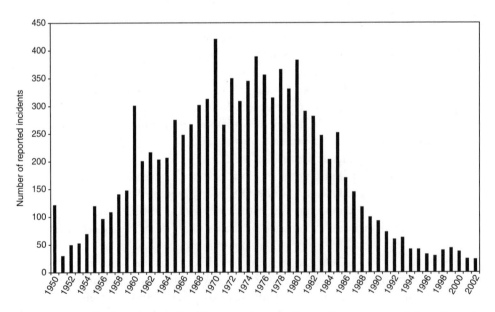

Figure 1. Distribution of alleged incidents of abuse by date of first instance of abuse (based on allegations between 1950 and 2002).

Fifth, the distribution of reported allegations shows a small but steady increase in allegations in the mid-1980s, sharp increases in allegations in 1992 and 1993, and an even more pronounced increase in 2002. Figure 2 depicts this distribution.[19] Note here the coincidence between the sharp increases in reported allegations and the Gauthe, Porter, and Geoghan cases. This data is consistent with anecdotal evidence from the previous chapter that these high profile cases encouraged victims to come forward in greater numbers. In chapter 5 we will further explore this mobilizing effect of the litigation on victims.

Sixth, the John Jay data reveal a delay in many cases between the occurrence of abuse and the reporting of abuse. Figure 3 depicts the pattern of delay between incident and report.[20] Note that many incidents are reported twenty or thirty years after the abuse occurred. This phenomenon of delayed reporting has increased over time. Before 1985, 85 percent of reported incidents were reported within a year and fewer than 2 percent were reported more than ten years later. By 2002, only 10 percent of reported incidents were reported within a year, and more than 95 percent were reported more than ten years later.[21] Former USCCB general counsel Mark Chopko recalls that in the late 1980s,

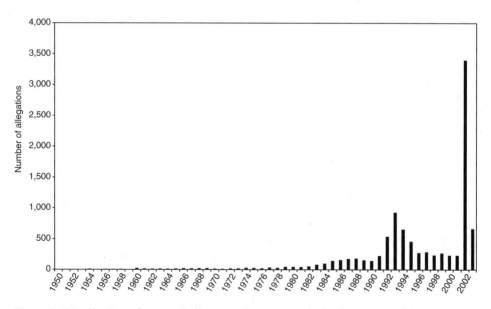

Figure 2. Distribution of reported allegations by year in which allegation was first made (based on allegations between 1950 and 2003).

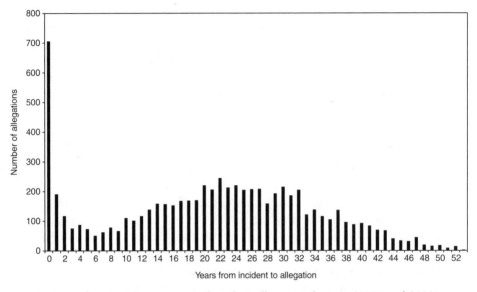

Figure 3. Time from incident to report (based on allegations between 1950 and 2002).

claims against the Church for clergy sexual abuse were increasingly based on incidents that had occurred many years previously. "When I started seeing cases in the 1980s," explains Chopko, "they were parents who were bringing their adolescents into chancery in real time: 'This happened to my son, my daughter last week. What are you going to do about it?' By the late 1980's . . . the cases overwhelmingly began to be dated. The allegations would date to the late '60s, '70s, '80s. They were not happening in real time . . . That's been very consistent over fifteen years . . . So we're dealing with an inventory of old cases."[22] This pattern of delayed reporting has had a significant impact on litigation because it has meant that in most cases the statute of limitations on the claim has expired. As Chopko explains, "from a defensive perspective we have used and we will continue to defend ourselves on the basis of the statute of limitations."[23] In order to avoid this defense, plaintiffs' lawyers often allege that the victim repressed his or her memory of the abuse— which in many jurisdictions tolls the statute—and recovered the memory only recently. As we shall see in the next chapter, the issue of repressed memory has been a focal point in controversy over the litigation.

Finally, the John Jay survey asked respondents to report claims that they considered false or that were withdrawn. (These claims were not counted in the estimates of allegations, accused priests, or victims.) Survey responses reflected that only 409 allegations (3.6 percent) were considered false and 286 (2.5 percent) were withdrawn.[24] The low rate of false allegations even by diocesan accounting sheds doubt on the suggestion by some commentators that fraudulent claims are common.[25] This is consistent with anecdotal evidence presented in the next chapter suggesting a low rate of false claims in litigation.

Trends in Clergy Sexual Abuse Litigation

The obstacles to estimating the total number of lawsuits against the Catholic Church for clergy sexual abuse are so daunting that few commentators have even ventured a guess. One might begin with court files. But even if one could comb files going back decades in thousands of local courthouses where lawsuits might have been filed, many court records have been discarded to conserve space, destroyed in fires and floods, or sealed by courts. Law office files would not be any better—they are even more geographically dispersed and prone to disappearance than official records. Electronic media such as Lexis/Nexis and Westlaw include only cases with some sort of published record. Press coverage is selective and misses altogether the many suits that have been quietly settled without attracting media attention. Diocesan records are perhaps the best place to look for comprehensive records of litigation against the Church for clergy sexual abuse. In fact, the John Jay survey asked respondents with regard to each reported allegation: "Was there any civil action taken against the cleric or the diocese for damages?" Unfortunately, because the John Jay research team asked the question at the beginning of a period of rapid increase in the number of lawsuits being filed, they did not consider the results reliable enough to report.[26]

A few commentators have nevertheless estimated the total number of clergy sexual abuse lawsuits against the Catholic Church. Canon lawyer Thomas Doyle and plaintiffs' attorney Steve Rubino suggested in a 2004 law review article that "[s]ince 1984, there have been about 3000 civil cases related to clergy sexual abuse throughout the United States." According to a footnote, this estimate was "obtained from unofficial consultations with attorneys and from press reports."[27] In a 2006 book, *Sex, Priests and Secret Codes: The Catholic Church's 2000-Year Paper Trail of Sexual Abuse,* Doyle and his coauthors estimate that "more than two thousand civil and criminal cases alleging sexual abuse of minors have been lodged against the Catholic Church and its representatives in the United States over the past two decades."[28] No evidence for this figure is cited. The John Jay study mentions "more than one thousand pending legal cases."[29]

Even without knowing the total number of lawsuits against the Church, we might still attempt to learn something about litigation trends over time based on more localized data. Let us examine three types of available data: (1) the number of new case files opened by three attorneys with a continuous national practice in clergy sexual abuse dating back to 1984, (2) a database of priest abusers maintained by a web-based clearinghouse for information on clergy sexual abuse, and (3) the volume and frequency of insurance claims for clergy sexual abuse from two insurance companies. It bears repeating that these data samples may not be representative and, at best, offer only an initial glimpse at possible trends. What we shall see is that the data from all of these sources display a similar pattern of increasingly dramatic rises in the number of lawsuits and insurance claims following the Gauthe, Porter, and Geoghan cases, a pattern that is consistent with anecdotal evidence from the previous chapter.

Let us consider first the number of new case files opened by three attorneys with a continuous national practice in clergy sexual abuse dating back to 1984. These three are plaintiffs' attorneys Steve Rubino and Jeff Anderson and former USCCB general counsel Mark Chopko. Rubino opened a total of 2,264 new client files from 1984–2005 involving allegations of clergy sexual abuse. Each file opened was the result of a client intake interview in which abuse was alleged, a perpetrator named, and a jurisdiction identified. The clients were from all over the country, referred by other lawyers based on Rubino's national reputation, and the interviews were conducted primarily by telephone. Only a few of the clients were from New Jersey where Rubino's office is located. The opening of a file did not necessarily result in any action beyond the initial interview.

Data from Anderson represent 1,012 case files opened during this same period. Anderson reported only case files where a client signed a retainer agreement. Anderson did not include in his count case files opened on clergy sexual abuse allegations that did not result in a retainer agreement or case files maintained by attorneys in other firms with whom Anderson collaborated as cocounsel. Moreover, the counts for years prior to 1987 are incomplete since many files opened in these years were not recorded on the firm's computerized case-file tracking system which was established in 1988. Thus, the Anderson data does not represent the total number of cases that Anderson worked on but only those where he had a retainer agreement and where he maintained the file in his office. Not all of the case files reported by Rubino and Anderson involved allegations against Catholic Church defendants.

The USCCB Office of general counsel (OGC), under the direction of Mark Chopko, opened 101 new case files during the 1984–2005 period. The OGC tended to open a file only when the USCCB was likely to be directly involved as a defendant or an amicus curiae. As with the Anderson data, the OGC data represents only a fraction of all of the legal work on clergy sexual abuse cases undertaken by the office.

The data from Rubino, Anderson, and the USCCB OGC are presented in Figure 4. The data from Rubino, with the largest sample of cases, reflects a dramatic rise in the number of case files opened in 1986–1987, 1992–1993, and 2002–2003, at the time of or just after the Gauthe, Porter, and Geoghan cases respectively. The data from Anderson shows a similar rise in 1992 at the time of the Porter case and 2002–2003 following the Geoghan case. It should be noted that while these data reflect a similar pattern of client intake activity at two of the leading firms litigating clergy sexual abuse claims, they do not provide in-

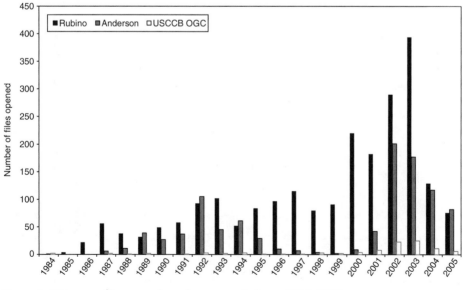

Figure 4. New case files opened on clergy sexual abuse, 1984–2005.

formation about the actual filing of lawsuits. The data from the USCCB OGC are based on legal filings, and they fit this pattern, but the rises are less dramatic and the sample of cases is much smaller.

A database of 2,895 priest abusers maintained by BishopAccount abilty.org records 998 lawsuits filed, 751 of them with filing dates. The BishopAccountabilty.org data is comprised of a database compiled by plaintiffs' attorney Sylvia Demarest and a database created by the web-based organization BishopsWatch.org, merged and updated. The Demarest data was derived largely from legal pleadings and the rest of the data comes primarily from press reports. Figure 5 presents the annual distribution of the 751 lawsuits with filing dates included in the BishopAccount ability.com database. Again, one sees a small rise in the years following the Gauthe case and more dramatic rises in the years following the Porter and Geoghan cases. It is worth noting that neither Demarest nor BishopAccountability.org make any claim that this data is representative.

Two insurance companies provided me with data concerning the number and frequency of insurance claims for clergy sexual misconduct filed under policies issued by them. Both wish to remain anonymous, so I will

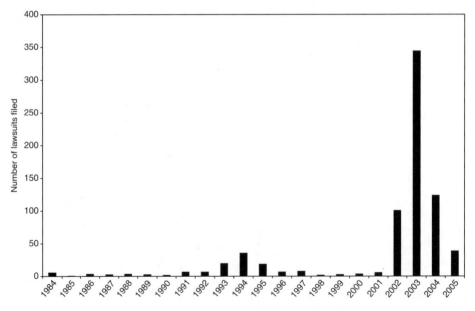

Figure 5. Lawsuits filed based on BishopAccountability.com data base.

refer to them as company A and company B. All of the coverage for clergy sexual misconduct issued by insurance company A between 1989 and 2005 was provided to U.S. Catholic dioceses. The national market share of clergy sexual misconduct coverage for Catholic dioceses issued by company A was 30 percent in 1990, 40 percent in 1995, 45 percent in 2000, and 50 percent in 2005. Between 1989 and 2005, a total of 275 clergy sexual misconduct claims were made against policies issued by company A. Figure 6 presents the annual distribution of these claims. Again, one sees a dramatic rise in the aftermath of the Porter case. A second dramatic rise at the time of the Geoghan case begins in 2001, before the unsealing of court documents and national coverage of the case starting in January 2002. Company A experienced this rise in claims because in that year it settled a large number of claims involving Geoghan. These claims aside, the distribution of claims reflects a second dramatic increase in 2002–2003 following public disclosure of the Geoghan files.

Company B issued liability insurance to Catholic and non-Catholic institutions up until the late 1980s that covered clergy sexual misconduct. Since that time, it has issued clergy sexual misconduct coverage only to non-Catholic institutions. Company B provided information

Figure 6. Number of clergy sexual misconduct claims, insurance company "A."

concerning the frequency of claims for clergy sexual misconduct under policies that it issued between 1984 and 2005. By "frequency" is meant the proportion of claims relative to the number of policies issued in any given year. Company B did not release to me the number of policies issued by it or the number of claims made in any given year. Figure 7 presents this data. Once again, we see the familiar pattern of dramatic rises in claims following the Gauthe, Porter, and Geoghan cases.

While each of these data sets has significant limitations, when taken together they suggest that the number of clergy sexual abuse victims seeking legal assistance and the amount of litigation-related activity rose dramatically following the Gauthe, Porter, and Geoghan cases. This is consistent with anecdotal evidence from the previous chapter suggesting that these cases served as a catalyst to increased litigation. In later chapters we will examine just what made these cases so influential on the course of litigation and, ultimately, on policy responses to the problem of clergy sexual abuse.

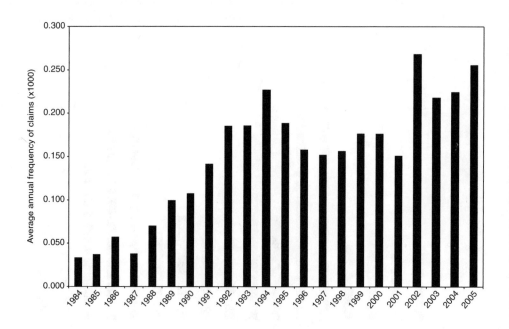

Figure 7. Frequency of clergy sexual misconduct claims, insurance company "B."

CHAPTER THREE

Legal Issues

Clergy sexual abuse lawsuits assert claims against individual priests who commit abuse and institutional defendants such as dioceses and religious orders. Claims against priests typically allege battery: intentional contact with the person of another that is harmful or offensive.[1] This is an uncontroversial theory of recovery, and these claims normally result in either an admission of liability or a relatively straightforward dispute over the facts of what happened. Most priests, however, lack sufficient assets to pay damages. They are named in civil suits primarily to bolster claims against institutional defendants.

Claims against institutional defendants seek to hold a diocese or religious order liable for church officials' failure to properly supervise a priest who commits abuse.[2] These institutional defendants have responded with a broad array of legal defenses. They have argued that church officials lacked knowledge of abuse and that abusers were acting outside the scope of their clerical duties. They have also asserted that claims are barred by statutes of limitation, that the First Amendment forbids courts from defining the supervisory duties of church officials, and that church institutions are protected from liability by charitable immunity. In some cases, defense lawyers have employed litigation tactics that have intimidated plaintiffs or worn them down. As we shall see, many of these defenses have successfully limited the Church's liability while at the same time tarnishing its public image.

Many clergy sexual abuse claims have been resolved through settlement. This is especially true where plaintiffs face significant legal obstacles and church defendants wish to resolve claims quickly without the media attention that normally attends court proceedings. Some dioceses have even established their own mediation and arbitration programs in order to facilitate settlement.

Clergy sexual abuse litigation has increasingly manifested features associated with mass torts: aggregation of claims, coordination among lawyers on both sides, collective settlements that include regulatory terms and administrative procedures for evaluating individual claims, and bankruptcy filings by defendants to limit future liability. These features of clergy sexual abuse litigation have emerged as it has matured, following patterns set by mass tort litigation involving asbestos, Agent Orange, Bendectin, the Dalkon Shield, silicone breast implants, tobacco, and guns. While the first and second waves of clergy sexual abuse litigation were characterized by traditional trials and individual settlements, one cannot understand the third wave without an appreciation for how clergy sexual abuse litigation has become a mass tort.

Another key feature of clergy sexual abuse litigation—one that tends to operate behind the scenes—is insurance coverage. The first wave of litigation took commercial insurance carriers by surprise, and they suffered heavy financial losses. By the 1990s, around the same time that the USCCB was formulating its Five Principles, insurers began to insist that dioceses implement personnel policies designed to reduce clergy sexual abuse as a condition of insurance coverage. Thus, to some degree, church reforms have been driven, or at least reinforced, by insurance carriers.

This chapter examines these various legal issues in lawsuits against dioceses. It examines claims and defenses, settlement practices, the transformation of clergy sexual abuse into a mass tort, and the hidden role of insurance coverage.

Theories of Liability

Theories of institutional liability for clergy sexual abuse fall into two general categories. First are theories of vicarious liability that seek to hold a diocese liable for the misconduct of a priest who commits abuse. Second are theories that focus on diocesan officials' own misconduct in improperly responding to clergy sexual abuse.

Respondeat Superior

Respondeat superior ("let the master answer") is the most common theory of vicarious liability in clergy sexual abuse claims against dioceses.

This doctrine subjects an employer to liability for the misconduct of an employee where (1) there exists a "master-servant" relationship between the employer and employee and (2) the employee was acting within the scope of his employment. In general terms, a master-servant relationship exists where an employer controls the conduct of an employee, for example, by assigning him to perform certain tasks in a certain manner. The law distinguishes between a servant and an "independent contractor," who is paid to perform a service but who controls the terms of his own employment and for whose misconduct the employer is not subject to liability. A shopkeeper who employs a clerk to attend to customers and hires a plumber to fix a leak in the shop has a master-servant relationship with the clerk, whereas the plumber is an independent contractor. The conduct of an employee is within the scope of employment if it is the kind of conduct he is employed to perform, it occurs within a time and space authorized by the employer, and its purpose is, at least in part, to serve the employer. Where the employee commits an intentional wrong, courts may additionally limit the employer's vicarious liability to foreseeable conduct.[3]

Plaintiffs have alleged that dioceses have a master-servant relationship with their priests and that a priest who uses his pastoral role to commit child sexual abuse is acting within the scope of his employment. The diocese, they argue, should therefore be vicariously liable under respondeat superior for abuse committed by a priest. Courts have rejected this theory in many jurisdictions. They have held that the abuse did not fall within the scope of employment because it was not in accordance with the principles of the Church, or it did not have the purpose of furthering the interests of the Church. In some cases, courts have rejected respondeat superior claims on the basis that the abuse was not foreseeable.[4] This theory has not, however, been entirely unsuccessful. The Oregon Supreme Court held that where a priest used his position as a youth pastor to gain access to a child whom he sexually abused, the archdiocese could be held vicariously liable.[5] There are also a handful of reported cases in which lower courts have refused to dismiss respondeat superior claims against dioceses for clergy sexual abuse and a number of jurisdictions where courts have held in other contexts that employers may be vicariously liable for the sexual misconduct of their employees.[6]

Since most litigation outcomes are unreported, it is impossible to know precisely what percentage of respondeat superior claims have resulted in favorable judgments or settlements for plaintiffs. These claims have failed in a majority of reported cases, and roughly half of the states have refused to impose vicarious liability on employers for the sexual misconduct of employees.[7] It is, however, the impression of some veteran lawyers on both sides of the litigation that by 2002, judges were more open to assertions that a priest who used his pastoral role to commit child sexual abuse was acting within the scope of his employment and that such abuse was foreseeable.[8]

Negligence

Under the tort doctrine of negligence, a person is subject to liability if he fails to exercise reasonable care and, as a result, injures another. Negligence liability is limited in two significant ways. First, negligence liability is, for the most part, limited to injuries that one could have foreseen and therefore could have taken care to prevent. Second, one is generally under no duty to prevent even foreseeable injuries where the risk of injury arises out of the conduct of a third party. For example, if an individual learns of a stranger's intention to harm another, the individual is normally under no duty to restrain the stranger or to protect the victim, even if it would be reasonable to do so. Courts do, however, impose such duties where there exists a special relationship between the individual and the injurer or between the individual and the victim. Such special relationships are characterized by the individual's unique capacity to control the risk of harm posed by the third party; for example, a parent's capacity to restrain a violent child or a landlord's capacity to protect tenants from intruders.[9]

In lawsuits against dioceses, plaintiffs have asserted that diocesan officials were negligent in hiring, supervising, and retaining priests with a record of sexual abuse and in failing to warn parishioners in communities where such priests were working. Plaintiffs have pointed to diocesan personnel records—including past allegations and psychiatric evaluations—to show that the risk of abuse was foreseeable. They have further argued that church officials' knowledge of a priest's past record of abuse and their authority over the priest's assignments constitute a special relationship between these officials and the priest that supports a duty to protect parishioners from the priest.[10]

Again, there is no way of knowing just how successful negligence claims have been. Defendants have prevailed in a majority of published cases. Some lawyers in the field, however, have the impression that by 2002, courts and juries viewed negligence claims more favorably. For example, one lawyer suggested that by the third wave of litigation signs of alcohol abuse or personality problems were sufficient to support a finding that sexual abuse by a particular priest was foreseeable.[11] According to plaintiffs' attorney Steve Rubino, "there has been a sea change in the way the judiciary understands this now."[12]

If there has, in fact, been a change over time in judicial attitudes toward clergy sexual abuse claims, it is probably due to some combination of media coverage, changing public attitudes, and the general direction of public policy in the area of sexual abuse. Such changes in judicial attitudes suggest a feedback effect. Just as litigation influences news coverage, public opinion, and policymakers, these in turn influence litigation.[13] We will return to this issue of feedback effects in chapter 8.

Other Theories of Liability

In addition to respondeat superior and negligence, plaintiffs have sued dioceses under theories of breach of fiduciary duty, ratification, and racketeering. A fiduciary duty consists of a legal relationship in which one party, the principal, places trust in the other party, the fiduciary, who is thereby obligated to act for the benefit of the principal. Plaintiffs have alleged that a bishop owes parishioners a fiduciary duty and that failure to protect a parishioner from a priest whom the bishop knows to have a record of sexual abuse is a breach of the bishop's fiduciary duty. Plaintiffs have prevailed in a handful of reported cases on this theory.[14] The doctrine of ratification "imposes liability on an employer when that employer adopts, confirms, or fails to repudiate the unlawful acts of an employee of which the employer is aware."[15] This theory prevailed in the O'Grady case.[16] Finally, plaintiffs have filed claims under the federal Racketeer Influenced and Corrupt Organizations (RICO) Act of 1970, designed to address organized crime. Section 1962(b) of the act prohibits maintaining "any interest in or control of any enterprise" "through a pattern of racketeering activity."[17] Plaintiffs have asserted in some cases that the diocese is an "enterprise" over which the bishop has maintained control through acts of bribery, extortion, mail fraud, and wire fraud in covering up clergy sexual abuse, amounting to a "pattern of racketeering activity."[18] To date, no plaintiff has prevailed on a RICO claim against the Church.

Defenses

In response to plaintiffs' claims, dioceses have asserted a number of affirmative defenses. Asserting these defenses has frequently helped the

Church fend off liability. As we shall see, however, vigorously defending itself in courts of law has cost the Church dearly in the court of public opinion.

Statutes of Limitation

A statute of limitation sets forth a period of time beyond which legal claims are barred. One justification for statutes of limitation is evidentiary—as time passes, memories fade and testimony becomes less reliable, evidence deteriorates or is lost, and witnesses are unavailable. A second justification is administrative—time limits encourage prompt filing of claims and relieve courts of the burden of adjudicating old cases. For most claims arising out of personal injury, the period of limitation begins at the time an injury occurs and runs between one and ten years.

The start of the limitation period may be delayed under certain circumstances. In cases where an injury victim is a minor, most states begin the limitation period when the victim reaches the age of majority. The start of the limitations period may be delayed further where the victim does not discover his or her injury until some time after the injury occurs. In cases of child sexual abuse, some jurisdictions start the limitations period at the time the victim discovers injuries resulting from the abuse or when the victim discovers the connection between those injuries and the abuse.[19]

As the John Jay study shows, most victims of clergy sexual abuse delay making allegations until many years after the abuse occurred. Church defendants typically argue that claims based on delayed allegations are barred by the statute of limitations. Explains former USCCB general counsel Mark Chopko, "most of the abuse that's alleged dates [back to the early 1970s], so we're dealing with an inventory of old cases, and that means that from a defensive perspective we have used and we will continue to defend ourselves on the basis of the statute of limitations."[20] According to plaintiffs' attorney Steve Rubino, statutes of limitation are "an overwhelming source of dismissal" in "thousands" of cases, and he estimates that, in his experience, 80 or 90 percent of claims are barred by the statute of limitations.[21]

For many dioceses, employing a statute-of-limitation defense is not designed to avoid liability altogether, but only to limit it. As former defense attorney (and now federal district judge) Patrick Schiltz explains, "I believe a church has a moral duty to help someone sexually abused by one of its pastors—no matter when the abuse occurred—but this does not mean it also has a moral duty to let a jury determine what it must pay to a plaintiff, or a moral duty to pay a defense attorney tens of thousands of dollars to defend the case, or a moral duty to pay a plaintiff's attorney tens of thousands of dollars for bringing the case."[22] Albany Bishop Howard Hubbard similarly explains that his diocese established a mediation program for clergy sexual abuse in order to "recognize and accept our moral responsibilities and provide an alternative to litigation, but at the same time, if people choose to go to the courts, then we certainly have exercised our right to invoke the statute of limitations."[23]

The success of statute-of-limitation defenses is a mixed blessing for church defendants. On the one hand, statutes of limitation have saved the Church from potentially devastating liability. On the other hand, they have opened up the Church to charges that it is using a legal technicality to avoid liability in cases where it is clear that abuse occurred and that church officials facilitated it. As Schiltz points out, "defending on the basis of the statute of limitations is not easy . . . Jurors dislike statutes of limitations; if a jury believes that a plaintiff was abused and that a church was negligent, it will usually hold the church responsible no matter what the statute of limitations provides." Thus, counsels Schiltz, when relying on a statute of limitation, the defense attorney should aim to have the case dismissed prior to trial.[24]

In order to avoid a statute-of-limitation defense, plaintiffs often allege that they only recently discovered injuries resulting from the abuse or traced those injuries back to the abuse. Legal allegations of delayed discovery are supported by expert opinion. Dr. Mic Hunter, a leading authority on the sexual abuse of boys, maintains that "[s]ome of the effects of sexual abuse do not become apparent until the victim is an adult and a major life event, such as a marriage or birth of a child takes place. Therefore, a child who seemed unharmed by childhood abuse can develop crippling symptoms years later and can have a difficult time connecting his adulthood problems with his past."[25]

In some cases, plaintiffs have invoked the controversial theory of recovered memory. This theory asserts that memories of a traumatic event may be repressed and later recovered in therapy or as a result of some event that triggers the memory. The reliability of memories that were allegedly repressed at the time of abuse and recovered many years later in therapy is a source of ongoing professional and public controversy.[26] Skepticism among psychologists about the recovered memory theory is frequently cited by commentators critical of clergy sexual abuse litigation. Dorothy Rabinowitz of the *Wall Street Journal* has suggested that allowing claims alleging recovered memory to go forward has "resulted in a system that rewarded false claims along with the true."[27] Alexander Cockburn of the *Nation,* in an editorial entitled "Back to Salem," denounced recovered memory theory as the "tool of [a] latter-day Inquisition."[28] Martin Gardiner of the *Skeptical Inquirer* concluded that "[w]hen claims are made about revived memories of pedophilia—recollections said to be repressed until uncovered decades later by suggestive therapy or by a triggering event—they should be considered fabricated fantasies unless they can be corroborated by a confession or by strong independent evidence."[29]

Concern about reliance on recovered memories and the danger of false accusations was heightened in 1994 by Steven Cook's withdrawal of his lawsuit against Cardinal Bernardin in Chicago amid revelations that his allegations were based on memories recovered under hypnosis with an unlicensed therapist. A 2004 settlement of $1.4 million with the Boston archdiocese in a lawsuit arising out of alleged sexual abuse by Father Paul Shanley, as well as Shanley's subsequent criminal conviction, were both based on recovered memories, and that case also became a lighting rod for criticism of clergy sexual abuse litigation.[30]

Skepticism over recovered memory has fueled a small backlash against clergy sexual abuse litigation that is part of larger reaction against zealous prosecution of child sexual abuse allegations that dates back to the mid-1980s. Fanciful accounts of ritual abuse given by children pressured to make allegations and bolstered by professional child sexual abuse experts have resulted in highly controversial convictions in a number of high profile cases. Journalist Debbie Nathan and lawyer Michael Snedeker have characterized these prosecutions as a "Modern American Witch Hunt."[31] Organizations such as Victims of Child Abuse Laws (VOCAL) and the False Memory Syndrome Foundation rose up in the 1980s and 1990s to support those accused of child sexual abuse and to advocate for law reforms that would prevent wrongful conviction.[32]

One must be careful not to overstate the role of recovered memory in clergy sexual abuse allegations or the incidence of false accusations. First, since claiming recovered memory is one way to overcome statute of limitations problems, clergy sexual abuse litigation makes the frequency of recovered memory among victims appear to be greater than it really is. Plaintiffs' attorney Sylvia Demarest explains that "the problems that were created by statutes of limitation led creative lawyers to try to do what they could to be able to help their clients . . . I don't think there's any question that to some degree recovered memory happens. But was it a true recovered memory situation or was it something where you just didn't want to think about it, but it was available to you?"[33] Second, most plaintiffs seeking to avoid dismissal of their claims under the statute of limitations do not allege recovered memory but rather delayed discovery of injury—claiming that, although they never forgot the abuse, they did not identify the damage that it caused or they did not attribute that damage to the abuse until much later. Third, responses by dioceses to the John Jay survey reflect a very low rate of false allegations. Respondents to the survey reported only 409 out of 10,667 allegations (4 percent) to be false.[34] Writes former defense attorney Schiltz, "In fewer than ten of the 500-plus sexual misconduct cases on which I worked did I even suspect the complaint was false. Plaintiffs will exaggerate and embellish, sometimes a great deal, but, if a plaintiff claims that she had sexual contact with a pastor, there is nearly a 98 percent chance that *something* happened. In the rare cases in which the allegations are completely false . . . the allegations are usually accompanied by such large red flags that the cases never reach trial."[35] Fourth, and finally, even the critical commentators quoted above are careful to point out that "Most of the cases against priests for sexual abuse against young parishioners are supported by full confessions or independent evidence of guilt," and that most allegations "had to do with charges all too amply documented . . . that involved true predators."[36]

In some jurisdictions, victims' groups and plaintiffs' attorneys have pursued a legislative strategy to overcome statute-of-limitation defenses. Many states have extended their statutes of limitation on child sexual abuse.[37] In 2002 the California state legislature retroactively suspended the statute of limitation on child sexual abuse claims for one year starting on January 1, 2003.[38] This led plaintiffs to file over 850 lawsuits in California courts. Delaware passed a similar measure in 2007.[39] Some states have made the statute of limitations defense more fact intensive—for example, by allowing a plaintiff's delayed discovery of harm to toll the statute. This has foreclosed early dismissal of claims based only on initial pleadings, motivating defendants to settle rather than face discovery.[40]

First Amendment

The First Amendment to the U.S. Constitution states that "Congress shall make no law respecting the establishment of religion, or prohibiting the free exercise thereof." The U.S. Supreme Court has held that this limitation on federal law applies also, through the principle of incorporation into the Fourteenth Amendment, to state law. Dioceses have asserted that the use of state tort law to hold them liable for clergy sexual abuse violates both the establishment and free exercise clauses of the Constitution.

The Supreme Court has held that the establishment clause prohibits laws that produce excessive government entanglement with religion.[41] Church defendants have asserted that allowing courts to determine the standards of reasonable conduct in the hiring, supervision, and retention of priests would put judges and juries in the business of determining how church officials should conduct their internal affairs. This, they suggest, would constitute excessive government entanglement with religion. Plaintiffs have countered that holding employers liable for failing to exercise reasonable care is part of the routine business of courts that does not rise to the level of excessive entanglement as defined by the Supreme Court. Some courts have dismissed claims on establishment grounds, while others have refused to do so.[42]

In evaluating free exercise claims, the Supreme Court distinguishes between laws specifically aimed at burdening religious practice and neutral laws of general applicability that only incidentally burden religious practice. Laws specifically aimed at burdening religious practice violate the free exercise clause unless they are narrowly tailored to advance a compelling governmental interest. Whether the government's interest is compelling depends, in part, on the value of the free exercise rights that the law infringes. In practice, such laws are normally struck down as unconstitutional. By contrast, neutral laws of general applicability need only be rationally related to a legitimate government interest, and they are, in practice, normally upheld. Neutral laws that are applied on the basis of a case-by-case individual assessment, however, are subject to the higher standard.

Church defendants assert that tort law, while a neutral law, is applied on a case-by-case basis. Thus, they argue, imposing liability on church defendants violates the free exercise clause unless plaintiffs can show that it is narrowly tailored to advance a compelling government interest and that that interest—the prevention of child sexual abuse—outweighs the value of the self-regulation of religious bodies free from government interference. Plaintiffs respond that respondeat superior and common-law negligence principles are neutral laws of general applicability. Again, some courts have struck down claims based on the free exercise clause, while others have refused to do so.[43]

The First Amendment also prohibits courts from resolving disputes on the basis of the court's own interpretation of religious doctrine. This prohibition is rooted in both the establishment and free-exercise clauses: were a court to decide matters of religious doctrine, this would constitute government establishment of a religious principle and suppression of alternative interpretations. Church defendants have argued that plaintiffs' claims require courts to interpret religious doctrine. For example, respondeat superior claims call on courts to define the nature of the relationship between a priest and his bishop and the scope of a priest's religious duties within the Church. Similarly, claims based on breach of fiduciary duty ask courts to define the duties owed by a bishop to the members of the diocese. According to defendants, resolving these claims would require a court to interpret canon law which defines the relationships between bishops, priests, and parishioners. Plaintiffs respond that the duties of employers and caretakers—religious or secular—are matters of common law that can be determined by courts without reference to canon law. Once again, some courts have dismissed claims based on the First Amendment prohibition on interpreting religious doctrine, while others have not.[44]

Church defendants have also raised the First Amendment in discovery. They have asserted that, under the free exercise clause, a bishop may not be compelled to produce documents in violation of a canon law requirement that he keep them secret. The results of this argument for the Church have been mixed.[45]

It is impossible to know whether First Amendment defenses have generally prevailed or gained or lost currency over the course of clergy sexual abuse litigation. The reported cases do not appear to favor either side or suggest a trend.[46] Some veteran lawyers on both sides have the impression that First Amendment defenses have become less successful over time. Plaintiffs' attorney Steve Rubino suggests that the Kos case was a "milestone" in terms of First Amendment defenses. "Prior to the Kos case," explains Rubino, "state trial judges were intimidated by First Amendment arguments raised by defendants." After the highly publicized Kos verdict, he asserts, courts were more willing to reject First Amendment defenses.[47] A defense lawyer who requested anonymity suggests that the Boston scandal "destroyed the First Amendment defense" beginning with a highly publicized decision in the Geoghan case and the negative media portrayal of Cardinal Law's attempts to use the First Amendment to protect the archdiocese from liability.[48]

Comparative Negligence and Assumption of Risk

Tort law reduces the recovery of plaintiffs whose own negligence contributes to their injury, and it bars recovery altogether by plaintiffs who knowingly assume the risk that caused their injury. In some cases, dioceses have suggested that victims were negligent or assumed the risk of abuse by spending time with a priest after being previously abused by him.[49] Dioceses have also argued that victims' parents were negligent in allowing their children to spend time in the unsupervised care of a priest, especially where there were indications of excessive interest on the part of the priest or unusual behavior on the part of the victim. In addition, dioceses have asserted that parents were negligent in subjecting their children to the trauma of litigation, thereby exacerbating the initial injury from the abuse.

In the Gauthe case, for example, defense attorney Bob Wright told jurors that Scott Gastals' parents were negligent for not having investigated Gauthe before allowing their son to spend the night with him in the rectory and for failing to intercede when Scott's behavior changed as a result of the abuse.[50] In court papers, Wright asserted that both parents "contributed to the damages allegedly sustained by their son, Scott Gastal, by their actions in deciding to publicize the matter, contrary to the specific advices of the treating psychologist at the time and the dictates of reasonable parental care."[51]

The Boston archdiocese raised a similar defense almost two decades later in a 2002 lawsuit brought by victims of Father Paul Shanley. However, when plaintiffs' counsel Eric MacLeish confronted Cardinal Law during a deposition with a pleading asserting comparative negligence, Law distanced himself from his lawyers and was unwilling to assert the defense with any conviction:

> *MacLeish:* Are you aware of any set of facts that could conceivably support the argument that a six-year-old child could in any way be responsible for his abuse by a Roman Catholic priest?

Law: As I indicated earlier, Mr. MacLeish, I have not seen this document before now. I was being represented in this document by counsel. I did not enter into the formulation of that response, and so I haven't a basis upon which to engage in a response on this. If you're asking me personally if a six-year-old child could have contributed negligence in a case like this, I would say the answer to that is clearly no.

MacLeish: What about the parents, Cardinal Law? Can you in any way conceive of a set of facts that would support the assertion that the parents of a six-year-old child could somehow be negligent with respect to the sexual abuse of their child by a Roman Catholic priest?

Law: Mr. MacLeish, I can answer that theoretically. I cannot answer that with specificity to the parents of this child because I have no facts concerning the parents of this child. But theoretically, I would suppose that one could presume that if parents were to put their child in the position of jeopardy for someone whom they suspected to be a risk, there would be some degree of negligence there. But I say that's a theoretical response. It in no way moves to the victim himself or herself, and it no way mitigates the responsibility of the person who would have committed the abuse. But could there be contributory negligence on the part of those who have supervision? I presume that, theoretically, that could be the case. But, again, I respond that under the terms of the specific case before us, I have no knowledge whatsoever of contributory negligence.[52]

Assertions of comparative negligence have done little to advance the Church's prospects in litigation, and they have caused considerable damage to its public image. As former defense counsel Schiltz put it, "Never, ever blame a child for being sexually abused. It is morally wrong, legally indefensible, and tactically moronic."[53]

Charitable Immunity and Damage Caps

Traditionally at common law, charitable institutions were immune from tort liability. Courts justified charitable immunity as necessary to prevent charitable donations from being used to satisfy tort judgments and to protect charities from potentially bankrupting liability. Beginning in the 1940s, state courts began to abolish common-law charitable immunity, and today only a minority of jurisdictions still have it. In some jurisdictions where courts overturned the doctrine, legislatures responded by providing statutory immunity or damage caps for charitable institutions.[54]

In some jurisdictions, courts have dismissed clergy sexual abuse claims based on charitable immunity.[55] Moreover, it is likely that charitable immunity and damage caps have discouraged many victims from filing suit in the first place. Victims' groups and plaintiffs' lawyers have actively lobbied state legislatures to abolish protections for charities against liability.[56] It is interesting to note, however, that even where these protections exist, they have not always prevented plaintiffs from securing favorable settlements. For example, although Massachusetts has a statutory cap of $20,000 on tort claims against charitable institutions, the Boston archdiocese has settled hundreds of claims for much more than $20,000 per victim.

Clergy-Communicant Privilege

All fifty states provide some form of statutory privilege for communications between clergy and those who confide in them. The clergy-communicant privilege has its roots in the seal of confession, a canon law principle that prohibits a priest from disclosing information communicated by a penitent as part of the sacramental confession of sins. The privilege was first recognized in an 1813 New York case, *People v. Phillips,* in which the court upheld a Roman Catholic priest's right not to testify based on his adherence to the seal of confession. Since that time, the privilege has been broadened to encompass non-Catholic clergy and those who confide in them. Most jurisdictions limit the privilege to communications made to a clergy member acting in his or her spiritual capacity in the context of a spiritual counseling relationship. In most states the privilege belongs to the communicant, but in a minority of states the clergy member holds the privilege. The privilege was originally justified in *Phillips* on the basis of the free exercise clause of the New York State Constitution. Since then, some commentators have suggested that it is grounded in the constitutional right to privacy, but most courts currently defend it on policy grounds as a means of fostering socially beneficial relationships between clergy and those who turn to them for help.[57]

In clergy sexual abuse litigation, accused priests and church officials have invoked the clergy-communicant privilege as a means of preventing discovery of conversations and diocesan files. For example, the L.A. archdiocese has asserted claims of privilege in resisting discovery requests and grand jury subpoenas for particular diocesan personnel files that include communications concerning sexual abuse and psychiatric evaluations. Cardinal Mahony has argued that confidentiality is essential to a bishop's ability to care for the physical, emotional, and spiritual well-being of his priests, as required by Catholic doctrine. Personal communications in the context of this pastoral relationship, he contends, are protected by a clergy-communicant privilege grounded in the free exercise clause, the right to privacy, and the social value of such relationships. In addition, diocesan priests have asserted a related psychotherapist-patient privilege to prevent the release of psychiatric evaluations in their diocesan personnel files.[58]

Litigation and settlement negotiations in California have been dominated by discovery battles involving claims of privilege. The courts have, by and large, been unsympathetic to these claims, especially given that the privilege—whether grounded in policy or the Constitution—must be weighed against the government's interest in protecting children from sexual abuse. Moreover, Cardinal Mahony's widely publicized assertions of privilege have done little to enhance the Church's reputation for transparency and contrition.[59]

Litigation Tactics

Tort litigation, even in the best of circumstances, takes a toll on plaintiffs. Under the rules of civil procedure, defendants have the right to request dismissal of claims, resist discovery, depose plaintiffs and witnesses, obtain documents, and countersue. These litigation tools are essential to defendants' ability to defend themselves against unfounded claims of liability and, in cases where they admit liability or are found liable, to limit damages. At the same time, defendants' use of motion practice, discovery, and counterclaims draws out litigation and subjects plaintiffs to unwanted scrutiny and counterallegations.

In some cases, church defendants have employed these tools to wear down and intimidate plaintiffs. Dioceses have fought aggressively to resist plaintiffs' discovery requests and delayed compliance with discovery orders. In depositions, defense attorneys have asked victims whether they enjoyed the abuse and have compelled victims to discuss embarrassing matters such as sexual affairs, substance abuse, criminal convictions, homosexuality, and abortions, the revelation of which cause irreparable harm to the victim's personal life and reputation. Dioceses have reportedly hired private investigators to uncover such embarrassing information by following victims, talking to their neighbors, contacting their employers, and going through their trash. Dioceses have also subpoenaed victims' therapy records. In several cases, dioceses have filed counterclaims against victims' parents, alleging that they were negligent in entrusting their child to the unsupervised care of a priest or in failing to uncover the abuse. In cases where plaintiffs have filed as "John Doe," in order to remain anonymous, dioceses have litigated to force them to refile using their real names. The father of one victim reports that diocesan attorneys subjected him to 120 hours of deposition, his wife to eighty hours of deposition, and his victimized ten-year-old son to several hours of aggressive videotaped deposition. Dioceses have also filed libel actions against plaintiffs for making allegations in the first place. Such tactics have caused plaintiffs to settle quietly or abandon their claims altogether.[60]

The use of hardball litigation tactics to wear down and intimidate victims is reported by both plaintiffs' and defense attorneys, and lawyers on both sides condemn it. Writes Villanova Law School dean Mark Sargent in an article offering advice about how to defend the Church in clergy sexual abuse lawsuits, "[w]here liability is clear and the damages sought are reasonable, resistance for the sake of intimidation of both present and future plaintiffs is unworthy of and dangerous for a religious institution that must seek the moral high ground."[61] Former defense attorney Schiltz asserts that hardball tactics are not only immoral but also imprudent: "a church must act like a church, and it is morally questionable for an attorney representing a church in essence to take advantage of the damage caused by one of the church's pastors. Moreover, from a tactical perspective, if the defense attorney is too aggressive about raising the plaintiff's problems, then he risks having the jury dislike him for attacking—'re-victimizing'—the plaintiff."[62]

While there is widespread agreement that defense attorneys have used hardball tactics, it is difficult to gauge how frequently they are employed. Plaintiffs' attorney Rubino estimates "in a majority of cases," while former defense attorney Schiltz asserts that they are "exceedingly rare."[63] One reason for this disparity may be that each side perceives defense efforts differently. Former USCCB general counsel Chopko explains that deposing plaintiffs and asserting affirmative defenses is necessary to verifying the legitimacy of plaintiffs' claims, preventing exaggeration of damages, and fulfilling church officials' duty to preserve the financial health of the diocese.[64] A libel action may be the only means for a priest or church official to publicly salvage his reputation in the aftermath of a false allegation. From the plaintiffs' perspective, questioning a victim's credibility in a deposition deprives the victim of the very need for validation that leads many, if not most, victims to litigate; scrutinizing the details of abuse and exposing personal information compounds the sense of shame, feelings of violation, and difficulties with intimacy that are among the deepest injuries of childhood sexual abuse; and prolonging the ordeal of litigation makes it harder for victims to obtain a measure of closure and move forward. Merely defending against a libel action can cost thousands of dollars in attorney's fees, and losing one can mean financial ruin.

Despite the difficulty of estimating the frequency of hardball tactics designed to wear down and intimidate plaintiffs, a few things are clear. First, while there is significant difference of opinion about what counts as hardball tactics, no one denies that litigation takes a toll on victims of clergy sexual abuse. Second, while no one admits to using hardball tactics—diocesan attorneys insist that only insurance company lawyers use hardball tactics, and insurance company lawyers insist that only diocesan attorneys do—everyone agrees that motion practice, discovery objections, depositions, and counterclaims have been used to wear down and intimidate victims. Third, while vigorously defending clergy abuse lawsuits has served dioceses well in the litigation arena, it has damaged the Church's public image. Fourth, and finally, the Church's efforts to defend itself in litigation—by invoking statutes of limitation and charitable immunity, asserting constitutional and common-law privileges, alleging comparative negligence and assumption of the risk, and employing aggressive litigation tactics—have angered victims and plaintiffs' attorneys, many of whom cite anger at the Church as a key motivation for filing lawsuits in the first place and litigating them aggressively.[65]

Settlement

In tort litigation, trials are relatively rare because 98 percent of tort claims are resolved by settlement or other nontrial dispositions.[66] The predominance of settlement does not mean, however, that tort law is irrelevant. Rather, scholars suggest, parties bargain "in the shadow of the law"—that is, settlement terms are influenced by how the parties think they would do if they decided to go to court.[67]

Clergy sexual abuse litigation departs from this norm insofar as dioceses have settled many claims that church lawyers believe would otherwise be dismissed based on the statute of limitations or charitable immunity. Dioceses are often motivated by a desire to put an end to the scandal as quickly as possible. As one attorney involved in the Boston litigation explained, "These cases in Boston were settled without regard to the cap and without regard to the fact that the insurance companies were disclaiming liability. They were settled on the basis that we cannot get past this scandal—we cannot get past this crisis and resume our role as a church ministering to people—until this goes away."[68] One might say that in clergy sexual abuse litigation, parties have bargained more in the shadow of scandal than in the shadow of the law.

Clergy Sexual Abuse as a Mass Tort

Mass tort litigation is characterized by a large number of claims arising from a common source—for example, an airplane crash, a hotel fire, a toxic chemical spill, or a harmful product. The similarity of individual claims and cooperation among plaintiffs' lawyers often leads to the aggregation of claims, either through formal mechanisms like class-action lawsuits or through less formal arrangements between attorneys who share information and coordinate their litigation strategies. Defendants, facing large numbers of claims and frequently uncertain future liability in cases where victims may develop or become aware of their injuries years after their exposure to a harmful chemical or product, may also seek to aggregate claims in order to facilitate a global and final settlement.[69]

Clergy sexual abuse litigation has developed many features characteristic of mass tort litigation. Since the first wave, there has been a great deal of coordination among lawyers on both sides. Experienced plaintiffs' attorneys such as Jeff Anderson and Steve Rubino have consulted in thousands of cases nationwide, and professional groups like the Child Sexual Abuse Litigation Group organized by the Association of Trial Lawyers of America (ATLA, now the American Association for Justice, AAJ) have served as clearinghouses for information and expertise. On the defense side, USCCB staff attorneys like Mark Chopko have been assisting diocesan attorneys around the country defending clergy sexual abuse claims, and the National Diocesan Attorneys Association has provided opportunities for mutual support. Among insurance counsel, insurance companies and industry groups facilitate communication among attorneys by hosting meetings and publishing materials on trends in clergy sexual abuse litigation and how to best handle claims.

Another related mass tort trend in clergy sexual abuse litigation is aggregation of claims. Some forms of aggregation are formal, such as the filing of class-action lawsuits against dioceses in Los Angeles; San Diego; Portland, Oregon; Chicago; Detroit; Philadelphia; Patterson, New Jersey; Louisville, Kentucky, and Covington, Kentucky. In California, pretrial proceedings in over 850 lawsuits have been coordinated into three geographic groups known as Clergy I (Los Angeles and Orange), Clergy II (San Diego and San Bernardino), and Clergy III (Northern California).[70] More frequent are informal methods of aggregation that rely on cooperation between plaintiffs' attorneys. For example, plaintiffs' attorneys in Boston and Los Angeles have teamed up in order to present a united front in settlement negotiations.[71]

Collective settlements with regulatory terms and administrative procedures for determining compensation are another mass tort feature of clergy sexual abuse litigation. In the first and second waves of litigation, dioceses typically entered into settlement agreements with individual plaintiffs that bound them to confidentiality. Collective settlement of sixty-eight Porter claims in 1992 was a notable exception and a precursor to the more frequent collective settlements that later became typical. The third wave brought hundreds of simultaneous claims against dioceses from Boston to Los Angeles, and these have been more typically settled en masse. These third-wave settlements have been highly publicized in the national media. A few settlements have also included regulatory terms, such as making church records public, requiring dioceses to establish procedures for reporting future abuse, and establishing victim counseling programs.[72] Many settlements employ administrative procedures for evaluating individual claims. These procedures include mediation and arbitration of claims, independent investigation, and valuation of claims using a chart that classifies claims according to variables such as the type, frequency, and duration of the abuse.[73] The use of such injury valuation grids are a standard tool in mass tort settlements.[74]

Bankruptcy has become yet another mass tort feature of clergy sexual abuse. In some cases, insurers have refused to cover claims, and dioceses fear financial ruin. In addition, injuries from clergy sexual abuse may not be discovered for many years. For defendants, this means that settling claims or paying judgments now does not foreclose future claims, and liability remains open-ended. This sort of uncertainty can undermine the operations of even the most secure and profitable institutional defendants. One means of staving off financial ruin and limiting future liability is to file for Chapter 11 bankruptcy.[75]

Chapter 11 bankruptcy entails court-supervised reorganization of a corporation's financial obligations with the goal of allowing the corporation to remain in business (as opposed to other forms of bankruptcy that liquidate a company's assets in order to satisfy creditors). Chapter 11 bankruptcy has been used in mass tort litigation to allow a corporate defendant to set up a trust fund out of which all existing and future liability will be paid. Bankruptcy reorganization thus enables a defendant to survive otherwise ruinous liability and to set a determinate limit on how much the defendant will have to pay in order to satisfy future claims.

The use of Chapter 11 bankruptcy to resolve mass tort claims was pioneered in asbestos litigation, and employed subsequently in Dalkon Shield and breast implant litigation. In response to clergy sexual abuse claims, dioceses in Tucson, Portland, Spokane, San Diego, and Davenport, Iowa, have filed for bankruptcy, and others may follow. In 2002, the Diocese of Tucson settled eleven lawsuits for $14 million. Two years later, facing a new wave of suits, the diocese filed for bankruptcy which resulted in the establishment of a $22 million trust fund for fifty victims and family members, including $5 million set aside for future claims. The Portland archdiocese, after paying out $56 million to settle 150 claims, filed for bankruptcy and eventually agreed to establish a $75 million fund to settle 177 lawsuits, with $20 million for future claims. Under similar circumstances, the Spokane diocese's bankruptcy produced a $48 million settlement with 170 victims and family members, with $1 million for future claims. In San Diego, a bankruptcy judge ruled that the diocese had improperly failed to disclose all of its assets and had not reported the fair market value of some of its property. The judge further ruled that forty-two claims could proceed to trial and scheduled a hearing on whether to reject the diocese's bankruptcy claim as meritless. Shortly thereafter, the diocese settled 144 claims against it for $198 million. The Davenport bankruptcy resulted in a $37 million settlement. Payouts to victims and family members in all of these bankruptcies ranged from $15,000 to $2 million.[76]

Bankruptcy can be a way of equitably distributing compensation among victims. Through litigation, the assets of a corporation can be depleted by those who sue first, leaving those who sue later with inadequate compensation. A bankruptcy-created trust can preserve funds for victims who are slow to make claims, and it can determine compensation based on the severity of harm rather than the order in which claims are filed.

Some plaintiffs and commentators, however, have argued that diocesan bankruptcy filings are not really about saving the church from financial ruin or ensuring equity for victims. Critics contend that church defendants are using bankruptcy to avoid litigation. A bankruptcy filing initiates an automatic stay of pending tort litigation against the debtor. Critics assert that church defendants have filed for bankruptcy in order to stop discovery, avoid high-profile trials in pending suits, and cause delays designed to wear down plaintiffs and pressure them to settle on terms more favorable to the church.[77]

Plaintiffs and commentators also argue that church defendants are using bankruptcy as an end run around the statute of limitations. Settlements arising out of bankruptcy cover future claimants, offering them compensation but barring them from filing suit, even where the statute of limitations on their claims has not expired. Critics of these settlements assert that this deprives victims of legal rights without their consent. It remains an open question whether a federal bankruptcy court can limit future claims that would otherwise be allowed under a state's statute of limitations.[78]

Finally, plaintiffs and commentators have suggested that church defendants are using bankruptcy to shield church assets. Dioceses have asserted that, under canon law, church properties belong to local parishes, not the diocese, and cannot therefore be used to compensate victims. While this claim could be made in state and federal trial courts in response to individual plaintiffs seeking to execute judgments against a diocese, a bankruptcy proceeding consolidates all such potential claims, gathers input from all stakeholders, and provides a single, definitive answer. Bankruptcy courts in the Portland and Spokane cases rejected the argument, but the Spokane decision was reversed on appeal, and the issue remains an open question with widespread implications for current and future litigants around the country.[79]

Insurance Coverage

Three commonly mentioned benefits of the tort system are injury compensation, risk reduction, and loss spreading. Behind the scenes, liability insurance plays a vital role in each of these three tasks. Liability insurance provides the funds necessary to compensate injury victims through settlements and judgments. Without liability insurance, many defendants simply could not afford to pay, and victims would be left undercompensated.

Liability insurance also facilitates tort law's ability to reduce risk. Most individuals are not trained in the law and are not aware of their liability exposure. Liability insurers, however, are in the business of estimating liability exposure, and they reduce the risks posed by their insureds by excluding certain activities from coverage, which puts insureds on notice that they are not covered and discourages them from engaging in those activities. Insurers also insist that insureds institute risk-reduction policies as a condition of coverage.

And finally, liability insurance spreads the cost of liability among all insureds who participate in an insurance pool created by the insurer. Insurance thus protects defendants from financial ruin as a result of liability. Insurance carriers themselves spread loss by purchasing their own insurance—known as "reinsurance"—against claims beyond what they could afford to pay.

Liability insurance for clergy sexual misconduct has been an important aspect of clergy sexual abuse litigation. The Gauthe case and the first wave of clergy sexual abuse litigation took insurance carriers completely by surprise. Insurers had long provided liability coverage to church institutions in the form of general liability and professional liability policies. So unexpected were clergy sexual abuse claims that they were not contemplated by underwriters when setting premiums. So large were the claims that they qualified for reinsurance. Explains Michael Bemi, president and CEO of The National Catholic Risk Retention Group, one of the primary liability insurance providers to the Catholic Church, "[T]he Gauthe claims, we've all since learned, were just the tip of the iceberg. But they were spectacular at the time and [reinsurance] underwriters at Lloyd's . . . took 100 percent loss ratios [i.e., zero profit on the coverage sold], simply based on sexual misconduct claims that they never expected to pay because they didn't think there were going to be sexual misconduct claims. Meanwhile they were paying for church fires, and for kids being run over in school yards by buses, grandma falling down the cathedral steps after Midnight Mass, or roof damage from ice and snow, so on and so forth. So they really took a beating."[80] Reeling from their losses and unable to predict the risk of future liability, commercial insurance companies excluded coverage for clergy sexual misconduct altogether in the late 1980s. To fill the gap, insurance brokers began to organize dioceses into self-insurance pools, known as risk retention groups. By the early 1990s, commercial insurers began once again to offer coverage for clergy sexual misconduct.

Risk retention groups and commercial insurers have offered this new coverage under special sexual misconduct insurance policies subject to a number of conditions. Policies provide limited coverage. For example, policies often exclude from coverage claims involving a previously identified perpetrator or abuse that occurred prior to a certain year. Many insurers also require that dioceses implement risk management programs that include policies for screening personnel, guidelines for interacting with children, and procedures for investigating and responding to allegations.[81]

Because so many clergy sexual abuse claims are based on abuse that occurred decades ago, liability insurance has not provided adequate protection for the Church. Church officials frequently cannot locate copies of old policies. Even when they can, the carriers that issued them may no longer be in business. And even when the carriers are still in business, exclusions or ambiguities in the policy language may embroil a diocese and its insurance carrier in time-consuming and costly litigation. And even when coverage is undisputed, claims may quickly exceed coverage limits. Newer policies, with their numerous exclusions and deductibles, do not provide adequate coverage. For example, The National Catholic Risk Retention Group, which is comprised of sixty-four dioceses and archdioceses, rejects the overwhelming majority of claims made by its members. Explains president and CEO Bemi, "of all of the sexual misconduct claims that have been reported to us historically, on average in any given year, in excess of 90 percent—most recently the average was about 93 percent—will be denied by us. And that is a function of the claims being pre-retro to us [i.e., based on abuse that occurred prior to 1988 and therefore excluded from coverage] . . . or . . . it was clear that the diocese had knowledge but did not report to us within the 120 days that our forms stipulate to report the claim to us or because we're an excess carrier and we don't [cover the first] $250,000 of loss from ground, . . . and the claim . . . is just not big enough to get to us."[82] In the case of risk retention groups, disputes over coverage are not merely conflicts between dioceses and their insurance carriers but also conflicts among dioceses. Risk retention groups deny or limit coverage when dealing with one diocese in order to protect the availability of coverage for the other dioceses within the group.[83] Current estimates indicate that of the more than $2.6 billion paid by the Church in response to clergy sexual abuse claims, less than 30 percent was covered by insurance.[84]

An appreciation for the role of insurance is essential to understanding the policy impact of clergy sexual abuse litigation. Risk management programs imposed by insurers as a condition of coverage appeared in the late 1980s and early 1990s—the same time that individual dioceses and the NCCB were developing new policies to respond to clergy sexual abuse. At the very least, these policies reinforced the efforts of reform proponents within the Church and, in some dioceses, they likely played an even more significant role in changing church policy.[85] The chapters that follow examine more closely the influence of tort litigation and insurance on policy responses to clergy sexual abuse.

PART TWO

Litigation and Policymaking

Private lawsuits have influenced the efforts of church officials, law enforcement, and legislators to craft policies aimed at addressing clergy sexual abuse. This part of the book examines three ways in which clergy sexual abuse litigation has influenced policymaking. Chapter 4 argues that litigation framed clergy sexual abuse as a problem of institutional failure on the part of church officials. Chapter 5 claims that litigation placed clergy sexual abuse on the policy agendas of church and government officials. And chapter 6 asserts that litigation generated information that has been essential to understanding the nature and scope of the problem.

CHAPTER FOUR

Framing Clergy Sexual Abuse as a Problem of Institutional Failure

This moral ineptitude in giving greater priority to the Church's image than to the protection of children has now become the scandal.

—BISHOP HOWARD HUBBARD

In lawsuits against the Catholic Church, plaintiffs have framed clergy sexual abuse as not merely a problem of child exploitation by individual clergy members but also as an issue of institutional failure on the part of church officials. This frame of institutional failure quickly became the dominant frame in news media coverage of the issue, and it was widely accepted among the general public, the Catholic laity, government officials, and church leaders. The USCCB's own National Review Board for the Protection of Children and Young People declared in its 2004 *Report on the Crisis in the Catholic Church in the United States* that "the number of incidents of sexual abuse of minors by Catholic clergy, at least over the past fifty years, is significant and disturbing. This is a failing not simply on the part of the priests who sexually abused minors but also on the part of those Bishops and other church leaders who did not act effectively to preclude that abuse in the first instance or respond appropriately when it occurred."[1] Porter victim Dennis Gaboury put it somewhat more crudely when he told CNN: "The Church is the real sodomist."[2]

Appreciating the influence of litigation on the framing of clergy sexual abuse is the first step in understating how litigation ultimately shaped the policies designed to address it. In this chapter I explain why plaintiffs' framing of clergy sexual abuse as an institutional failure by church officials became the dominant news frame. My analysis reveals a correlation between certain features of litigation and news production that accounts for the influence of clergy sexual abuse lawsuits on press coverage. Complaints provided dramatic narratives with clear moral implications that made for gripping news stories. Discovery documents, deposition transcripts, and trial testimony were perceived by journalists as especially reliable sources of information. The litigation process provided a steady flow of new developments that supported ongoing coverage. And intensive coverage encouraged increasing numbers of victims to sue, which in turn gave rise to more coverage, thereby creating a self-reinforcing news theme and the perception of a "wave" of litigation and a "crisis" in the Church.

I begin the chapter by introducing the concept of framing, which is central to both law and journalism and to my account of the relationship between litigation and news production. Next, I analyze more closely the particular features of litigation and news production that explain the plaintiffs' influence on media coverage of clergy sexual abuse. I support theoretical claims about the correlation between litigation and news production with empirical evidence from interviews of lawyers and journalists, content analysis of news stories, and statistical data. Finally, I explain why in the case of clergy sexual abuse the plaintiffs' frame of institutional responsibility dominated news media coverage of the issue despite efforts by the Church's defenders to frame the issue differently.

Frame Analysis

My analysis of the influence of litigation on news media coverage of clergy sexual abuse relies heavily on the concept of framing. In order to understand and communicate our experience of the world, we must select, organize, and contextualize our perceptions. Thus facts are always presented within some larger conceptual frame. These frames allow us to make sense of the world by focusing on aspects of our experience that we consider relevant, putting them together into a coherent whole and relating them to things we already know in order to make experience meaningful. Framing is the selection, organization, and presentation of issues, events, or people that places them within a context with the aim of promoting a particular interpretation or evaluation.[3] Frames are the principles of selection, organization, and presentation that guide framing.[4]

Individuals often frame the same event or issue differently, and many disputes arise out of these differences in framing. For example, whether

Bernard Goetz's shooting of an unarmed assailant constitutes a justified act of self-defense or a deplorable instance of gun violence depends on how one frames it. Indeed, any particular characterization of the event—in this case, mentioning that the victim was "unarmed" (or, in this last sentence, identifying him as a "victim")—itself implies a choice of frame.

Frames can be combined in different ways. A frame can be reused repeatedly to draw connections between different events in order to suggest a pattern. A number of shootings can all be framed as similar instances of gun violence in order to suggest a gun violence "problem" or, if there are enough instances, a gun violence "epidemic." Different frames can be used to emphasize distinctions between events. Instead of reusing the same frame of gun violence to characterize all fatal shootings, one might frame some as assaults, some as accidents, and some as suicides, suggesting an array of quite dissimilar phenomena. A frame can itself be placed within another frame in ways that affect how the initial frame is viewed, as when gun control advocates frame assertions of a gun violence epidemic as social science findings, or when gun rights advocates frame the same assertions as a propaganda campaign aimed at promoting gun control.[5]

Frames often suggest a particular course of action.[6] Thus framing the rate of highway fatalities as caused by unsafe driving suggests stricter enforcement of traffic laws, whereas framing it as due to poor automobile design suggests imposing more rigorous design standards on car manufacturers. Framing fatalities as a "problem" in the first place— as opposed to merely a necessary cost of widely accessible highway travel—itself implies that some course of action is necessary.

As the above examples suggest, frames often compete. The ability of one frame to predominate over others depends on a number of factors.[7] First, the *cultural resonance* of a frame contributes to its persuasive power. A frame has a high degree of cultural resonance when the language and images that it employs reinforce widely-held views or evoke shared values. Frames that resonate with popular political principles, moral commitments, or worldviews will be more convincing. Second, the *prominence* of a frame also enhances its persuasive power. Early articulation of a frame soon after an event gives a frame prominence, as does adoption of the frame by a respected person or institution. Third, *repetition* of a frame enhances its persuasive power. Repetition creates a perception of widespread acceptance and leads some people to adopt it out of a desire to conform and may even result in a reality of widespread acceptance.[8]

Information travels between people in frames, and the persuasiveness of a frame determines how readily facts in it are accepted and how widely they are disseminated. The widespread diffusion of a frame has the quality of a *cascade,* building momentum and developing cumulative force as it flows.[9] Successful diffusion of culturally resonant frames reinforces the cultural values that made them persuasive in the first place, which in turn makes these frames even more persuasive over time. So too, as frames become more widely accepted, they are more likely to be championed by prominent figures and repeated more frequently, and this leads other prominent figures to promote them, increasing their prominence and the frequency with which they are repeated. As the momentum of a frame builds, individuals may accept it based on deference to the opinions of experts and authorities, reliance on common sense and conventional wisdom, and social pressure to conform. Successful frames thus tend to become more pervasive and persuasive as they cascade.

Frame analysis is helpful in understanding the relationship between tort litigation, media coverage, and policymaking. Clergy sexual abuse litigation illustrates how the litigation process is capable of generating persuasive frames that are promulgated by the news media and ultimately shape policy. We turn next to a detailed examination of why the litigation process led plaintiffs' lawyers to frame clergy sexual abuse as an issue of institutional failure and why the nature of news production led journalists to promulgate this frame.

The Influence of Litigation Frames on Media Frames

Tort litigation attracts media coverage because it has many of the ingredients that make a story newsworthy: tort claims are framed in terms of personal drama about injury and wrongdoing, legal documents are readily available and viewed as highly credible sources of information, and the litigation process provides a steady stream of episodic developments as claims move forward. Tort litigation thus provides ready-made news frames. In the case of clergy sexual abuse litigation, plaintiffs' frames dominated media coverage because the plaintiffs presented frames that more closely matched the demands of the news production process.[10]

The Complaint's Compelling Narrative and Cultural Resonance

Both the litigation process and the news production process provide incentives to frame issues in terms of dramatic narratives with clear moral implications. Consider first the litigation process. Most tort causes of action require that plaintiffs assert their claims in terms of wrongdoing that causes injury. The need to convince judges and jurors of the claim's merit leads plaintiffs to dramatize this basic narrative structure as a morality tale about right and wrong.[11] The value of plaintiffs' claims can be enhanced by portraying injuries as severe and wrongdoing as egregious, and one's chances of recovery are increased by naming defendants capable of satisfying judgments, who are often well-known figures or institutions. Thus stories of innocent victims injured by uncaring and unaccountable corporate officers are familiar in tort litigation.

For their part, defendants seek to reframe plaintiffs' allegations in doctrinally significant and culturally familiar terms of consensual risk taking, the plaintiff's own or some third party's carelessness, or just bad luck. In arguing before a jury, defense lawyers often counter plaintiffs' stories of corporate malfeasance with their own narratives about undeserving plaintiffs seeking to hold innocent business defendants liable for normal misfortunes.[12] These defense frames, which have gained widespread cultural resonance thanks to public campaigns for tort reform, can be just as persuasive as plaintiffs' frames.[13]

Like filing a claim, reporting news is an act of framing.[14] Sources, reporters, editors, publishers, and broadcasters frame events, issues, and people in order to create news stories. One powerful influence on the construction of news is audience demand. Newsmaking is a business that depends on advertising revenue, and advertising rates are determined by circulation.[15] News organizations are thus sensitive to what readers want. Media scholars have identified criteria that journalists use in selecting and framing news stories based on their perception of what readers want. These criteria define what makes a story newsworthy.

The newsworthiness of a story depends largely on its form. First, a story is more likely to be considered newsworthy if it can be framed as a *dramatic narrative* that involves active characters and exciting events.[16] Personal conflict provides a common premise for such dramatic narrative, and groups and institutions are commonly personified in order to increase dramatic effect.[17] A central event, or "peg," provides an attention-getting image around which the narrative can be organized.[18] Second, the *magnitude* of an event and the extent of its impact influence its newsworthiness.[19] All things being equal, the more powerful the storm and the more widespread its destruction, the more newsworthy it is. The magnitude and impact of an event can be increased by framing it as a part of a larger trend or crisis, such as the worst hurricane season of the century. Third, a narrative with clear implications and straightforward *moral lessons* is considered more newsworthy than one open to many different interpretations.[20] Fourth, the news media favor stories that are set in frames that are *culturally familiar* to readers.[21] This familiarity allows readers to understand and relate to a news story without the need for extensive background information. A story's cultural familiarity may be enhanced by the use of stereotypes or by telling the story is a way that readers expect or want it to unfold.[22] Fifth, a story that portrays the *unexpected or unusual* within familiar frames is considered more newsworthy.[23] Events that are surprising or shocking attract more attention than those that are routine. A story that is old or stale is not newsworthy—as one scholar explains, news is "a depletable consumer product that must be made fresh daily."[24] Sixth, a story about *elites* or well-known figures is considered more newsworthy.[25] Sometimes the media create well-known figures—most commonly crime victims or perpetrators—to enhance the newsworthiness of a story.[26] Newsworkers use these criteria in both selecting and shaping news stories.[27]

On a theoretical level, there is a close correspondence between the doctrinal, rhetorical, and strategic considerations that shape the framing of tort claims on one hand and the criteria of newsworthiness on which journalists rely in constructing the news on the other hand. This should come as no great surprise. After all, even though they work in very different institutional settings, both lawyers and journalists are in the business of constructing persuasive frames for audiences that include both elites and members of the general public.

This correspondence between litigation and news production is especially clear in clergy sexual abuse litigation. The Gauthe case is a good place to begin. In that case, the complaint named as defendants:

ARCHBISHOP PHILIP M. HANNAN; BISHOP GERALD L. FREY; VICAR GENERAL RICHARD VON PUHL MOUTON; MONSIGNOR HARRY E. BENEFIEL; MONSIGNOR H. A. LARROQUE; THE ARCHDIOCESE OF NEW ORLEANS, D/B/A THE

ROMAN CATHOLIC CHURCH; THE ROMAN CATHOLIC CHURCH FOR THE DIOCESE OF LAFAYETTE; THE ROMAN CATHOLIC CHURCH; ST. JOHN PARISH REPRESENTING THE COMMUNITIES OF ESTHER AND HENRY, VERMILLION PARISH, LOUISIANA; CERTAIN UNDERWRITERS AT LLOYD'S OF LONDON; IN-TERSTATE INSURANCE COMPANY AND FATHER GILBERT GAUTHE.

By listing first well-known church officials and institutions, including "THE ROMAN CATHOLIC CHURCH," the title of the case began the process of framing the sexual abuse committed by Gauthe as an institutional failure.[28]

The complaint alleged that Gauthe "recruited, enticed and coerced numerous young children of the congregation of the aforementioned Parishes to engage in sex initiation rings under the guise of religious initiation rites, training and tutelage."[29] This characterization must have had great cultural resonance against the background of the highly publicized allegations around the country in the early 1980s of childcare workers running child sex rings and engaging in ritual child sex abuse.[30] These allegations would have been well known to the judge as well as to many, if not most, prospective jurors.

The most detailed allegations, however, were against church officials, whom the plaintiffs asserted "made possible" the abuse by failing to remove Gauthe from ministry or inform parishioners even after the officials knew of his repeated sexual abuse of children.[31] A supplemental complaint filed by plaintiffs' attorney J. Minos Simon further alleged that "church officials made a studied effort to conceal and withhold . . . information concerning Gauthe's misconduct from members and families of the church," and that church officials "having full knowledge . . . of his tendencies to sexually abuse young children," moved him from one parish to another. In doing so, Simon's supplemental complaint concluded, church officials "knowingly created an environment which operated to maximize opportunities for Gauthe to further wantonly sexually abuse innocent young children."[32] The complaint also referred to church officials as "corporate officers," undermining feelings of personal allegiance to them and making the allegations sound like a typical story of corporate malfeasance and cover-up.[33]

Answers filed by the Church and insurance defendants simply denied the allegations, and they make for much less compelling reading than the complaint.[34] Gauthe's answer alleges that he was "insane at all times material" and therefore "not legally responsible" for any of the conduct alleged in the complaint.[35] His answer also argues that he successfully deceived church officials by concealing his sexual activity with children—that the Church, like the children and their parents, was one of Gauthe's victims.[36]

The first print coverage of the Gauthe litigation was published in a local weekly, the *Times of Acadiana,* by Barry Yeoman, on November 1, 1984. It was entitled "Is Nothing Sacred?"[37] The article places the Gauthe affair within the context of rising local awareness of child sexual abuse and community responses to it, and it features a sidebar focusing on the litigation itself. The sidebar essentially adopts the frame presented by the plaintiffs' pleadings. The only photograph in the sidebar is of plaintiffs' attorney Simon with a caption that states in large bold type, "Church officials made a studied effort to conceal Gauthe's misconduct"—a direct quote from Simon's supplemental complaint.[38] Of the thirty-one paragraphs in the sidebar, thirteen discuss the plaintiffs' case, quoting extensively from the original and supplemental complaints. Only five paragraphs are dedicated to the defense, all of them based on the assertions of insanity and deception in Gauthe's answer. In contrast to two colorful quotes from an interview with Simon, the sidebar states that "Neither the Diocese of Lafayette nor the Archdiocese in New Orleans would comment on the suit."[39]

Reading Yeoman's sidebar in light of our previous examination of the pleadings provides insight into why the news media adopted the frame presented by the plaintiffs. To begin with, the plaintiffs' complaint offers a dramatic narrative of ritual child sex rings and corporate cover-up, a stark morality tale with innocent children victimized by an evil sexual predator and callous corporate officials. The cultural resonance of this frame with contemporaneous stories from around the country about child sex rings, ritual child sex abuse, and corporate wrongdoing and cover-up made the frame all the more compelling. By contrast, the flat denials in answers by the Church and insurance defendants did not offer much in the way of alternative frames. Gauthe's assertions of insanity and deception did provide an alternative frame, although one with less drama and cultural resonance than that provided by the plaintiffs. Moreover, Simon's readiness to speak to the press allowed him to advocate for his version of events, whereas the defense attorneys' refusal to comment did little to promote their views in the press.

The final paragraph of the sidebar ends by not only reinforcing the plaintiffs' frame but at the same time highlighting the importance of drama and cultural familiarity in Yeoman's adoption of it. "The most interesting aspect of the Gauthe case," Yeoman concludes, "stands to be the church's role in the civil case. Like Paul Newman in 'The Verdict,' attorney Simon will be trying to establish not only Gauthe's guilt but also the guilt of a seemingly omnipotent institution."[40] The plaintiffs' frame is compelling, according to Yeoman, because it has all the drama of a blockbuster Hollywood film.

The second print article, "Church Knew of Abuses, Sex Case Depositions Show," by John Pope, appeared on the front page of the *New Orleans Times Picayune* on November 9, 1984. The headline's adoption of the plaintiffs' frame was reinforced by the opening paragraph reporting that "Catholic Church officials knew for almost seven years about the Rev. Gilbert Gauthe's sexual activities with boys at churches in southwest Louisiana, according to two depositions filed this week in a court case."

Examination of subsequent press coverage illustrates how this frame of institutional failure cascaded throughout the media, growing in significance as the plaintiffs' version of the Gauthe litigation itself came to frame the larger phenomenon of clergy sexual abuse. An Associated Press report of January 25, 1985, was entitled, "Bishop says he got word of Gauthe's actions 10 years ago" and began, "The bishop of the Catholic Diocese of Lafayette, in sworn testimony, says he first learned of the Rev. Gilbert Gauthe's sexual activities with little boys about 10 years before ordering him suspended." Details of Gauthe's actions and mention of his criminal indictment are relegated to five short paragraphs near the end of the article. The *Times of Acadiana* in May and June 1985 introduced a three-part in-depth investigation of the Gauthe litigation by Jason Berry with an editorial suggesting that "At issue in the final stages of this tragedy are the troubled lives of dozens of Acadiana families, millions of dollars in damages claims and *the responsibility of the Roman Catholic Church's Lafayette Diocese for the actions of one of its priests.*"[41]

Regional coverage projected the frame of institutional failure to a larger audience. A May 26, 1985, *Dallas Morning News* article on the front page of the Sunday edition reported the litigation as a "Child abuse scandal" and quoted plaintiff Glen Gastal saying "As far as I'm concerned, I would like to see the Bishop behind bars. He was an accessory to the crime. He knew about it back in 1973 . . . If he had done something then, this wouldn't have happened to my child."[42] The next day, the *Houston Post* ran a story titled "Parents Say Church Knew Priest was Child Molester," which opened with the same quote from Gastal.[43] The lengthy *Dallas Morning News* story only briefly mentioned the defendants' assertion that they were themselves deceived by Gauthe, and this alternative account is missing altogether from the shorter *Houston Post* article. The *Dallas Morning News* article also used the Gauthe litigation to frame a listing of similar cases around the country—in Rhode Island, Pennsylvania, Idaho, Minnesota, and Oregon—provided by plaintiffs' attorney Simon.

National coverage began with two investigative articles in the June 7, 1985, edition of the *National Catholic Reporter* (NCR). A front-page editorial introduces the articles.[44] The opening sentence of the editorial explains that "[i]n cases throughout the nation, the Catholic Church is facing scandals and being forced to pay millions of dollars in claims to families whose sons have been molested by Catholic priests," lending a sense of magnitude to the issue by suggesting that clergy sexual abuse was national in scope. The second paragraph goes on to place responsibility for this national problem on church officials, suggesting that, beyond the harm suffered by victims and damage to the Church's reputation, "a related and broader scandal seemingly rests with local bishops and a national episcopal leadership that has, as yet, no set policy on how to respond to these cases." The last paragraph emphasizes the primacy of institutional failure over individual instances of abuse: "[T]he tragedy, and scandal, as NCR sees it, is not only with the actions of the individual priests—these are serious enough—but with church structures in which bishops, chanceries, and seminaries fail to respond to complaints, or even engage in cover-ups; sadly, keeping the affair quiet has usually assumed greater importance than any possible effect on the victims themselves."[45] This frame of institutional failure presented by *National Catholic Reporter* editors was itself derived from their knowledge of specific cases in the two investigative articles, in which the Gauthe litigation was the most extensively researched and the most prominently featured.[46] And, as we have seen, the version of the Gauthe case in the news media was that of the plaintiffs. Thus, the plaintiffs' framing of clergy sexual abuse in the Gauthe case came not only to dominate local, regional, and national press coverage of that particular case, but of the whole nationwide phenomenon of clergy sexual abuse.

The *National Catholic Reporter* coverage began a frame cascade through the national media.[47] On June 9, the *Washington Post* ran a story on the Gauthe litigation, borrowing heavily from prior coverage by the *Times of Acadiana* and the *National Catholic Reporter*.[48] On June 20, the *New York Times* published a story on the Gauthe litigation, quoting the *National Catholic Reporter* editorial emphasizing institutional failure over Gauthe's individual actions.[49] In its July 1 issue, *Time* magazine published a short item on the Gauthe litigation, citing the *Times of Acadiana* series and the *National Catholic Reporter* coverage as its primary sources.[50] Thus, the use of other news organizations as sources, themselves highly influenced by the plaintiffs' framing of the issue, fueled the cascading of this frame throughout the national media.

In later coverage of the issue over the next two decades, the Gauthe litigation acquired special status as "the seminal case" of clergy sexual abuse.[51] As national coverage of the scandal reached its peak in late 2002, the Associated Press published a list of "key dates in the abuse crisis in the U.S. Roman Catholic Church," the first significant entry being the Gauthe case in 1985.[52] The Gauthe litigation is still the invariable first term in frequent litanies of notorious cases.[53]

The focus on church officials' institutional responsibility rather than on the individual culpability of abusive priests remained a dominant theme in later coverage. For example, one of the first *Boston Globe* stories on the Porter case was entitled "Some Fault Church on Sex Abuse by Priests," and it began "Despite continuing disclosures about sexual misconduct by its priests . . . the Catholic Church is not responding to the problem as aggressively or as uniformly as other religious denominations."[54] The *Globe* followed this article with another a few days later, characterizing clergy sexual abuse as an instance of corporate misconduct. The article quoted a Porter victim who, in explaining his reason for filing suit against the diocese, opined that "we all know that huge corporations—and that includes the Catholic church—often don't change their behavior until they get hurt financially."[55]

Television coverage of the Porter case also emphasized the Church's institutional responsibility. In February 1993, ABC's *Nightline* aired the first of many examinations of clergy sexual abuse. Host Ted Koppel introduced the broadcast by stating that "For years, the Church looked the other way."[56] In a subsequent *Nightline* broadcast in December of that year, host Chris Wallace began the show by suggesting that while Porter's abuse of children was shocking, "[e]ven worse . . . the Catholic Church transferred him from one parish to another, finally into treatment, and then back to a church."[57] In March 1993, the CBS show

60 Minutes broadcast a segment on clergy sexual abuse in the Archdiocese of Santa Fe entitled, "The Archbishop: Cover Up by Roman Catholic Church of Pedophilia by its Priests." Host Mike Wallace pointedly asked the mother of two boys abused by a New Mexico priest, "Do you hold the archbishop responsible for all of this?" to which she replied, "A hundred percent."[58] Similar examples can be found on ABC's *Primetime Live* and a CNN special report.[59]

The frame of institutional responsibility was even more pronounced in coverage of the Geoghan case and its aftermath in Boston. A January 2002 *Boston Globe* article, entitled "Church Allowed Abuse by Priest for Years," is typical: "Now, as Geoghan faces the first of two criminal trials next week, details about his sexual compulsion are likely to be overshadowed by a question that many Catholics find even more troubling: Why did it take a succession of three cardinals and many bishops 34 years to place children out of Geoghan's reach?"[60]

In television coverage, ABC's *Nightline* led the field in hammering away throughout 2002 on the theme of the Church's institutional responsibility. In a January episode on the Geoghan case, host Chris Bury invoked the familiar frame of corporate misconduct, suggesting that "parallels to the Enron debacle are striking."[61] He suggestively asked USCCB general counsel Mark Chopko, "How much responsibility does the Catholic Church have for the actions of its priests?"[62] In a February broadcast, host Ted Koppel began with the question, "What can be done that will restore confidence in the ability of the institution to clean house?"[63] In March, Bury introduced the show by stating that "At one time, the Roman Catholic Church could confidently proclaim that individual cases of sexually abusive priests were just that: Bad apples, aberrations, isolated examples. That argument is getting harder to make."[64] A second program on the topic in March focused on the claims of "critics" arguing that "[f]or too long . . . the Roman Catholic Church protected its priests."[65] In April, Bury introduced an episode titled "Turning a Blind Eye: Victims and Families of Sex Abuse by Catholic Priests hold Boston Cardinal Law Responsible" by asserting that "the cover-up can be far more damaging than the crime."[66] During a second show on the scandal in April, Koppel peppered Washington, D.C., Archbishop Cardinal Theodore McCarrick with questions about "responsibility among the princes of the church and among the bishops," their active participation "in a cover-up, moving priests from one location to another," and "the general public perception, now, . . . of a church that has handled this thing very poorly."[67] In June, Koppel opened the program by summarizing the current state of the scandal in Boston in this way: "Former priest, John Geoghan, imprisoned. Former priest, Paul Shanley, charged with child rape. Cardinal Law, accused of cover-up."[68] This placed Cardinal Law on par with the nation's most notorious clergy sexual abusers. Indeed, Cardinal Law eventually eclipsed Geoghan as, what ABC's *Good Morning America* called, "the man at the center of the Catholic Church's sexual abuse scandal."[69] On a June *Nightline* episode, Koppel lectured Minneapolis Archbishop Harry Flynn, chairman of the USCCB Ad Hoc Committee on Sexual Abuse, on the feelings of American Catholics about the scandal: "The disappointment, Your Excellency, if I may suggest, it seems to be not so much about the behavior of the priests themselves—of course there is great anger about that—but about the failure of the establishment of the American Catholic—of the Catholic Church in America to do something about it." To which the archbishop replied, "And I would agree one hundred percent with that."[70] In a second June program on the issue, Koppel concluded that in developing policies to detect and punish abusive priests, the bishops had "finessed" the issue of disciplining bishops who had facilitated abuse.[71] In December, *Nightline* wrapped up its 2002 coverage of the issue with a program on Cardinal Law's resignation and its implications for other bishops.[72] The frame of institutional responsibility also appeared prominently on ABC's *Good Morning America* and *20/20* and CBS's *60 Minutes, 60 Minutes II,* and *Sunday Morning.*[73]

Aside from this extensive anecdotal evidence, there is some statistical confirmation of the predominance of the institutional responsibility frame. A Lexis/Nexis search of *New York Times* news stories on clergy sexual abuse in 1993, during intensive coverage of a number of cases around the country sparked by the Porter case, found reference to the role of bishops in 24 of 32 articles (75 percent).[74] A similar search for 2002 during media coverage of the Geoghan and other cases found reference to the role of bishops in 488 of 604 articles (76 percent).[75]

A number of factors sustained this frame of institutional responsibility over two decades of news stories. First, news coverage of the Gauthe litigation provided a template for later coverage.[76] For example, in a June 2002 broadcast of *60 Minutes II,* host Ed Bradley opened the program with the question, "Why is it taking the Roman Catholic leadership so long to make the church safe for its children?" "We found some answers," Bradley suggested, "in Louisiana, in a case which could have taught the church nearly everything it needed to know about that nineteen years ago." The program then combined old news footage of the Gauthe case and interviews with parties to the litigation and their attorneys to frame the bishops' response to clergy sexual abuse in 2002.[77]

Second, many news stories relied for expertise on individuals involved in the Gauthe case, most notably journalist Jason Berry, whose analysis of clergy sexual abuse was shaped by his own coverage of the case. Berry was quoted extensively throughout the print media.[78] A Lexis/Nexis search of the *New York Times, Washington Post, Chicago Tribune,* and *Los Angeles Times* between 1990 and 2004 produced 82 quotations by Berry and citations to his work.[79] A 2002 *Washington Post* article referred to Berry as "a figure of legend in the coverage of sexual abuse by priests."[80] Berry appeared on *Nightline* as an expert on clergy sexual abuse in 1993, twice in 2002, and then once again in 2003.[81]

Third, a steady flow of subsequent legal claims that highlighted the failures of church officials provided the basis for news stories. Following the Gauthe case, hundreds of clergy sexual abuse lawsuits between 1984 and 2002 named church officials as defendants.[82] The Porter, Kos, O'Grady, and Geoghan cases discussed in Chapter 1, all named church officials as defendants. As we shall see next, litigation documents and interviews with plaintiffs' attorneys provided the primary sources for coverage of clergy sexual abuse.

Reliance on Litigation Documents and
Plaintiffs' Attorneys as News Sources

Audience demand is not the only ingredient of newsworthiness. In order to get published, a story must also be credible. According to one British broadcaster, "Credibility . . . is the *sine qua non* of news."[83] Credibility is the key to the power of news as an authoritative source of information.

Journalists rely on sources to provide information and promote the credibility of their stories. Sources that are themselves perceived as credible are especially attractive to journalists. Hence, news stories commonly quote official documents.[84] Pleadings, depositions, discovery documents, and trial transcripts—either filed in court and available as public documents or provided directly to reporters by lawyers—are treated by journalists as authoritative sources of information. Journalists and the public at large tend to view legal documents as especially credible. Perhaps one explanation for this phenomenon is that pleadings are supposed to contain only facts with a sufficient evidentiary basis, and depositions and trial testimony are given under oath. It may also be that filing documents in a court gives them an official status that inspires confidence in the truthfulness of their contents. In addition, there may be an element of naive belief that individuals involved in legal proceedings do not lie. And finally, legal filings may provide the factual basis necessary to defend against a libel suit or political cover for a news organization. (As one editor told a reporter covering the clergy sexual abuse scandal, "Get a lawyer to file it, and I'll print it.")[85] Whatever the case may be, litigation documents provide the credibility that journalists seek and are thus often the source of news frames.

In the search for credible sources, journalists regularly rely on experts and officials.[86] The media not only rely on experts, they also create them, and sources themselves gain credibility by being cited as experts in the media.[87] Expert opinion ratifies a news story, and media coverage ratifies the expert's opinion. Using experts to boost the credibility of news stories enhances the prominence of news media frames by attributing them to respected figures.

Media coverage of clergy sexual abuse relied heavily on litigation documents supplemented by interviews with plaintiffs' attorneys quoted as experts. As Arthur Jones, an editor at the *National Catholic Reporter,* suggested to Jason Berry during his early coverage of clergy sexual abuse, "The real story should be told from legal documents."[88] One regularly finds news stories based on pleadings, depositions, discovery documents, and trial transcripts. As we have seen, Barry Yeoman's initial print coverage of the Gauthe litigation in the *Times of Acadiana* was based almost entirely on the plaintiffs' pleadings. In a recent interview, Yeoman recalled that "there was a sense in the newsroom that we should cover the story responsibly . . . to write about childhood sex abuse as a broader issue and discuss the civil case in a factual, dispassionate sidebar." The sidebar was "written almost entirely from pleadings as a way to give the community a sense that we were just reporting the facts, rather than inflaming passions." "The editor," he explained, "was a stickler for using the court record as the primary source [based on] a sense that if you quote from court documents you are less open to a libel suit than if you quote an individual." Yeoman suggested that in "hewing to the structure of the lawsuits," the story was "based on the plaintiffs' original assertions" and "framed by the plaintiffs' framing of the issue."[89]

John Pope's subsequent story in the *New Orleans Times Picayune* was based on and quoted extensively from depositions that were filed by plaintiffs' attorney Simon precisely in order to put them into the public record and make them accessible to the press.[90] In an interview, Pope suggested that he was merely reporting what he found in the public record. You just go out and "see what you find," he explained, "you don't go into a story with an *idée fixe.*" Of his heavy reliance on the depositions, he said: "It is sworn testimony, testimony under oath, not just someone on the street talking about vague details. You want information that you feel you can take to the bank."[91] Subsequent local, regional, and national coverage of the case regularly cites the same pleadings, depositions, and, in later coverage, trial testimony.[92] In the *National Catholic Reporter*'s early investigative articles, information about cases of clergy sexual abuse from around the country was based almost entirely on litigation documents.[93]

In later coverage of clergy sexual abuse, one finds frequent reliance on litigation documents and proceedings. For example, the *Boston Globe*'s first article on the Porter case relied heavily on a demand letter written to the diocese by plaintiffs' attorney Eric MacLeish on behalf of a group of nine victims.[94] The *Globe*'s Pulitzer prize–winning coverage of clergy sexual abuse in 2002 was based largely on sealed court files in the Geoghan case that the paper successfully litigated to have unsealed.[95]

A Lexis/Nexis search of *New York Times* news stories on clergy sexual abuse in 1993 found explicit reference to litigation documents or proceedings in 22 out of 44 articles (50 percent).[96] A similar search for 2002 found explicit mention of litigation documents or proceedings in 312 out of 692 articles (45 percent).[97] Of course, these figures under-represent reliance on litigation as a news source since they include only stories that *explicitly* mention litigation documents or proceedings.

The leading books on the clergy sex abuse scandal—written by journalists—also rely heavily on litigation documents. Jason Berry states in the introduction to *Lead Us Not Into Temptation,* "[c]ivil lawsuits provided the documentation on most of the cases I wrote about," "a baseline of information," and he discloses in the prologue, "[m]y primary sources were transcripts of civil testimony given under oath by Bishops and priests in lawsuits across the country."[98] Frank Bruni, a *New York Times* reporter, and Elinor Burkett, a free-lance journalist, in their book *Gospel of Shame* acknowledge, "J. Minos Simon, who actually let us take three fifty-pound boxes of his files to a hotel room for the weekend."[99] The notes to their book suggest that they relied most heavily on news reports, which were themselves largely based on litigation documents.[100] The investigative staff of the *Boston Globe,* who won a Pulitzer prize for their coverage of the scandal, explain in the notes to their book *Betrayal* that they relied heavily "on a large number of Church documents filed in connection with criminal and civil court cases."[101] David France, who covered the story for *Newsweek* magazine, states in the notes to his book *Our Fathers,* "[m]y key resource for this book was tens of thousands of pages of court documents . . . [especially] the extensive record of court depositions."[102]

In both news stories and books, these documentary sources are supplemented with interviews. As we have seen, interviews with plaintiffs' attorney Simon were often quoted in news stories about the Gauthe litigation, and he is acknowledged as a key source in the books by Berry, Bruni, and Burkett. Plaintiffs' attorneys figure prominently in news stories and in lists of attorneys interviewed for the books.[103] These plaintiffs' attorneys function as what media scholars call "parajournalists"—organizational spokespersons whose job it is to provide ready-made news stories to journalists.[104] In perhaps the most extreme example, in April 2002, plaintiffs' attorney Eric MacLeish held a previously announced news conference in the ballroom of the Sheraton Boston Hotel and Towers, lasting over two hours, complete with victim testimonials and a PowerPoint presentation of 87 documents relating to claims against Father Paul Shanley, at the end of which MacLeish distributed 800-page document packets to dozens of journalists in attendance.[105] Plaintiffs themselves are also frequently quoted in news stories, either in sworn testimony or personal interviews. By contrast, defense attorneys, especially church and insurance company attorneys, regularly refuse comment, as do church officials.[106]

In general, plaintiffs' lawyers, and to a lesser degree plaintiffs themselves, are eager to speak with reporters and publicize their cases— providing ready-made frames for the press—because it serves their litigation goals.[107] Favorable publicity in the media can influence potential jurors. When news stories adopt the plaintiffs' frames, they make those frames more familiar, and hence more persuasive to jurors exposed to them in media coverage. The long-term effects of such publicity are especially powerful. Whereas once it might have been difficult to convince judges and juries that a Catholic priest could be capable of sexually abusing children, in the wake of twenty years of highly publicized litigation this is no longer the case. Press coverage can also in-crease settlement pressure on defendants eager to staunch the flow of embarrassing information to the public. Throughout the scandal, the Church has entered into confidential settlements in order to avoid neg-ative publicity. Press interviews also enable plaintiffs to air their claims against the Church publicly, a common goal of plaintiffs in clergy sex abuse litigation. Finally, plaintiffs' attorneys often seek to enhance their reputation, and getting the plaintiffs' stories reported in a favorable light serves this end. As Jason Berry puts it, "[a] symbiosis often devel-ops between journalists and lawyers in a high-profile case."[108]

By contrast, the Church has throughout been eager to avoid press coverage altogether for fear initially of igniting and later fueling public scandal.[109] This reluctance of defendants and their attorneys to speak with the press has made defendants' compulsory testimony in litigation documents such as depositions and trial transcripts all the more influ-ential as a source for media coverage. This further benefits plaintiffs, as this testimony is elicited by plaintiffs' attorneys seeking to use it to sup-port their frames.

Litigation as an Unfolding Drama

In the news production process, a news story with *continuity*, that un-folds over time and can be released in episodes, is considered more newsworthy.[110] Such an ongoing story is said, in news jargon, to "have legs."[111] The protracted and dramatic nature of the litigation process lends litigation frames continuity and enhances their newsworthiness.

The litigation process gave the clergy sexual abuse story legs because it generated a steady flow of litigation events that each provided new revelations and pegs for news stories. In the Gauthe litigation, for ex-ample, the filing of pleadings, the taking of depositions, hearings on motions, trial events, appeals, and settlements all gave rise to media sto-ries.[112] In this manner, subsequent lawsuits since 1985 have supported coverage of clergy sexual abuse for more than twenty years.

At times, the drama of litigation itself—the competition between attorneys—has generated coverage. Part two of Berry's 1985 three-part investigative series in the *Times of Acadiana* examines the "legal dra-mas unfolding as a result of [Gauthe's] crimes," and features on the first page side-by-side photos of plaintiffs' attorney Simon and defense at-torney F. Ray Mouton.[113] Next to each photo is a bold caption in large type. The one next to Simon reads: "Attorney Minos Simon's suit on behalf of the Gastals rests on the premise that church officials not only had prior knowledge of Gauthe's crimes but also had long tolerated homosexuality among other clerics in the sprawling diocese," and the one next to Mouton states that "Defense attorney F. Ray Mouton has entered an insanity plea to Gauthe's criminal indictment. The jury will have to decide if the priest was capable of telling right from wrong at the time he molested his victims." The photos and their captions illustrate nicely that litigation is essentially a frame competition in which articulate attorneys engage in drawn out and, at times, dramatic conflict, all of which makes for an attractive news story.

Subsequent coverage also played up the drama of litigation. CNN anchor Bonnie Anderson characterized the filing of a countersuit for defamation against a plaintiff as "just the start of the Archdiocese counterattack."[114] Videotaped depositions of Cardinal Law in the Geoghan and Shanley cases were posted on the web by the *Boston Globe* and dramatic excerpts were played on the evening news and included in newspaper stories.[115]

Clergy Sexual Abuse as a News Theme

In addition to audience demand and credibility, editorial concerns influence news production. In composing the daily paper or news program, editors must select and organize news stories. In order to do so, they employ themes that provide selection criteria and principles of organization. "A news theme," explains media scholar Mark Fishman, "is a unifying concept. It presents a specific news event, or a number of such events in terms of some broader concept . . . A news theme allows journalists to cast an incident as an *instance* of something."[116] The extent to which a particular story fits within a theme makes it more newsworthy. The development of themes over time enhances the continuity of the news and allows news organizations to frame individual stories as episodes within an unfolding drama.[117]

The tendency to select news stories that fit a theme applies not only within a particular news organization but also among news organizations as a whole. Once one media outlet has identified a theme, other news organizations are likely to view it as newsworthy and to report on it as well. As already mentioned, news organizations rely heavily on each other's judgments of newsworthiness. Expanding coverage of the theme is self-reinforcing. As Fishman explains, "when a . . . theme is beginning to spread through more and more media organizations, the 'reality' of the theme is confirmed for the media organizations who first reported it. They now see others using the same theme. Moreover, as the theme persists, news organizations already using the theme will not hesitate to report new instances . . . Thus, each use of the theme confirms and justifies its prior use."[118] Moreover, official and public reaction to the theme further confirms it and generates additional stories. Sources seeking to attract media coverage frame the information they provide in terms of the theme. Fishman's analysis of news themes describes a kind of frame cascade that further helps to explain the persuasiveness and pervasiveness of news media frames.[119]

One reason for the news media's adoption of the plaintiffs' framing of clergy sexual abuse is that the filing of numerous claims against the Church created and sustained a news theme. Filing multiple claims simultaneously or aggregating many claims into class-action or government entity litigation has become an increasingly common strategy among tort plaintiffs that intensifies pressure on defendants to settle.[120] This strategy increases the magnitude of the alleged wrongdoing and harm, as well as the litigation itself, and it frames individual claims as part of a larger trend, which provides a news theme. As the news theme cascades among news organizations and grows, it often leads the media to portray the claims as part of a larger crisis.

As originally reported by Yeoman, the Gauthe litigation was framed as part of a larger news theme of child sexual abuse in general. The multiple claims filed against the Church by Gauthe's victims and his subsequent criminal indictment, however, generated enough stories to make the Gauthe litigation a news theme in its own right. As Berry and others uncovered and reported on other clergy abuse litigation around the country, the theme became clergy sexual abuse in the Catholic Church. As we have seen, these initial news frames cascaded throughout the media, and media coverage encouraged more victims to come forward and file suit, in turn generating more media coverage. By June 1985, the *National Catholic Reporter* called clergy sexual abuse a national "crisis" in the Catholic Church. In 1991, *Time* magazine referred to it as "[w]ithout doubt . . . the worst wave of moral scandals ever to beset Roman Catholicism in North America," and by 2002 the press was regularly characterizing it as what "may be the greatest scandal in the history of religion in America and perhaps the most serious crisis Catholicism has faced since the Reformation."[121]

It is significant, according to the John Jay study, that the rate of sexual abuse by Catholic clergy rose in the 1950s and 1960s, peaked in the 1970s, and began a steady decline starting in the early 1980s, all before the scandal broke publicly.[122] If this finding is correct, then it was the commencement and growth of litigation, rather than any rise in the rate of abuse, that supported the news theme of a crisis in the Church.

Explaining the Dominance of Plaintiffs' Framing of Clergy Sexual Abuse

So far in this chapter, I have argued that tort litigation framed clergy sexual abuse as an issue of institutional failure and that this became the dominant frame for news media coverage. The dominance of plaintiffs' framing of the issue, however, was by no means inevitable. Beginning with the Gauthe litigation, defense lawyers, church officials, and commentators constructed and promoted alternative frames. I will canvas the most prominent contenders and then suggest why the plaintiffs' frame ultimately prevailed.

In pleadings at trial and in statements to the press, defense counsel in the Gauthe case, Bob Wright, suggested that the Gastal parents were partly responsible for the harm done to their son by subjecting him to a public trial.[123] In a statement to the press during the trial, Wright said "The boy's psychologist . . . advised the Gastal family not to bring the matter to trial. He told the Gastals that publicity would only make their son's condition worse. We contend that exposing the matter in a trial has interfered with his chances of recovery."[124] Wright and the plaintiffs' original attorneys, Bencomo and Hebert, insisted that secret settlements were necessary to protect the privacy of the victims.[125] Wright also told the press that the Gastal parents sought an excessive recovery, implying that they were using the litigation for financial gain.[126] Speaking generally of the phenomenon of clergy sexual abuse litigation against the Church, scholarly commentator Philip Jenkins similarly asserts that high damage awards are a primary motivation for pursuing the litigation. "[T]he potentially lucrative rewards of church litigation," he writes, "are an obvious temptation."[127] According to this frame, the litigation process itself is a form of child exploitation.

A related defense frame offered by the Church is that parents have been contributorily negligent in allowing their children to spend so much time in the unsupervised care of a priest, especially where there might have been indications of excessive interest on the part of the priest or unusual behavior on the part of the victim. Defense lawyers and church officials are somewhat reticent to promote this frame as it implies common knowledge of clergy sexual abuse—and therefore toleration of it by church officials—and it smacks of blaming the victim.[128]

Defenders of the Church also frequently blame lawyers on both sides for exacerbating the crisis. They suggest that the mishandling of clergy sexual abuse was originally just an honest mistake. According to this account, church officials dealing with abuse allegations in the 1960s, '70s, and '80s did the best they could with the resources available at the time. They relied on what we now know in hindsight to be erroneous advice that the best response to child sexual abuse is confidentiality to protect victims and psychotherapy to rehabilitate offenders. "Some of the mistakes that bishops made," asserts former defense attorney Patrick Schiltz, "would have been made by just about any of us at that time. Those mistakes did not reflect bad faith, but an honest misunderstanding of the nature of sexual abuse and the impact on its victims—an honest misunderstanding shared by most Americans at the time."[129] Between 1992 and 2002, according to Schiltz, the Church could have preempted the post-2002 storm of litigation by admitting its mistakes, holding accountable the priests who committed abuse and the officials who facilitated it, and compensating victims. The Church failed to do this, asserts Schiltz, because diocesan attorneys and insurance company lawyers took an adversarial approach to the problem and advised bishops to share no information, make no apologies, offer no assistance to victims, and impose no punishments on abusers since any of these actions could be construed as an admission of wrongdoing and could be used by plaintiffs to support their legal claims.[130] The post-2002 litigation boom has also been fueled, continues Schiltz, by plaintiffs' attorneys seeking to profit from clergy sexual abuse who discourage any contact between victims and the Church that might lead to reconciliation and who encourage victims to inflate the extent of their injuries.[131]

Since the very beginning of the litigation, the Church has portrayed itself as a victim of abusive priests who concealed their crimes from diocesan officials. In a deposition statement widely reported in the press, Lafayette bishop Gerald Frey referred to Gauthe in the following terms: "I think you have to understand the man we're talking about . . . He's a very, very unique person. He's got a sort of Dr. Jekyll and Mr. Hyde personality, where he can fool people very easily. And he certainly deceived me."[132] In 1997, twelve years later, church officials were quoted as insisting that "they lacked knowledge about pedophiles' incurability until the early 1990s and now are moving to flush out 'wolves in sheep's clothing.'"[133]

Defenders of the Church have also portrayed the Church as the victim of an oversexed popular culture in the United States that has eroded priests' commitment to celibacy and led them to commit child sexual abuse. The real problem, suggested Vatican spokesman Joaquin Navarro-Valls in 1993, is "a society that is irresponsibly permissive, hyperinflated with sexuality and capable of creating circumstances that can induce into grave moral acts even people who have received for years a solid moral formation and education in virtue."[134]

Church officials have attempted to downplay the magnitude of the problem. In the wake of revelations concerning Porter, Cardinal Law suggested that priests who sexually abuse children are "the rare exception."[135] Ray Flynn, the former Boston mayor and U.S. ambassador to the Vatican, began a 2002 interview on *Nightline* by suggesting, "Let's not just try to bring down the Catholic church here because of a handful of bad apples in the barrel."[136]

The Church and its defenders have consistently represented the Church as a victim of an anti-Catholic press. In 1985, the *Daily Advertiser of Lafayette* criticized the *Times of Acadiana* in a stinging editorial, proclaiming that "[i]t's time to call a halt to the exploitation of the Gilbert Gauthe affair," and denouncing the rival paper's coverage of the affair as an "attempt to blacken the reputation of our entire religious community."[137] Similar sentiments were expressed at a 1992 meeting of 500 Boston-area priests who met to discuss reforms proposed by the Boston archdiocese. One priest reportedly said that press coverage of clergy sex abuse was "just like in Germany when the Nazis crushed the church."[138] Also in 1992, Cardinal Law himself issued an angry denunciation of press coverage of the Porter affair. "The good and dedicated people who serve the church deserve better than what they have been getting day in and day out in the media," he declared, "[b]y all means, we call down God's power on the media, particularly the *Globe!*"[139] Commentator Philip Jenkins alleges that the press unfairly singled out the Catholic Church in its coverage of clergy sexual abuse, and that press framing and rhetoric grow out of a tradition of centuries-old anti-Catholic polemic.[140] Onetime religion correspondent for the *New York Times*, Peter Steinfels, laments "just how antagonistic to Catholicism the media culture has become."[141]

Defenders of the Church have combined efforts to minimize the problem with claims of anti-Catholic bias by characterizing the incidence of clergy sexual abuse as low compared to the incidence of child sexual abuse in other social institutions. In a 2006 advertisement on the Op-Ed page of the *New York Times,* Catholic League president William Donohue, citing data that there were only nine credible allegations of sexual abuse committed in 2005 by Catholic priests—".02 percent of priests"— argued:

> It is highly unlikely that there are many institutions or demographic groups with a better record than this (e.g., it is estimated that the rate of sexual abuse of public school students is more than 100 times the abuse by priests). Obviously, one victim is too many. But when 99.98 percent of priests today are not under suspicion—and indeed most are good men—it is outrageous that they continue to be subjected to vile depictions in the media, sneering remarks by educators and inequitable treatment by lawmakers. Stereotypes do not die easily, but it is high time our cultural elite began to treat priests with the degree of respect they've earned. Sweeping condemnations of any group is rightly regarded as bigotry. Including Catholic priests.[142]

On this account, the Catholic Church is in fact a leader in addressing the problem of child sexual abuse and a victim of widespread anti-Catholic bias.

Individuals on both sides of the issue have blamed homosexuality among priests for clergy sexual abuse of children. Plaintiffs' attorney in the Gauthe case, J. Minos Simon, believed that pedophilia was "a species of homosexuality" and that "homosexuality *per se* was a risk-producing activity." Based on these beliefs, he argued that "knowledge on the part of church officials concerning the existence of homosexual activity would result in a duty on the part of the church officials to take affirmative steps to protect altar boys from homosexual priests."[143] The relationship between homosexuality and pedophilia in the Gauthe case was analyzed and debated in early media coverage of the litigation.[144] Berry suggested that hypocritical tolerance within the Church of homosexual activity among priests contributed to a clerical culture that turned a blind eye toward other forms of sexual activity also forbidden by church doctrine.[145] American bishops and Vatican officials as well sought to frame clergy sexual abuse as a result of accepting homosexuals within the priesthood.[146] In late 2005, in response to the scandal, the

Vatican issued a new policy banning candidates for the priesthood "who are actively homosexual, have deep-seated homosexual tendencies, or support the so-called 'gay culture.'"[147]

Church officials have also framed clergy sex abuse as a matter of sin, a moral failing that is best addressed by church doctrines of repentance and forgiveness, rather than as a crime or a civil wrong to be turned over to the secular justice system.[148] In explaining why he failed to check on Gauthe's behavior as a parish priest, even after he knew of Gauthe's sexual misconduct with children at a previous parish, diocesan official Monsignor Richard Mouton explained, "I am trained to forget people's sins, as a priest."[149] As Cardinal Law explained in a 1992 *Boston Globe* article, "we live out our life as a community of faith, very much like a family. My hope is that we can evolve a policy that can effectively deal with the issue without gearing it into a legal mode."[150]

Commentators and church officials have attempted to downplay the scandal by drawing a distinction between sexual molestation of prepubescent children ("pedophilia") and postpubescent adolescent children ("ephebophilia"), noting that cases of the former are relatively rare among reported cases of clergy sexual abuse while the latter are more common.[151] Framing the abuse of prepubescent children as a distinct phenomenon from abuse of adolescents allows church defenders to portray pedophilia as a relatively minor problem within the Church and divert attention to less scandalous sexual relations between clergy and postpubescent adolescents. Relying on this distinction, Jenkins suggests that "[i]n the prevailing psychiatric opinion of the 1970s and early 1980s, it would have been quite appropriate to return to a parish setting a man who had been successfully treated for ephebophilia but not for pedophilia, and it was precisely this issue of the employment of past offenders that led to such scandal following the Gauthe case." He goes on to quote a Canadian Bishop who framed a clergy sexual abuse scandal in Nova Scotia in the following terms: "We are not dealing with classic pedophilia. I do not want to argue that homosexual activity between a priest and an adolescent is therefore moral. Rather it does not have the horrific character of pedophilia." Jenkins himself concludes that "[s]uggesting that the church concealed or tolerated pedophiles is much more destructive than the charge that it granted a certain degree of tolerance to priests involved in consensual relationships with older boys or young men. In Catholic Church law, the age of heterosexual consent is sixteen rather than the eighteen common in most American jurisdictions."[152]

As these alternative frames suggest, there has been a great deal of frame competition over how to characterize clergy sex abuse. One could plausibly frame it as a matter of parental neglect and exploitation of abused children, excessive litigiousness by lawyers on both sides, victimization of the Church by a small number of deceitful priests, anti-Catholic bias in the media and society at large, homosexuality in the priesthood, the corrosive effects of an oversexed popular culture, the appropriateness of treating child sexual abuse as a sin rather than a crime or a tort, or largely an issue of consensual sexual relations between priests and adolescent boys and young men.[153] The dominant news media frame, however, is clearly that of plaintiffs, who portray the issue as one of institutional failure and episcopal responsibility for child sexual abuse by clergy.

Drawing on our earlier analysis, we can identify four reasons that explain the news media's adoption of plaintiffs' framing of clergy sexual abuse as an issue of institutional failure. First, the plaintiffs' complaint in the Gauthe case employed the kind of frame appealing to news audiences: a narrative drama with a clear moral lesson involving personal conflict between innocent children, a compulsive pedophile, and allegedly uncaring elites in positions of power. Against the background of widespread news reports in the early 1980s of ritual child sexual abuse among daycare workers, this frame offered a culturally familiar story with a novel clerical element. The Gauthe case's dramatic narrative provided a template for subsequent litigation over the next twenty years, enhancing the cultural familiarity of the frame over time.[154]

Second, the media's desire for credible sources led it to rely heavily on litigation documents, which it viewed as providing, in the words of John Pope, "the kind of information you feel you can take to the bank."[155] The media supplemented these documentary sources with interviews of plaintiffs' attorneys who acted as parajournalists. Once adopted by the media in early coverage, the plaintiffs' framing was perpetuated in later coverage by frequent reliance on journalists—often presented as experts—who had previously covered the story.

Third, a steady flow of litigation events provided news pegs and facilitated continuous episodic coverage of the story. The protracted drama of the litigation itself attracted attention, as illustrated by such news items as the side-by-side photos and quotes of attorneys Simon and Mouton in the Gauthe case.

Fourth, the continuous supply and growing volume of litigation provided the basis for a news theme, portrayed eventually as a "crisis" in the Church. True to the dynamics of news themes, this "crisis" grew in magnitude and significance as time went on, becoming an increasingly salient theme for news editors. At the outset of the litigation in the mid-1980s, there was considerable ambivalence, and in some cases resistance among editors about criticizing church officials.[156] Nevertheless, the initial newsworthiness of the story and eventual momentum of the theme as it cascaded through the media overcame most of this reticence, until the media gave the frame of institutional failure a place of clear predominance.

I do not mean to suggest that the frame of institutional failure originated in litigation. It is probably impossible to determine where it first arose and, for our purposes, it does not matter. My point is that a number of competing frames have been offered to characterize the problem of clergy sexual abuse and that tort litigation made the frame of institutional failure more persuasive and pervasive than it would otherwise have been. It is because of litigation that clergy sexual abuse is so widely considered a problem of institutional failure requiring institutional reform.

CHAPTER FIVE

Placing Clergy Sexual Abuse on Policy Agendas

> It would be silly not to concede that the gravity of the
> litigation wasn't a motivating factor in keeping the
> Church's attention focused on . . . the problems with
> the children.
>
> —J. MICHAEL HENNIGAN, ATTORNEY FOR THE L.A.
>   ARCHDIOCESE

At the June 2002 meeting of the U.S. Conference of Catholic Bishops in Dallas, the only item on the agenda was clergy sexual abuse. *Boston Globe* reporters described the atmosphere as "the kind of circus that normally attends a presidential convention."[1] Seven hundred journalists attended the meeting. Outside the Fairmont hotel, where the meeting took place, hundreds of protesters greeted the bishops as they arrived. Fearing that the situation might get out of control, Dallas police, including SWAT teams, stood by on high alert.[2] Inside, USCCB president Bishop Wilton Gregory opened the meeting by explaining that "[t]he task that we bishops have before us these days in Dallas is enormous and daunting. We are called upon to put into place policies that will insure the full protection of our children and young people and to bring an end to sexual abuse in the Church."[3]

Clergy sexual abuse occupied a prominent place on the agendas of other policymaking institutions as well. That same year, prosecutors convened grand juries to investigate dioceses in Westchester, Long Island, Philadelphia, Cleveland, Cincinnati, Dayton, Phoenix, and Los Angeles. Attorneys general in Massachusetts, New Hampshire, and Maine launched extensive inquiries into clergy sexual abuse in their states. State legislatures across the country considered bills designed to make it easier to hold church officials legally accountable for clergy sexual abuse.

In this chapter, I examine the essential role played by litigation in making clergy sexual abuse a top priority for church and government policymakers. As we have seen, litigation led the news media to report clergy sexual abuse and to frame it as an issue of institutional failure. Once publicized, litigation raised concern about the issue among large segments of the general public and the Catholic laity. Litigation and news coverage also mobilized victims, lawyers, and activists who joined forces to advocate for policy reforms. Pressure from all of these groups, along with genuine concern among policymakers themselves, increased over time. By 2002, efforts to address clergy sexual abuse consumed the USCCB, became an area of major interest among law enforcement officials, and were taken up by state legislatures around the country. Litigation and the media coverage it generated thus placed clergy sexual abuse on the agendas of key policymaking institutions.

I begin the chapter by introducing the concept of a policy agenda. Scholars have developed this concept to explain how and why certain issues attract the attention of policymakers. Next, I examine how litigation increased concern over clergy sexual abuse among the general public and the Catholic laity and how it mobilized victims, lawyers, and activists. I then look at how public concern and mobilization of activists brought clergy sexual abuse to the attention of church and government policymakers. My claims about the influence of litigation on the public, activists, and policymakers are informed by agenda theory and supported by a variety of empirical data. Finally, I explore why litigation has been such an effective strategy for achieving agenda access for clergy sexual abuse.

Agenda Access

Policy debate can be viewed as a contest of frames. In analyzing competition between frames within the policymaking process, scholars have developed the idea of an agenda. Roger Cobb and Charles Elder distinguish between two distinct but related types of agendas. The first type is *public agendas*, consisting of "issues that are commonly perceived by members of the political community as meriting public attention and as involving matters within the legitimate jurisdiction of existing governmental authority." The relevant political community can be either all members of a polity or some political subdivision. The second type of agenda is *institutional agendas*, consisting of "that set of items explicitly up for the active and serious consideration of authoritative decision-makers."[4] In analyzing the impact of clergy sexual abuse litigation, I distinguish between the public agendas of the general public and the Catholic laity and the institutional agendas of church officials, law enforcement, and state legislatures.

The presence of an issue on a public agenda may create pressure to place that issue on an institutional agenda. In other words, public pressure may attract the attention of policymakers and spur them into action. Thus raising public concern over an issue is a good first step in getting policymakers to take notice. As Cobb and Elder put it, "the expansion of issues to larger publics acts as a prelude to formal agenda consideration."[5]

The key to raising public concern is persuasive framing. Public policy scholars have identified a number of features that make issue frames persuasive to larger publics. Elaine Sharp suggests that frames are more likely to attract public attention when they have a *dramatic character, personal relevance,* and elements of *novelty.*[6] Sharp explains widespread public concern with drug abuse based on the use of dramatic stories of personal tragedy used to frame the issue, widespread personal experience with the negative social consequences of drug abuse, and the periodic appearance of new drugs. Ellen Frankel Paul observes that framing issues in the context of dramatic, *catastrophic events* increases their salience, and public attention to them can be sustained by subsequent recurrent events of a similar nature.[7] National concern with hurricane response in the wake of hurricane Katrina in New Orleans and subsequent hurricanes in Houston and Florida offers a recent example. Frank Baumgartner and Bryan Jones point out that framing issues in *relation to other currently salient issues* also attracts attention.[8] For example, framing airline regulation in terms of safety may make it more salient if transportation safety is already on the public agenda. All of these findings complement the frame analysis of litigation and news production which suggests that dramatic narratives with momentous events and familiar themes enhance the persuasiveness of frames. That is, the same features that make frames persuasive to judges and juries and appealing to journalists also attract the attention of larger publics.

Expanding Concern over Clergy Sexual Abuse to Larger Publics

Litigation and the media coverage it generated raised concern about clergy sexual abuse among the general public and the Catholic laity and mobilized victims, lawyers, and activists around the country. According to the agenda theory, one way to achieve this is through persuasive framing. As we have seen, litigation framed the issue of clergy sexual abuse in terms of dramatic narratives with momentous events, familiar themes, and well-known elites, which the media adopted and publicized.

Empirical evidence further supports the claim that litigation raised public concern about clergy sexual abuse and mobilized activists. Survey data, press coverage, and activity among activists reveal a correlation between landmark cases on one hand and increases in public concern and mobilization on the other hand. While each of these types of evidence has significant shortcomings, when taken together they provide a reliable basis for asserting that litigation played a decisive role in expanding the issue of clergy sexual abuse to larger publics.

The General Public

In examining general public awareness of and concern about clergy sexual abuse, I turn first to survey data, the most direct measure. Unfortunately, there are no relevant survey data prior to 2002. In order to supplement this limited survey data, I look at the venues and volume of media coverage of the issue over a longer period, between 1984 and 2004. While not a direct measure of public awareness and concern, the venues and volume of media coverage during this period indicate the public's exposure to the issue, which may be viewed as a "surrogate indicator of what issues the public is likely to believe are important."[9] I look also at the volume of letters to the editor, which provides a more direct measure of public awareness and concern but for which there is less data available.

SURVEY DATA

Surveys conducted in 2002 suggest a high level of public awareness of and concern about clergy sexual abuse. A February *ABC News* poll of a random national sample of 1,008 adults found that 60 percent of them agreed with the characterization of clergy sexual abuse as "a major problem that requires immediate attention," 26 percent viewed it as a "less immediate problem," 12 percent saw it as "not much of a problem at all," and only 3 percent had no opinion.[10] A subsequent March *Washington Post/ABC News/*Beliefnet poll of a random sample of 1,086 adults found that those viewing it as a "major problem" had risen to 76 percent, with 16 percent characterizing it as a "less immediate problem," 6 percent "not much of a problem at all," and only 2 percent had no opinion.[11] Eighty percent of respondents in this poll characterized the issue as a "crisis" for the Church. Subsequent *ABC News, Washington Post,* and Beliefnet polls in April, June, and December register similarly high levels of concern about the issue, and they report disapproval of the Church's handling of clergy sexual abuse ranging from between 59 and 77 percent.[12] A May *New York Times/CBS News* poll of a random national sample of 1,172 adults asked them, "How closely have you been following the news about the recent charges against Catholic priests involving sexual abuse of children and teenagers?" Twenty-eight percent responded "very," 41 percent "somewhat," 21 percent "not very," 9 percent "not at all," 0 percent "no opinion."[13] Finally, Associated Press readers selected the clergy abuse scandal as the third most important news story of 2002.[14]

Together these polls in 2002 suggest a high degree of public awareness, with between 96 and 100 percent of respondents offering some opinion on the matter. They also suggest a relatively high level of concern about the issue, with between 60 and 76 percent of respondents in the early polls characterizing it as a "major problem that demands immediate attention," and 80 percent calling it a "crisis." Recall that 2002 was the year that litigation documents in the Geoghan case were unsealed and widely reported in the media, abuse allegations skyrocketed, and the volume of litigation exploded from Boston to Los Angeles. Unfortunately, poll data can tell us nothing about the levels of general public awareness and concern prior to 2002. For this, we will have to rely on the venues and volume of press coverage, for which there is data available back to the initial coverage of the Gauthe litigation.

MEDIA COVERAGE

The venues and volume of press coverage may be used to gauge the level of public awareness and concern about an issue. Media scholars Shanto Iyengar and Donald Kinder, based on studies of television coverage, have shown that "those problems that receive prominent attention in the national news become the problems the viewing public regards as the nation's most important."[15] Political scientists Roy Flemming, John Bohte, and Dan Wood point out that "[r]elations between the media and the public are obviously reciprocal in nature. The media faces market incentives to follow events and develop stories that attract audiences. At the same time, public concerns over issues reflect in part the media's coverage."[16] Regardless of the direction of influence, however, media coverage of an issue—which can be measured by the placement, or venue, and the volume of stories—offers a proxy for public awareness and concern.

Consider first the venues in which stories about clergy sexual abuse appeared. As we have seen, the Gauthe litigation generated stories in national news venues such as the *New York Times*, the *Washington Post*, *Time* magazine, and the AP and UPI wire services. It was also the basis for an episode of the CBS news magazine *West 57th*, and it inspired the 1990 Home Box Office movie *Judgment*. The Porter case also attracted significant national media attention in 1992 and 1993, including stories in the *New York Times*, *Newsweek*, and *People*; segments on *Prime Time Live* and *60 Minutes*; and episodes of *Geraldo*, *Oprah Winfrey*, *Phil Donahue*, and *Sally Jessy Raphael*.[17] Between 1992 and 1994, stories on clergy abuse were also published or broadcast in *Time*, *The Nation*, the *New Yorker*, the *National Review*, *Ms. Magazine*, *Redbook*, *McCall's*, *Playboy*, *Rolling Stone*, *ABC's Primetime Live*, *Dateline NBC*, *CNN Reports*, Arts and Entertainment Network's *Investigative Reports*, and Court Television.[18] Another surge of media occurred at the time of the Geoghan case in Boston, generating thousands of newspaper articles in 2002 and placing the issue on the covers of *Newsweek*, *Time*, and *U.S. News and World Report*, "a journalistic trifecta usually reserved for war, politics, plane crashes and colossal natural disasters."[19]

A sense of the volume of press coverage can be obtained by tracking newspaper and magazine coverage for each of the years from 1984 to 2004. Table 1 presents the number of stories published in thirteen major newspapers and nine popular magazines each year during this period.[20] These news outlets all have relatively large audiences and are available on the Lexis/Nexis and Westlaw databases back to 1984 or 1985. For almost all of these news outlets, there is a sharp increase in the number of stories in 1992 and again in 2002. During the peak years of 1993 and 2002, press coverage was heavy in several of the news outlets examined. For example, in 1993, the *New York Times*, *Washington Post*, *Los Angeles Times*, *Boston Globe*, and *St. Louis Post Dispatch* each ran between forty and eighty-six articles. The *Chicago Tribune* in that year ran 111 stories. These numbers are even more dramatic in 2002, when they each ran between 337 and 773 articles. The heavy volume of news stories continued in 2003 and 2004.

Beyond media exposure, another measure of public awareness and concern is letters to the editor. Table 2 presents the number of letters to the editor concerning clergy sexual abuse in these same publications

Table 1. Newspaper and magazine articles reporting on clergy sexual abuse

	1984	1985	1986	1987	1988	1989	1990	1991	1992
Boston Globe	2	4	3	0	1	0	3	6	104
New York Times	1	2	3	3	9	0	6	2	19
LA Times[a]	0	4	14	12	14	7	21	18	29
Chicago Tribune[b]	0	6	6	12	6	1	7	24	91
St. Louis Post Dispatch	0	0	0	0	2	1	8	5	16
Washington Post	0	1	1	1	9	3	9	8	24
Miami Herald	0	2	4	3	7	3	11	1	16
Philadelphia Inquirer	1	0	0	0	6	4	3	1	12
San Jose Mercury News[c]	0	0	3	8	13	1	12	0	30
Seattle Times	0	0	0	0	0	4	1	3	17
San Francisco Chronicle[d]	0	0	0	0	0	1	0	2	19
Christian Science Monitor	0	0	1	0	0	0	0	0	0
Newsweek	0	0	0	1	0	0	0	1	2
U.S. News & World Report	0	0	0	0	0	0	0	0	2
Time	0	1	0	0	0	0	0	0	2
Wall St. Journal Abstracts	0	0	0	0	0	0	0	0	3
People	0	0	0	0	0	0	0	0	1
The Nation	0	0	0	0	0	0	0	1	0
Cosmopolitan	0	0	0	0	0	0	0	0	0
Esquire	0	0	0	0	0	0	0	0	0
Harpers	0	0	0	0	0	0	0	0	0
Forbes	0	0	0	0	0	0	0	0	0
TOTAL FOR YEAR:	4	20	35	40	67	25	81	68	387

Identical or nearly identical articles that appeared in multiple editions of the same newspaper were not counted in these tallies.

a. LA Times coverage begins January 1, 1985.
b. Chicago Tribune coverage begins January 1, 1985.
c. San Jose Mercury News coverage begins June 1985.
d. San Francisco Chronicle coverage begins February 9, 1985.
   Source: See Appendix 1.

1993	1994	1995	1996	1997	1998	1999	2000	2001	2002	2003	2004
86	43	26	16	24	22	12	14	25	773	372	222
44	18	11	12	9	16	5	10	11	692	297	142
74	42	22	10	16	10	6	14	17	469	288	171
111	54	23	13	19	13	8	12	10	410	178	155
57	49	17	6	6	6	8	5	3	354	138	130
40	10	30	11	8	6	6	2	3	337	127	107
19	12	15	6	18	12	3	4	14	265	126	70
25	15	10	1	4	3	0	1	4	234	89	87
35	12	12	8	5	5	3	11	3	196	57	41
19	7	10	5	9	8	3	6	3	180	64	75
17	17	27	13	3	5	7	18	4	116	37	38
0	0	0	0	0	0	0	0	0	36	14	12
4	1	0	0	0	0	1	0	0	35	4	6
0	1	0	0	0	0	0	0	0	23	7	2
2	2	3	0	1	2	0	0	1	22	6	5
2	1	0	0	0	0	0	0	0	8	4	2
0	0	0	0	0	0	0	0	0	5	2	2
0	0	0	0	0	0	0	0	0	2	3	1
0	0	0	0	0	0	0	0	0	1	0	0
0	0	0	0	0	0	0	0	0	0	0	0
0	0	0	0	0	0	0	0	0	0	0	0
0	0	0	0	0	0	0	0	0	0	4	0
535	284	206	101	122	108	62	97	98	4158	1817	1268

Table 2. Letters to the editor discussing clergy sexual abuse

	1984	1985	1986	1987	1988	1989	1990	1991	1992
New York Times	0	0	0	0	0	0	0	0	2
Boston Globe	0	0	0	0	0	0	0	0	0
St. Louis Post Dispatch	0	0	0	0	0	0	0	0	0
LA Times[a]	0	0	0	0	0	0	1	3	3
Chicago Tribune[b]	0	0	0	0	0	0	0	1	14
Washington Post	0	0	0	0	0	0	1	0	1
Seattle Times	0	0	0	0	0	0	0	0	0
San Francisco Chronicle[c]	0	0	0	0	0	0	0	0	0
Newsweek	0	0	0	0	0	0	0	0	0
People	0	0	0	0	0	0	0	0	0
Wall St. Journal Abstracts	0	0	0	0	0	0	0	0	0
Time	0	0	0	0	0	0	0	0	0
Cosmopolitan	0	0	0	0	0	0	0	0	0
Esquire	0	0	0	0	0	0	0	0	0
Harpers	0	0	0	0	0	0	0	0	0
Miami Herald	0	0	0	0	0	0	0	0	0
Philadelphia Inquirer	0	0	0	0	0	0	0	0	0
San Jose Mercury News[d]	0	0	0	0	0	0	0	0	0
Christian Science Monitor	0	0	0	0	0	0	0	0	0
Forbes	0	0	0	0	0	0	0	0	0
The Nation	0	0	0	0	0	0	0	0	0
U.S. News & World Report	0	0	0	0	0	0	0	0	0
TOTAL FOR YEAR:	0	0	0	0	0	0	2	4	20

a. LA Times coverage begins January 1, 1985.
b. Chicago Tribune coverage begins January 1, 1985.
c. San Francisco Chronicle coverage begins on February 9, 1985.
d. San Jose Mercury News coverage begins June 1985.
   Source: See Appendix 2.

1993	1994	1995	1996	1997	1998	1999	2000	2001	2002	2003	2004
3	0	1	1	0	0	0	0	0	89	24	8
0	0	0	0	0	1	1	2	2	75	24	17
2	3	0	0	0	0	0	0	0	60	5	8
6	2	0	0	0	1	0	0	3	42	11	11
8	1	0	1	1	0	0	0	0	38	7	6
5	1	3	0	0	0	1	0	0	13	2	1
0	0	0	0	1	0	0	0	0	22	1	1
2	1	0	0	0	0	0	0	0	8	3	1
0	0	0	0	0	0	0	0	0	4	0	0
0	0	0	0	0	0	0	0	0	2	0	0
0	0	0	0	0	0	0	0	0	1	3	0
1	1	0	0	0	0	0	0	0	1	0	0
0	0	0	0	0	0	0	0	0	0	0	0
0	0	0	0	0	0	0	0	0	0	0	0
0	0	0	0	0	0	0	0	0	0	0	0
0	0	0	0	0	0	0	0	0	0	0	0
0	0	0	0	0	0	0	0	0	0	0	0
0	0	0	0	0	0	0	0	0	0	0	0
0	0	0	0	0	0	0	0	0	0	0	0
0	0	0	0	0	0	0	0	0	0	0	1
0	0	0	0	0	0	0	0	0	0	0	0
27	9	4	2	2	2	2	2	5	355	80	54

and period as Table 1.[21] Again, one finds sudden increases in 1992 and 2002 and peaks in 1993 and 2002, although they are less dramatic than the increases in the volume of news stories in most cases. The volume of letters in 2002 is especially notable: the *New York Times* (89), *Boston Globe* (75), *Los Angeles Times* (42), *St. Louis Post Dispatch* (60), and *Chicago Tribune* (38).

The high volume of media coverage and letters to the editor in 1992–1993 and 2002—which reflects a high level of public concern in those years—coincides with the Porter and Geoghan cases respectively. These two landmark cases provided what policy scholars call *focusing events*. Thomas Birkland defines focusing events as sudden, rare events that affect a relatively large number of people and thereby attract media coverage and capture the attention of larger publics and policymakers.[22] Typical examples include natural disasters or political crises. Focusing events influence policy agendas by expanding awareness of issues to larger publics and by spurring the mobilization of groups seeking policy change. The Gauthe, Porter, and Geoghan cases served as focusing events: they suddenly exposed what were thought to be rare instances of clergy sexual abuse involving large numbers of victims. The Porter and Geoghan cases each reportedly involved over 200 victims and gave rise to dozens of lawsuits.[23] Thus, the suddenness and magnitude of these two cases sparked intensive media coverage and captured public attention. They also, as we shall see, captured the attention of lay Catholics and facilitated the mobilization of victims, lawyers, and activists seeking policy change.

Peaks in media coverage coinciding with the Porter and Geoghan cases are highlighted in Figure 8, which graphs the annual total number of articles and letters in all of the publications surveyed. One can see also a less dramatic increase in newspaper and magazine articles in 1997 and 1998 that coincides with the Kos and O'Grady cases, and can also be explained by viewing these cases as focusing events.[24]

A number of factors explain reduced media coverage and public concern in the years between the Gauthe, Porter, and Geoghan cases, despite substantial amounts of litigation during those periods. In the 1985–1991 period, most claims were settled quietly with confidentiality agreements that bound the parties to secrecy, and case files were commonly sealed by trial judges. The drop in coverage between 1994 and 2002 was due not only to the continuing use of confidentiality agreements and the sealing of court files but also to media reticence to cover the issue in the wake of the widely publicized allegations against Chicago's Cardinal Bernardin that were subsequently withdrawn.

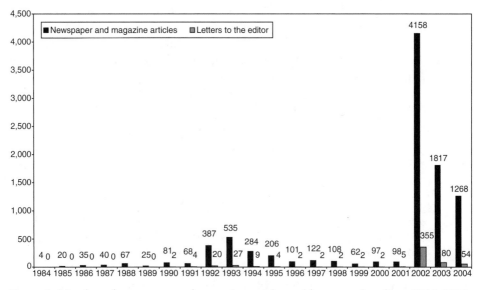

Figure 8. Number of newspaper and magazine articles and letters to the editor, 1984–2004.

Catholic Laity

Evidence that clergy sexual abuse has featured prominently on the agenda of lay Catholics can similarly be found in survey data and media coverage. Concern among lay Catholics was a significant source of pressure on church officials to take up the problem of clergy sexual abuse. As former USCCB general counsel Mark Chopko explains, the key to understanding the Gauthe case's impact was "the energy that it gave to the people in the pews . . . [I]t's not a problem for bishops if the *New York Times* gets excited about it. It's a real problem for bishops to know that their people are outraged by it, and both of these things were happening at the same time."[25]

SURVEY DATA

Survey data shows that clergy sexual abuse has been a major concern among the Catholic laity at least since the Porter case. A 1992 *Boston Globe* poll of 401 self-identified Massachusetts Catholics found that 96 percent said that "they were aware of recent news stories about 'inappropriate sexual contact' between priests and young people" and that 69 percent agreed with the statement that "the church has not done enough to address these kinds of incidents."[26] A 1993 *National Catholic*

Reporter/Gallup poll of 800 Catholics found that according to 50 percent of respondents, reports of clergy sexual abuse "weakened their faith and commitment" to the Church.[27] The newsletter *Emerging Trends* reported in 1993 that "nearly half of U.S. Catholics (48 percent) believe that sexual abuse of young people by priests is a widespread problem" and that "a majority of 53 percent believe the Catholic Church has done a bad job of dealing with the problem, and 64 percent say it has been more concerned with protecting its own image than with solving the problem."[28]

Subsequent polls in 2002 also indicate concern among the laity. A February *ABC News* poll of 231 Catholics from around the nation found that 48 percent considered clergy sexual abuse a "major problem," 29 percent a "less immediate problem," 21 percent "not much of a problem at all," and 2 percent had no opinion.[29] A follow-up *Washington Post*/*ABC News*/Beliefnet poll of 503 Catholics from around the nation found that 71 percent now considered it a "major problem," 19 percent a "less immediate problem," 9 percent "not much of a problem at all," and 1 percent had no opinion.[30] A February *Boston Globe*/WBZ-TV poll of 800 Boston Catholics asked respondents "How closely have you been following recent news stories detailing instances of sexual abuse of children by priests?" Forty-nine percent responded "very," 43 percent "somewhat," and 8 percent "not."[31] A May *USA Today*/CNN/Gallup poll of 256 Catholics from around the nation found that 75 percent of respondents thought that the Catholic Church has "done a bad job in dealing with the problem of sexual abuse committed by its priests," 20 percent thought the Church was doing a good job, and 5 percent had no opinion.[32] A June *Washington Post* poll of 355 self-identified Catholics from around the nation found that 70 percent disapproved of "the way the Catholic Church has handled the issue of sexual abuse of children by priests," 27 percent approved, and only 3 percent had no opinion.[33] A similar December *ABC News*/*Washington Post* poll found this rate of disapproval steady at 69 percent.[34]

More recent surveys suggest that the Catholic laity remains concerned about clergy sexual abuse. For example, in a 2003 *Boston Globe* survey of 400 Boston Catholics, 41 percent said that they considered "addressing clergy sexual abuse" to be "the most important problem facing the Boston Catholic archdiocese today."[35] An April 2005 Quinnipiac University poll of 500 Catholics from around the nation found that 86 percent thought that "under the next Pope, . . . the Catholic Church [should] do more to combat sexual abuse of young people by priests," while 11 percent thought that the Church's "current position about right," and only 4 percent had no opinion or didn't know.[36] While polls in 2005 and 2006 have suggested that faith among Catholics in the leadership of the Church may be rebounding, awareness and concern about clergy sexual abuse remains high.[37]

This survey data suggests that, as early as 1992 among Massachusetts Catholics there was widespread awareness (96 percent) of the issue and concern among the great majority (69 percent) that the Church was not doing enough. National surveys in 1993 reflect serious concern about the problem among roughly 50 percent of Catholics. Polls in 2002 show that by mid-year, an overwhelming majority of Catholics nationwide considered the issue a major problem, and that no more than 5 percent in any poll had no opinion on the matter. Polls since 2002 consistently suggest ongoing concern about the problem.

MEDIA COVERAGE

Aside from survey data, another indication that clergy sexual abuse holds a prominent place on the agenda of the laity are the venues and volume of coverage in the Catholic media. The issue has been covered in such widely read Catholic and Christian periodicals as *America, Commonweal, U.S. Catholic, Church and State, Episcopal Life,* and *Christian Century.* The *National Catholic Reporter* which, as we have seen, began its coverage of the issue in 1985, has provided sustained coverage since that time.[38] A computer search for "clergy sex abuse" in the weekly's online archives yielded 423 items in the twenty-two weeks between February 6, 2004 and July 15, 2005—an average of nineteen articles or references to the topic per week.[39] A similar search in the recent online archives of the Catholic News Service, an independent division of the USCCB used frequently as a news source by the approximately 170 U.S. Catholic newspapers and broadcasters, yielded 297 news items in the thirteen weeks between April 1 and July 29, 2005—an average of twenty-three items per week.[40] These two publications are among the most prestigious and widely read Catholic news outlets, and although these figures are far from comprehensive, they do provide evidence of heavy exposure to the issue among the Catholic news media audience.

A sense of the volume of Catholic media coverage since 1984 can be obtained by tracking the number of articles on clergy sexual abuse listed in the *Catholic Periodical and Literature Index* between 1983 and 2004. Sixty-four Catholic periodicals listed in the index published 1,130 stories on clergy sexual abuse during this period. The volume of stories increased dramatically (125 percent) in 1993 to fifty-four stories and even more so (2,460 percent) in 2002 to 512 stories, with an additional increase (81 percent) in 1998 to forty-nine stories, rising to sixty-six stories (thirty-three of which were published in the *National Catholic Reporter*) in 1999. These data are presented in Figure 9.[41] Again, the 1993 and 2002 peaks in news volume coincide with the Porter and Geoghan litigation and the peak in 1999 coincides roughly with the Kos and O'Grady cases.

Evidence of not only exposure to but also engagement with the issue of clergy sexual abuse among the laity may be gleaned from a search for web pages on the Internet. A Google search for web pages including the terms "sex" and "abuse" and either "church," "clergy," or "priest" produced 3,250,000 web pages.[42] The same search terms produced a listing of 89,300 discussion groups (many with multiple comments by multiple authors) in Google's online discussion group service.[43] This last figure includes only those online discussion groups sponsored by Google, so the number of comments posted to online chat sites is likely

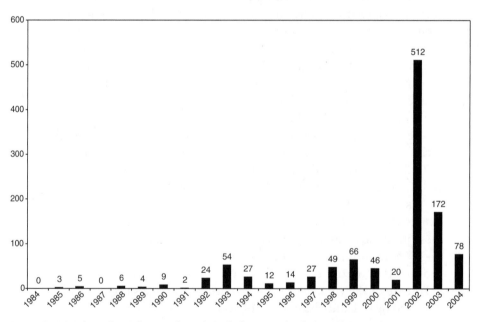

Figure 9. Number of articles in selected Catholic periodicals, 1984–2004. Source: See Appendix 3.

to be considerably larger. There have been several websites dedicated entirely to clergy sexual abuse, providing news, analysis, documents, and studies of the issue, such as bishop-accountability.org, bishops watch.org, and many others that offer extensive and sustained coverage of the issue. These latter include websites of the *Boston Globe* and the *National Catholic Reporter*, as well as beliefnet.com.

Victims, Lawyers, and Activists

Victims, their lawyers, and activists make up a third significant public that exerted pressure to put clergy sexual abuse on the institutional policy agendas of church and government officials. Litigation often has the effect of mobilizing such groups. Lawsuits personalize and dramatize social issues, and resulting press coverage disseminates information about them. Lawsuits and the publicity they generate embolden victims to speak out, educate lawyers about how to litigate more effectively, and provide activists a flag around which to rally.[44] Greater mobilization leads to more litigation, which in turn increases mobilization. Clergy sexual abuse litigation has been a central force in mobilizing victims, lawyers, and activists.

The mobilizing effect of clergy sexual abuse litigation on victims has been dramatic. The Gauthe, Porter, and Geoghan cases were each followed by increases in the number of victims who reported abuse. Figure 2 (page 47) reflects increases in the number of abuse reports to dioceses in 1985 after the Gauthe case, in 1992–1993 in the wake of the Porter case, and in 2002 following the Geoghan case. Victims and their families also contacted lawyers. Figure 4 (page 51) shows increases in the number of case files opened by plaintiffs' attorneys Jeff Anderson and Steve Rubino in 1992 and 2002.

Litigation has helped plaintiffs' attorneys learn how to litigate against the Church more effectively. As we saw in chapter 1, during the first wave of litigation, plaintiffs' attorneys learned to subpoena secret archives and to use the *Official Catholic Directory*, which enabled them to piece together a priest's assignment history. They also began to exchange information through a growing national network of lawyers interested in clergy sexual abuse litigation. For example, the Child Sexual Abuse Litigation Group organized by the Association of Trial Lawyers of America (ATLA, now the American Association for Justice, AAJ) was founded in 1986 and has served as a clearinghouse for information and expertise. The second wave of litigation saw growing nationwide cooperation among plaintiffs' attorneys, and by the third wave they were coordinating collective settlement talks involving dozens and sometimes hundreds of plaintiffs.

Litigation has fueled the growth of victim advocacy and church reform groups. Jeanne Miller's unsuccessful suit against the Chicago archdiocese in the early 1980s led her to found Victims Of Clergy Abuse Linkup (VOCAL, later renamed the Linkup and again renamed The Healing Alliance) in the early 1990s.[45] SNAP national director David Clohessy recalls that his group, founded in 1989, underwent dramatic increases in membership following the Porter and Geoghan cases.[46] Voice of the Faithful, a Boston-based church-reform group with thousands of supporters and chapters nationwide, was formed in response to the Geoghan case.[47] Activists not only responded to litigation; they also used it. As Porter victim Frank Fitzpatrick explains, by being "armed with the credibility of legal representation," reform groups could more effectively generate public concern for their cause.[48]

Placing the Issue on the Policy Agendas of Church Officials

There are at least three clear indicators that litigation helped place the issue of clergy sexual abuse on the policy agenda of the Catholic Church in the United States. The first is the attention paid to it by bishops, both individually and as a group. The second are public statements by Pope John Paul II and Vatican officials. The third is widespread concern about the issue among clergy. As we shall see, heightened attention to the issue by these three groups coincides with the Gauthe, Porter, and Geoghan cases as well as the heightened concern that these cases raised among the general public, the Catholic laity, and activists advocating policy reform.

The Bishops

The United States Conference of Catholic Bishops (USCCB) is a membership organization of U.S. bishops headquartered in Washington, D.C., with a 350-person staff. According to its corporate charter, the purposes of the USCCB are "[t]o unify, coordinate, encourage, promote and carry on Catholic activities in the United States; to organize and conduct religious, charitable and social welfare work at home and abroad; to aid in education; to care for immigrants; and generally to enter into and promote by education, publication and direction the objects of its being."[49] In 2001, the USCCB was created out of a merger between the United States Catholic Conference (USCC) and the National Conference of Catholic Bishops (NCCB), both founded in 1966. The NCCB was also a membership organization of bishops created to coordinate their activities nationwide. The USCCB, like the NCCB before it, holds semiannual meetings every June and November and has various committees that meet throughout the year.

In response to the Gauthe case and the growing revelation of a nationwide problem, NCCB staff began to research the problem of clergy sexual abuse and to offer advice to bishops facing allegations within their dioceses.[50] At a June 1985 NCCB meeting in Collegeville, Minnesota, the bishops dedicated an entire day of executive session to examining the psychological, legal, and moral aspects of clergy sexual abuse within the Church. They also considered nonbinding recommendations for how individual dioceses could best respond to the problem, and they formed committees to explore the issue further. Following the meeting, NCCB staff conducted research on the spread of clergy sexual abuse litigation around the country. NCCB staff also helped dioceses develop training programs to prevent child abuse, policies for reporting it, and protocols for assisting victims and their families. Some individual bishops took it upon themselves and investigated abuse in their own dioceses, issued reports, and created new procedures for dealing with claims.

The Porter case in 1992 put the issue of clergy sexual abuse back at the top of the NCCB's agenda. At their June meeting, the bishops dedicated most of their eight-hour closed executive session to the question of whether priests who had sexually abused children should be allowed to return to ministry.[51] They also formally endorsed a nonbinding set of "Five Principles" to guide diocesan responses to clergy sexual abuse: (1) prompt response to allegations, (2) immediate suspension of accused priests and investigation of allegations, (3) compliance with reporting requirements under civil law and cooperation with criminal investigations, (4) victim outreach, and (5) greater transparency in dealing with the issue.[52] At the November 1992 NCCB meeting, the bishops created a subcommittee to study the problem of clergy sexual abuse, and in February of 1993 the subcommittee convened a two-day think tank in St. Louis, that included a broad variety of experts discussing the issue.[53] At their June 1993 meeting, the bishops issued public statements of remorse, created an Ad Hoc Committee on Sexual Abuse, and adopted a brief nonbinding resolution pledging an "appropriate and effective" response to the problem.[54] As in the wake of the 1985 Collegeville meeting, the issue continued to receive attention in committees and individual dioceses.[55]

If clergy sexual abuse first appeared on the NCCB agenda in 1985 and rose to the top of it in 1992 and 1993, it is fair to say that it completely dominated the bishops' agenda in 2002. The Geoghan case and its aftermath consumed the bishops throughout the year. As already mentioned, the only item on the agenda for the June 2002 meeting in Dallas was clergy sex abuse.[56] After highly publicized proceedings, the bishops adopted the *Charter for the Protection of Children & Young People,* a binding policy that proclaimed "zero tolerance" for clergy sexual abuse within the Church, along with a set of *Essential Norms for Diocesan/Eparchial Policies Dealing with Allegations of Sexual Abuse of Minors by Priests or Deacons* to guide implementation of the Charter. The Charter created lay review boards in each diocese to assess claims and make recommendations to the bishop, a National Review Board charged with overseeing compliance with the policy and commissioning a comprehensive study of the problem, and an Office of Child and Youth Protection to assist with implementation of the policy.[57] Subsequent revisions to the Charter and Norms demanded by the Vatican, ongoing debate over its provisions and implementation, and publication of the comprehensive study have maintained clergy sexual abuse on the USCCB's agenda. Throughout 2002, individual bishops in their dioceses also implemented additional reforms.[58]

The prominence of clergy sexual abuse on NCCB/USCCB's meeting agendas in 1985, 1992–1993, and 2002 coincides with the Gauthe, Porter, and Geoghan cases. As we saw earlier, these three cases increased concern over clergy sexual abuse among the general public, the Catholic laity, and activists advocating policy reform. These findings suggest that litigation may have influenced the bishops' policy agenda by providing focusing events that expanded concern over clergy sexual abuse to larger publics, thereby creating pressure to place the issue on the bishops' institutional agenda. Indeed, there are specific examples of activists applying pressure for reform at key moments. Mouton, Doyle, and Peterson wrote their report and contacted influential bishops, including Cardinal Law, prior to the 1985 Collegeville meeting to impress upon them the gravity and magnitude of the issue.[59] A group of activists from Survivors of Porter and VOCAL met with a number of bishops, including Cardinal Mahoney, at the November 1992 NCCB meeting to lobby for reforms.[60] And, of course, activists staged protests outside and delivered speeches inside the 2002 USCCB meeting in Dallas.

We should be careful not to overstate the case. It would be inaccurate to say that there was no policymaking activity among the Bishops in the years between the Gauthe and Porter cases (1985–1991) and the Porter and Geoghan cases (1994–2001). NCCB staff and subcommittees were busy gathering information and assisting individual dioceses in developing new policies during both of these periods. The momentary rise of clergy sexual abuse to the top of the NCCB/USCCB's agenda in 1992 and 2002, and the flurry of policy initiatives that followed, might best be characterized as what political scientist John Kingdon calls policy windows. These are "occasions during which a problem becomes pressing, creating an opportunity for advocates of proposals to attach their solutions to it."[61] Focusing events, explains Kingdon, often open a window of opportunity for policy change.[62] Successful proposals for change do not merely appear when a policy window opens. Rather, those actively pursuing policy change—"policy entrepreneurs"—push steadily for consideration of proposals and increase their salience with the public and policy elites so that when a policy window does open, conditions are ripe for adoption of the policy. Kingdon calls this "softening up the system."[63]

I would like to suggest that the Gauthe, Porter, and Geoghan cases served as focusing events that opened up policy windows which policy entrepreneurs—victims' advocates, plaintiffs' attorneys, and reformers within the Church—used to promote policy change. Ongoing litigation in the periods between these cases played an essential role in softening up the system.

The Vatican

Clergy sexual abuse also made it onto the Vatican's policy agenda. Responding to intense media coverage of the Porter case, Pope John Paul II made his first public statement about the issue in 1993 while addressing a group of visiting U.S. bishops in Rome, saying that he shared their "sadness and disappointment when those entrusted with the ministry fail in their commitment, becoming a cause of public scandal," and denouncing "sensationalism" in the news media.[64]

At the height of press coverage about the issue in 2002, papal spokesman Joaquín Navarro-Valls made statements to the press blaming the crisis on homosexuality among priests.[65] Shortly thereafter, and just prior to the Dallas meeting, the pope summoned the American cardinals to Rome for two days in April 2002, and suggested that the Church was leading an effort to grapple with a general crisis in sexual morality: "The abuse of the young is a grave symptom of a crisis affecting not only the Church but society as a whole. It is a deep-seated crisis of sexual morality, even of human relationships, and its prime victims are the family and the young. In addressing the problem of abuse with clarity and determination, the Church will help society to understand and deal with the crisis in its midst."[66] Vatican attention to the issue continued after the Dallas meeting, with successful efforts in the summer of 2002 to revise The Dallas Charter and Norms.[67] Just as we saw in examining the bishops' agenda, the appearance of clergy sexual abuse on the Vatican's agenda in 1993 and 2002 coincides with the Porter and Geoghan cases.

The Priesthood

Clergy sexual abuse also found a prominent place on the agenda of priests as a group. A 1993 *Los Angeles Times* poll of 2,087 Catholic priests in eighty dioceses found that 41 percent said they considered "pedophilia within the priesthood" a "very serious problem," and another 31 percent ranked it as "somewhat serious," while 18 percent called it "not too serious" or "not at all serious."[68] A subsequent 2002 *Los Angeles Times* poll of 1,854 priests found that 69 percent agreed, in reference to clergy sexual abuse, that "The Catholic church in America is now facing its biggest crisis in the last century" and 18 percent ranked it as the most important problem facing the Church.[69]

Clergy sexual abuse has also been prominent on the agenda of the National Federation of Priests Councils (NFPC), a national organization of priests founded in 1968. At national conventions and regional convocations, former NFPC president Father Robert Silva often discussed the problem. At the organization's 2003 fall convocation in Cincinnati, he addressed "how priests are coping with the scandal."[70] Following the public release of the John Jay study in 2004, he issued a public statement calling it "downright scandalous" and said that it "shows the failure of a system of silence and secrecy that allowed such abuse to take place."[71] At his address to the 2005 annual convention in Portland, Oregon, he listed clergy sexual abuse sixth in a list of eight issues on the "agenda for the priests of the United States in the circumstances of the Church today."[72] According to a 2004 national survey of NFPC member diocesan councils, "Sex abuse has jumped up to the top of the list as a key agenda item."[73]

While limited, these findings suggest that concern about clergy sexual abuse among priests has run high in the wake of the Porter and Geoghan cases.

Placing the Issue on the Policy Agendas of Government Officials

Litigation also placed clergy sexual abuse on the agendas of law enforcement and state legislatures. In the wake of civil litigation, law enforcement officials have often been more willing to investigate and prosecute child sexual abuse by clergy and to address it as a serious policy concern. Legislatures have also taken up proposals to eliminate clergy exclusions in mandatory reporting laws and remove barriers to litigation such as statutes of limitation.

Investigations and Prosecutions

Tort litigation and the public concern it generated increased efforts to investigate and prosecute clergy sexual abuse. Of course, it would be a gross overstatement to suggest that in all cases civil litigation was responsible for increased investigation and prosecution. Indeed, in some cases, secrecy agreements in civil settlements were a hindrance. Nevertheless, there is evidence that civil litigation placed clergy abuse litigation on the agenda of many law enforcement officials and agencies.

Accounts of the Gauthe, Porter, and Geoghan cases offer anecdotal evidence that tort litigation increased criminal investigation and prosecution of clergy sexual abuse. Jason Berry relates that the criminal prosecution of Gauthe did not occur until after civil suits were filed and reported in the news media.[74] Plaintiffs' attorney Simon suggests in his account of the Gauthe affair that district attorney Nathan Stansbury was reluctant to prosecute Gauthe and that press coverage of the civil suits provided the pressure, or at least the political cover necessary to proceed against the Church.[75]

National press coverage of the Gauthe litigation influenced law enforcement officials beyond Lafayette, Louisiana. As Philip Jenkins writes:

> Before 1984, there was a conspicuous lack of public agencies with a desire or ability to intervene officially in cases, and police and prosecutors were usually reluctant to offend so powerful a constituent as the local Catholic church . . . The Gauthe case shaped reporting of a series of scandals that broke between 1984 and 1986, in which Catholic priests or religious had sexual contacts with minors, sometimes children who were in their charge in the capacity of pupils or altar boys. Nationwide

there were at least forty instances in those years in which Catholic priests would be charged with multiple acts of molestation and outright rape. Courts now showed themselves more willing to intervene in the thitherto confidential disciplinary proceedings of the Catholic church. Prosecutors also became increasingly prepared to press criminal charges in such cases, and in 1985 and 1986 notorious criminal trials ensued in some strongly Catholic communities . . . After 1985 . . . criminal justice agencies realized that traditional qualms about embarrassing church authorities were increasingly questionable, and restraint that once seemed politically wise would now be legally dangerous.

Jenkins also documents how, after 1985, reluctance to prosecute clergy or to challenge the Church could even become a political liability for prosecutors facing reelection.[76]

Plaintiffs' attorney Eric MacLeish's use of the press, without even filing a formal complaint, provided essential pressure for prosecution of James Porter by the local district attorney.[77] Having been rebuffed by the district attorney more than once, several Porter victims came to MacLeish, who helped them attract media coverage of their story in leading media venues such as the *New York Times, Newsweek, People, Prime Time Live, 60 Minutes, Geraldo, Oprah Winfrey, Phil Donahue,* and *Sally Jessy Raphael.* With an entourage of press, they then filed a complaint with the local police, and ten days later the district attorney launched an investigation that eventually culminated in the prosecution and conviction of Porter. For Bruni and Burkett, the Porter case in 1992 "marked a change in the reactions of secular authorities to cases of priests who molest . . . America's prosecutors and judges and reporters seemed to awaken on a national level . . . Authorities stopped trusting the Church to handle its own malfeasants." As proof for this contention, they offer examples of prosecutions immediately following the Porter revelations in Massachusetts, Missouri, and Illinois.[78]

In addition to individual prosecutions, public concern surrounding the Geoghan litigation in 2002 motivated law enforcement officials to issue reports on clergy sexual abuse and to offer policy reforms for dealing with the problem. In 2002, grand juries were convened in Westchester and Suffolk counties in New York, both of which issued highly publicized official reports containing detailed findings and policy recommendations. The Suffolk grand jury report is 181 pages and proposed twenty-one legislative reforms. Both the Suffolk and the Westchester grand juries recommended elimination of the statute of limitations for the sexual abuse of a minor, mandatory reporting by clergy of possible sexual abuse, criminal liability for supervisors who allowed employees with a known record of child sexual abuse access to minors, and prohibition of confidentiality agreements in civil settlements involving sexual abuse of a minor.[79]

Grand jury proceedings in Hillsborough, New Hampshire, that same year resulted in an agreement between New Hampshire attorney general Peter Heed and the Diocese of Manchester whereby the attorney general agreed not to press charges in exchange for mandatory reporting by diocesan personnel of possible sexual abuse; the development and implementation by the diocese of policies, procedures, and training to address the problem of sexual abuse; an annual audit of the diocese by the attorney general; public disclosure of the agreement; and publication by the attorney general of a report on the investigation.[80] In 2003, a Philadelphia grand jury issued an 800-page scathing critique of archdiocesan officials, asserting that "the Archdiocese's 'handling' of the abuse scandal was at least as immoral as the abuse itself."[81] Grand juries were also impaneled to investigate clergy sexual abuse in Cincinnati, Cleveland, Phoenix, and Los Angeles.

Massachusetts attorney general Thomas Reilly published a lengthy report in 2003 on clergy sexual abuse in the Archdiocese of Boston following grand jury proceedings and additional investigation.[82] Although the report concluded that the investigation "did not produce evidence sufficient to charge the archdiocese or its senior managers with crimes under applicable state law," it did detail misconduct by archdiocesan officials such as failing to respond to or report clergy sexual abuse and transferring known abusers to new parishes in the wake of allegations.[83] It also recommended specific reporting and disciplinary policies to be adopted by the archdiocese.[84] In a cover letter to the report, Reilly suggested that the purpose of publishing the report was to "confirm . . . that this tragedy was real," and "to create an official public record of what occurred so that this type of widespread abuse of children might never happen again here or elsewhere."[85] In 2004, Maine attorney general G. Steven Rowe issued a similar report on clergy sexual abuse allegations in the Catholic Church in Maine.[86]

The impact of clergy sexual abuse litigation on official investigations and criminal prosecution is difficult to quantify. Based on reports from private attorneys and a review of news coverage, Doyle and Rubino suggest that, "Although there are isolated instances of criminal and civil court actions prior to 1984, the [Gauthe] case appears to have opened a wide gate. Since that time there have been several hundred criminal prosecutions of Catholic clerics throughout the United States. Charges have varied from child endangerment to alienation of affection and aggravated rape. Sentences have varied from probation, to multiple life terms. It is estimated that perhaps 250–300 Catholic clerics have received sentences through the criminal justice system."[87] Consistent with this estimate, the John Jay study counted 252 priests convicted of child sexual abuse between 1950 and 2002.[88]

Legislation

Since the Geoghan case in 2002, litigation and the public concern it has generated have placed the issue of clergy sexual abuse on the agendas of state legislatures across the country. News stories posted on a SNAP webpage mention state legislative activity in Arizona, California, Colorado, Connecticut, Florida, Hawaii, Illinois, Indiana, Iowa, Kentucky, Maryland, Massachusetts, Minnesota, New Hampshire, New Jersey, New York, Ohio, Pennsylvania, South Carolina, Virginia, West Virginia, Wisconsin, and Washington.[89] Legislative proposals would extend or eliminate statutes of limitation for child sexual abuse, remove clergy exemptions in mandatory child abuse reporting laws, create child endangerment provisions that would make diocesan supervisors criminally liable for assigning known abusers to positions where they will have access to children, and remove civil damage caps for charitable organizations in cases of sexual abuse.[90] In California and Delaware, plaintiffs' attorneys and victim advocates lobbied successfully for a one-year suspension of the statute of limitations for child sexual abuse. While some of these proposals have fared better than others, they are powerful evidence that clergy sexual abuse was placed on state legislative agendas in response to heightened public concern beginning in 2002.

Litigation as an Effective Strategy for Agenda Access

Sometimes, agenda access and policy change are hotly contested. Those seeking to preserve the status quo or to promote private, in-house solutions may seek to keep issues off of public and institutional agendas. Public policy scholars Roger Cobb and Marc Ross have developed a theory of what they call "strategies of agenda denial" that are deployed against "initiators seeking consideration of a new issue" by "opponents who want to keep that issue off the agenda."[91] This theory can help us analyze the efforts of some defenders of the Church to prevent public disclosure of clergy sexual abuse and to prevent law enforcement officials and legislatures from getting involved. These efforts were, in the end, largely unsuccessful. What emerges is a better understanding of why litigation has proven to be a highly effective strategy to achieve agenda access.

Cobb and Ross divide strategies of agenda denial into four categories. First are "strategies that stress *nonrecognition of the initiator position*" such as refusing to recognize or denying the existence of a problem or refusing to recognize the groups advocating a response to it. This strategy was most commonly used prior to 2002. In many instances bishops refused to disclose that the reason for removal of a pastor was allegations of sexual abuse, and they failed to report abuse to law enforcement. As we have seen, this was the case in the Gauthe, Porter, and Geoghan cases. Bishops also withheld recognition of individuals or groups advocating reform. For example, some bishops refused even to meet with victims seeking to air their grievances. Similarly, some bishops ignored calls for reform by Voice of the Faithful and banned local chapters from meeting on church property.[92]

Second are "strategies aimed at *attacking the proposed policy* of the initiating group" such as discrediting the initiating group, dismissing initiators' concerns as isolated incidents, reversing roles by claiming that opponents are being victimized by initiators, and raising public fears that the solutions proposed by initiators will have detrimental effects. One sees these strategies not only in the earlier years of the scandal, but also more recently. As we saw in the previous chapter, some defenders of the Church have sought to discredit advocates of policy change by denouncing them as anti-Catholic. Defenders of the Church have also attempted to minimize the problem of clergy sexual abuse, chalking it up to "a handful of bad apples."[93] They have suggested that reform proposals for intervention by law enforcement officials and legislatures would violate constitutional guarantees of religious freedom and constitute government interference in the internal workings of the Church.[94] Church defenders have called plaintiffs and their attorneys money-hungry, and they have asserted that litigation is a threat to the financial survival of the Church.[95]

Third are "strategies intended to *symbolically placate the initiating group*" such as recognizing the issue but postponing action and invoking public trust in and loyalty to institutions charged with addressing the problem while doing little or nothing to address it. One might characterize the slow pace of reform and the nonbinding nature of NCCB policies in the years prior to the 2002 Dallas meeting as serving the desire of some within the Church to preserve the status quo by dragging their feet until public attention to clergy sexual abuse subsided. Priests and bishops have also exploited victims' loyalty to the Church and to the hierarchy in order to convince them to drop their claims. Recall from chapter 1 the exhortation of Father John Thomas to Maryetta Dussourd urging her not to report Father Geoghan to the police and to let diocesan officials handle the matter in order to spare the Church from scandal. Recall also the assurances of Boston Archbishops Medeiros and Law to Dussourd's sister, Margaret Gallant, that they would take appropriate action in the matter, even though neither removed Geoghan from parish work with children.

Fourth are strategies that are *costly to both sides,* but more costly to initiators than to opponents. These include threatening or carrying out social, political, economic, legal, or violent retaliation. Hardball litigation tactics, such as employing unnecessarily aggressive deposition techniques, using private investigators to uncover embarrassing personal information, and filing countersuits for defamation, while they contradict the mission and damage the image of the Church, have been, in the end, effective means of intimidating and silencing plaintiffs.

Despite the use of these different strategies, advocates of policy reform succeeded in increasing public concern about clergy sexual abuse and placing the issue on the policy agendas of church and government institutions. Litigation, as we have seen, played a key role. In order to better understand why litigation has proven to be such an effective strategy for achieving agenda access, let us return for a moment to frame analysis.

As a frame is disseminated, it is often placed within another frame, especially when it passes from one institutional setting to another. A different institutional setting creates a new context for the frame. That is, the frame is itself placed within another frame, and this subsequent framing of the initial frame can affect our response to the information contained within the initial frame.[96] The placement of a frame within another frame may be used to validate or undermine the original frame. This can occur repeatedly, creating a *nesting* effect with subsequent frames containing prior frames. The outermost frame defines the status of the prior frames within it.

For example, consider allegations that frame an individual's actions as murder. We would view these allegations differently if they were presented within a frame of gossip than if they were made within a frame of sworn testimony. And we would view the same allegations made in sworn testimony differently if reported in the news media than if portrayed within a play. And again, our view of the same allegations made in sworn testimony reported in the news media would be different if framed in the context of a documentary on media inaccuracy. Whether we view the allegations as merely gossip, sworn testimony, fictitious portrayal of sworn testimony, news about sworn testimony, or misleading news about sworn testimony will depend on the outermost frame.

Litigation not only framed clergy sexual abuse as an issue of institutional failure; it also placed that frame within a second frame of legal proceedings. Because of the authority and respect that legal institutions command, placing frames within the contextual frame of legal proceedings makes them more persuasive. As we have seen, allegations that church officials facilitated clergy sexual abuse are much more likely to be viewed as credible if contained in a complaint filed with a court or made under oath during deposition or trial. The enhanced credibility of these frames makes the news media more likely to report them, and framing them as news further validates and disseminates the allegations. That is, the nesting of a frame within the frame of legal proceedings leads to its further nesting within the frame of news, and this nesting process makes the initial frame more persuasive and fuels its dissemination. It also enables proponents of the frame to harness the power of the courts to promote the frame. I shall refer to this as "legal nesting."

Cobb and Ross suggest that in a contest over agenda access, "[t]he contestant that does a better job of linking its issue position to culturally rooted worldviews is usually victorious. This involves the use of cultural strategies, associating a proposal with powerful values and symbols."[97] As we have seen, plaintiffs in clergy sexual abuse litigation framed their claims in terms of dramatic narratives with momentous events, well-known elites, and culturally familiar themes. They invoked widely shared values such as child welfare, they named church leaders, and they employed powerful symbols such as corporate corruption. The same, however, is true of those seeking to deny them agenda access. Church defenders also drew on culturally resonant values such as religious liberty and symbols such as greedy plaintiffs. So why did the plaintiffs ultimately prevail?

What I have called "legal nesting" helps to explain the success of reform advocates in overcoming church defenders' strategies of agenda denial. First, legal nesting was an effective way to overcome nonrecognition strategies of agenda denial. Filing a lawsuit provided a level of state, and subsequently media, recognition of the plaintiffs' claims that aired them publicly and compelled church officials to respond. Failure to respond ran the risk of default judgments in the courts and further damage to public image in the press. Exposure of the general public, the Catholic laity, and activists to litigation and news coverage that validated the plaintiffs' frame of institutional responsibility created pressure to place clergy sexual abuse on church and government policy agendas.

Second, legal nesting also diffused attacks on the policy proposals for reform. Making claims in legal documents filed in courts and in testimony under oath enhanced their credibility. The willingness of courts to let plaintiffs' claims proceed and to give them careful consideration made it harder to dismiss the problem as the product of anti-Catholic bias, and the increasing volume of claims over time undermined suggestions that the problem consisted merely of isolated incidents. The vindication of plaintiffs' claims in court and the rejection of First Amendment defenses also made many people less sympathetic to church defenders' pleas of financial hardship and weakened their appeals to religious liberty.

Third, legal nesting fueled public outrage, increasing impatience for real reform and making efforts to symbolically placate pro-reform constituencies harder. It also undermined the unquestioning trust and obedience of many Catholics that had been exploited by some to deflect allegations. Fourth, and finally, legal nesting raised the cost to the Church of hardball tactics, and it equipped plaintiffs with tools to defend themselves and fight back.

Clergy sexual abuse lawsuits thus highlight that litigation can be a powerful strategy for achieving agenda access. Victims and their lawyers have used this strategy effectively. Due in large measure to their efforts, addressing clergy sexual abuse has become a top priority within the Catholic Church and a matter of significant concern to law enforcement and state legislatures around the country.

CHAPTER SIX

Uncovering Concealed Information

The facts are that secrets *are* being kept, and litigation
is the only tool in this democracy that pries out
corporate secrets.

— STEVE RUBINO, PLAINTIFFS' ATTORNEY

The litigation process has forced us to go into the
archives and uncover the way personnel problems like
this were dealt with in the past, and it's been an
education for everyone.

— J. MICHAEL HENNIGAN, ATTORNEY FOR THE
L.A. ARCHDIOCESE

Allegations that bishops have attempted to cover-up clergy sexual abuse
have persisted throughout the scandal. The most notorious allegations
were made by Governor Frank Keating of Oklahoma. The bishops selected Keating at their June 2002 Dallas meeting to chair the newly created National Review Board, charged with overseeing implementation
of the *Charter for the Protection of Children & Young People*. Keating's
appointment was announced with great enthusiasm and portrayed as
the start of a new, tougher attitude toward clergy sexual abuse. "From
this day forward," proclaimed USCCB president Bishop Wilton Gregory, "no one known to have sexually abused a child will work in the
Catholic Church in the United States. No free pass. No second chance.
No free strike."[1] Keating, a devout Catholic and former prosecutor, began his tenure by characterizing the Church's response to clergy sexual
abuse up to that point as "intolerable" and "horrifying," and he suggested that church officials who transferred known abusers were "aiders,"
"abettors," and "obstructers of justice."[2]

By September, Keating was openly criticizing Cardinal Law in the press
for his handling of the Geoghan and Shanley cases and calling on Boston
Catholics to withhold donations and attend Mass in a different diocese.[3]
In March of the following year, Keating publicly denounced Cardinal
Mahony's assertion of First Amendment and privacy objections in response

to the subpoena of church documents by the Los Angeles County district attorney's office. "It's just so sad," Keating told the press, "that the front pages are still filled with stories of avoidance and denial and coverup."[4]

Keating's allegations of cover-up reached a crescendo in June 2003. In response to resistance among California bishops to participating in the John Jay study commissioned by the National Review Board under the terms of the charter, Keating compared the bishops to the mafia: "To act like La Cosa Nostra and hide and suppress, I think, is very unhealthy." He added that "there are a number of bishops—and I put Cardinal Mahony in that category—who listen too much to his lawyer and not enough to his heart."[5] In frustration, Keating resigned from the board. In his letter of resignation, he refused to back down: "My remarks, which some bishops found offensive, were deadly accurate. I make no apology. To resist grand jury subpoenas, to suppress the names of offending clerics, to deny, to obfuscate, to explain away; that is the model of a criminal organization, not my church."[6]

While Governor Keating's characterizations are certainly extreme, they do reflect a widely held perception that some bishops have been—and continue to be—less than entirely forthcoming. As one Catholic lay minister put it, "I believe the Church is guilty of trying to cover-up any incidents that occur. This is a very serious mistake and the reason why many people don't trust the Church regarding this issue."[7]

There are, however, those who deny any cover-up. Attorney for the L.A. archdiocese J. Michael Hennigan suggests that "the plaintiffs like to use the term 'cover-up,' and, of course, there's no such thing. When you're dealing with a child and his family, you've got several people who are fully aware of the circumstances. [T]he fact that the Church didn't choose to publicize it was typical if we go back before 1985. These problems were typically covered up by everybody involved. The child, the family, the police departments, the Church, nobody wanted to talk about it and understandably so." Disclosure of past abuse has been slow, suggests Hennigan, because, by 2002, much of the information being demanded by plaintiffs and grand juries was buried in hard to locate archived church files dating back decades.[8]

While there is disagreement about whether church officials have engaged in a cover-up, there is one thing on which everyone seems to agree: litigation has played an essential role in generating information about clergy sexual abuse. In many cases, discovery has uncovered hidden (or merely hard to access) information and made it publicly available. Other aspects of litigation have also generated information. Through framing and agenda setting, litigation has prompted efforts by church officials, activists, and law enforcement to conduct investigations and publish reports on clergy sexual abuse. And settlement has been used to force dioceses to release information.

In this chapter, I examine the role of litigation in generating information about clergy sexual abuse. I begin by introducing the theory of stubborn information, which offers a general account of why some organizations conceal information in ways that are harmful to public health and safety and why litigation may be necessary to obtain this information. I then analyze why church officials failed to disclose information about clergy sexual abuse. Next, I examine the methods that some Bishops used to actively conceal information and the discovery techniques that plaintiffs' lawyers used to uncover it. After that, I look beyond the discovery process to consider the role of litigation in prompting internal church, grand jury, and attorney general investigations. I look also at the use of settlement to force disclosure of church documents. And finally, I present a brief survey of the information generated by clergy sexual abuse litigation.

Stubborn Information

Reliable information is essential to effective policymaking. Recently, there has been growing scholarly interest in understanding the unique ability of lawsuits to uncover information hidden from the public and government regulators. Legal scholars have analyzed the success of breast implant litigation in revealing inadequate safety testing, of tobacco litigation in disclosing the manipulation of nicotine levels in cigarette manufacturing, and of gun litigation in uncovering industry research on safer gun designs.[9] A leading scholar in this area, Wendy Wagner, has developed a theory of "stubborn information" that explains inadequate information disclosure by regulated industries. "Stubborn information," she explains, "arises when information is privately held and there are no incentives or subsidies to encourage its production or sharing." Instead, there are private costs, often substantial, from sharing information. "As a result, the information is closely guarded and deliberately withheld from other participants in the policy-making process."[10]

Stubborn information is the product of asymmetrical information, according to Wagner. "Actors who create risks to health and the environment amass specialized private expertise about the ways their activities or products could cause harm." They guard this information since disclosure "often threatens to lead to increased liability or regulation."[11] For example, manufacturers are especially well-situated to acquire knowledge of risks associated with their products or to develop alternative designs that would make their products safer. They have a powerful reason to conceal this information when disclosure could make them vulnerable to tort liability or give rise to calls for greater regulation of their products.

Industrial actors are able to prevent disclosure of stubborn information, asserts Wagner, because of their influence within the regulatory process. For example, many regulatory programs allow regulated parties the option of having information they are required to submit classified as "confidential business information" on the basis that it could be used by a competitor to the economic detriment of the regulated party. Agencies regularly allow manufacturers and polluters to classify health and safety research as confidential business information on the basis of claims that its release would cause them economic harm. So lax are current standards for classifying this information in some agencies that such claims require no substantiation and there are no penalties for facially frivolous claims. This arrangement—allowing regulated parties to prevent public disclosure of heath and safety information—reflects the influence of those parties on agency rulemaking and regulatory practice.[12]

Wagner suggests that litigation is often an effective way to overcome the asymmetry of information and the industry influence over government regulatory agencies that cause stubborn information. The discovery process, backed by the threat of contempt sanctions, offers plaintiffs a powerful tool with which to force disclosure of concealed information. Moreover, the monetary rewards of successful litigation provide a powerful incentive for plaintiffs and their attorneys to pursue information disclosure. And they are largely immune from the political pressure that industry applies to prevent government officials from making information public that an industry wishes to keep secret.[13]

Why the Church Failed to Disclose Information

The theory of stubborn information provides a useful starting point for analyzing the failure of church officials to disclose information about clergy sexual abuse. As the theory suggests, asymmetry of information gave church officials the opportunity to conceal information, and fear of liability provided a powerful reason to do so. Former defense attorney (now federal district judge) Patrick Schiltz explains that, in many cases, fear of liability motivated the failure of church officials to disclose abuse allegations. According to Schiltz, defense counsel regularly advised bishops to "say nothing that could be construed as an admission that the abuse occurred, even if there was no doubt it occurred"; "make no apology, because an apology could be construed as an admission of fault"; "refuse to meet any victim, at least without an attorney present, so that the victim could not later claim that the bishop made an admission or a legally enforceable promise"; "take no immediate action against the pastor"; and "say nothing publicly about the case."[14] The National Review Board's 2004 report on the crisis suggests that in the early 1990s, the USCCB considered gathering nationwide data on clergy sexual abuse allegations, but the bishops voted against doing so on the advice of diocesan attorneys who feared that any results could be used against the Church in future litigation.[15]

It would, however, be a gross mischaracterization to suggest that liability exposure was the only, or even the primary, reason for church officials' concealment of information about clergy sexual abuse. It would also be unfair to suggest that in all instances the failure to disclose information was the result of a conscious decision to conceal it. In applying stubborn information theory to clergy sexual abuse, we must expand it beyond Wagner's focus on the profit-maximizing behavior of industry actors to take into account a broader set of concerns that motivated church officials.

Some commentators suggest that doctrinal commitments explain church officials' failure to disclose information. Clinical psychologist John Gonsiorek points to three church doctrines in particular. First, he asserts that Catholic doctrine regarding the nature and purpose of human sexuality blinded some church officials to the damage done to victims of child sexual abuse. "If one perceives sexual expression as illegitimate, except for the purpose of procreation, and elevates celibacy even above that, it is difficult to appreciate the reality of sexual abuse on a fundamental level. The essential spoiling of sexuality that typically accompanies sexual abuse cannot be comprehended if sexuality is not seen as valuable in its own right." Second, Gonsiorek contends that belief in ordination as a purification and transformation that empowers individuals occupying the priestly role to avoid sin led some church officials to believe that reengaging offenders by reassigning them would help them overcome sexual temptation. "[T]he implicit assumption in the Roman Catholic tradition," explains Gonsiorek, "is that the flawed priest should be able to return to priestly functioning once he has fully reengaged his priestly role." Third, Gonsiorek argues that doctrinal commitment to the aristocratic prerogatives of the hierarchy produced a top-down managerial culture that did not encourage accountability.[16]

Church doctrine to avoid scandal among the faithful—the disclosure of information that might erode ordinary Catholics' respect for the Church—has also been cited as a reason for church officials' failure to disclose information about clergy sexual abuse.[17] Journalists Frank Bruni and Elinor Burkett quote Bishop Thomas Gumbleton of Detroit: "We were taught that the Church is the perfect society and the Church is a divine institution and part of our tasks as bishops was to make sure people respected the institution. If you allowed it to be defamed and tarnished, you were failing as a bishop. You weren't living up to your pledge to protect the mystical body of Christ."[18] Declared USCCB president Bishop Wilton Gregory at the 2002 Dallas meeting: "We . . . are the ones who worried more about the possibility of scandal than in bringing about the kind of openness that helps prevent abuse."[19]

Related to this concern about scandal, it has also been suggested that church officials have failed to disclose clergy sexual abuse because they fear that accusers will expose widespread sexual activity among clergy. "The reasons for bishops' and priests' inaction," write Thomas Doyle, Richard Sipe, and Patrick Wall, "may be that so many of them themselves are sexually active, although not necessarily with children." "Priests who abuse minors," they assert, "are part of a much larger group, an anonymous network of the clergy who are aware of each other's sexual proclivities, behaviors, and activities and are capable of blackmailing each other."[20]

Other commentators suggest that institutional culture accounts for the manner in which church officials approached disclosure. *New York Times* columnist Peter Steinfels argues that the insularity of the priesthood contributed to a lack of transparency: "priest abusers and their superiors operated within an enclosed, self-protected clerical culture bonded by years of seminary formation and reinforced by celibacy." Steinfels points also to personnel practices: "priests moved from assignment to assignment without the open process of inquiry, interview, and evaluation that was characteristic of many other religious groups as well as professional appointments." In addition, Steinfels argues that a culture within the Church of deep respect and extreme deference to priests made it easier to suppress information: "[A] powerful aura of being consecrated surrounded the Catholic priesthood, making these crimes all the more unthinkable to most people." Finally, Steinfels asserts that the highly deliberative and bureaucratic nature of decision making in the Church accounts for the slow pace of disclosure. "If there is one thing that the Catholic Church is not built for, it is speed. Decisions about even noncontroversial matters creep through multiple stages of deliberation."[21]

There is also within the Church a firm commitment to keeping government out of the Church's internal affairs, and this led many bishops to handle abuse allegations in-house rather than reporting them to state authorities. This aversion to government interference is often mixed with a suspicion that state interference may be motivated by a long tradition of anti-Catholic bias. In reference to criminal investigations of bishops for their role in facilitating clergy sexual abuse, law professor John Baker warns of "a lynch-mob mentality" and asserts that "the Church must defend its doctrine and jurisdiction against the intrusions of the state."[22]

Finally, commentators have suggested that particular perceptions of the problem arising out of a Catholic perspective explain the failure of church officials to disclose information. Bruni and Burkett argue that church officials' own discomfort with sex led them to suppress information: "Projecting their own sense of shame onto victims, they often assumed that those children and their families had no more desire or inclination to discuss what had happened than bishops themselves did. They assumed as well that families wanted the matter handled quickly and quietly, without the intrusion of police officers, lawyers and the news media."[23] Journalist John Allen suggests that suspicion of those calling for disclosure also affected church officials' reaction to the problem. He explains that, from the Vatican down, it was widely believed among church officials that lawsuits by victims were simply a financial shakedown of the Church by greedy plaintiffs and their lawyers, that allegations were simply attempts fueled by anti-Catholic prejudice to discredit the Church, and that dissidents within the Church were inflating the scandal in order to use it as a vehicle for their own reform agenda.[24]

How the Church Concealed Information

The stubborn information theory suggests that we look at the influence of church officials in explaining how they managed to prevent disclosure of information about clergy sexual abuse. According to many accounts, church officials used their influence with law enforcement officials, legislators, and the media to prevent disclosure of abuse allegations. For example, David France tells the story of a woman in a Boston suburb who in 1979 went to the local police station to file a complaint against Father Geoghan for molesting her son. "Because her allegation involved a Roman Catholic priest," explains France, "it was directed to the attention of the chaplain of the police department. The disposition of the case was left up to him. No other information was reported back, either to the police officials or to the complainant."[25] Bruni and Burkett relate that in 1987, Bishop John McCarthy of Austin, Texas, assigned a priest who admitted sexually molesting a child to a parish on the condition that the priest sign a document stating that if he ever molested again, he would leave the priesthood. When the priest was arrested for child sexual abuse a year later, "McCarthy phoned the district attorney, arranged a meeting and pleaded for the priest not to be charged. 'You can move against him,' McCarthy said to the D.A., 'and my church in that area will be hurt.' McCarthy pulled out the document with the priest's signature. 'Look,' he said, 'he's out of the priesthood.' The D.A. acquiesced."[26] Historian Philip Jenkins describes how in 1988 a New Orleans district attorney took no action against a local priest, Dino Cinel, who produced pornographic videos recording sexual encounters in the parish rectory between himself and several teenage boys, so as not to embarrass what the D.A. called "Holy Mother the Church."[27]

Church officials have also exercised influence in state legislatures. Statewide organizations, called Catholic conferences, represent bishops and the interests of the Church in the political process. They formulate policy, mobilize voters, make public statements, and lobby state legislatures. Their efforts are complemented by national organizations such as the USCCB and the Catholic League for Religious and Civil Rights. In many states, these organizations have lobbied successfully to exempt clergy from statutes mandating that professionals who provide services for children report child abuse to state authorities. Most recently, they have helped to defeat attempts to repeal these clergy exemptions in mandatory reporting laws. Those representing the Church have argued that elimination of clergy exemptions might require priests to violate Catholic doctrine by revealing information received during confession. State Catholic conferences and national organizations have also lobbied hard to oppose legislation that would extend or eliminate the statute of limitations for child sexual abuse. Bishops have often taken a leading role in efforts to defeat these two legislative responses to clergy sexual abuse.[28]

This is not to say that there is anything wrong with bishops or Catholic organizations formulating policy, mobilizing voters, and lobbying legislatures. My aim is only to point out that successful lobbying is one means by which church officials have managed to prevent the disclosure of information about clergy sexual abuse. And in fairness, it should be noted that in at least three states—California, Washington, and Wisconsin—the Church supported adding priests to the list of those required to report child abuse.[29]

Influence over the media also contributed to church officials' ability to prevent disclosure of clergy sexual abuse. Journalist Jason Berry recounts how there was "incredible resistance from the mainstream print media in '84 and '85" to covering the Gauthe story. The *Lafayette Daily Advertiser,* the local daily newspaper, initially refused to cover the story and blasted the alternative weekly *Times of Acadiana* for printing Berry's three-part expose and thereby "blacken[ing] the reputation of the entire religious community."[30] David France tells of how church officials called *Boston Globe* publisher Bill Taylor to complain about a Sunday magazine article on the Porter case, and how Taylor called in his top editor, Matt Storin, who pledged that from thenceforth, "the chancery would find an editorial environment more attentive to the church's point of view," after which Storin reprimanded the author of the article.[31] Phillip Jenkins asserts that there is a long tradition dating back to the 1930s of fear among journalists that news articles critical of the Catholic Church would elicit potentially ruinous readership and advertising boycotts. He suggests that the remarks of a journalist on one suppressed scandal in Massachusetts in the mid-1970s could be applied to virtually any community with a strong Catholic presence: "If any priest had any sexual problems or was involved in a compromising incident—even if it involved an arrest—the diocese could prevail upon the local papers not to write about it and upon the district attorney's office not to prosecute. To reveal a priest's shortcomings was akin to blasphemy in the eyes of diocesan officials, and they were ever vigilant against such disclosures." The suppression of stories critical of the Church was, Jenkins explains, not merely a result of specifically Catholic influence but also of a more general reticence prior to the 1980s to embarrass public figures and stir up public scandal.[32] The particular power of church officials to suppress media coverage of clergy sexual abuse was thus supported by this broader cultural deference to public figures and established institutions.

Litigation and Information Disclosure

Consistent with stubborn information theory, tort litigation has been an effective means of generating information about clergy sexual abuse. Plaintiffs' lawyers have used civil discovery to compel church officials to disclose information. But we should be careful not to oversimplify. Plaintiffs' lawyers, especially during the first two waves of litigation, also frequently opted for settlements that included secrecy agreements, making it even less likely that information about allegations would ever be disclosed.

Secret settlements resulted from a mix of factors that varied from case to case. First, some plaintiffs' attorneys were eager to maintain cordial relations with church officials and reluctant to stir up scandal. Second, some plaintiffs' attorneys shared church officials' view that secrecy was best for victims and their families. Third, some plaintiffs' attorneys agreed to secrecy in order to obtain money from the Church for their clients and for themselves. And finally, in some cases, plaintiffs' attorneys were likely merely responding to the wishes of their clients.[33]

The prevalence of these secret settlements complicates Wagner's assertion that litigation is an effective means for uncovering stubborn information, because it suggests that plaintiffs' lawyers are not always immune from political influence and may sometimes have financial incentives to pursue litigation in ways that do not promote information disclosure. In the first two waves of litigation, plaintiffs' attorneys were sometimes less than zealous out of deference to the Church and faced financial incentives to suppress information. In order to understand how litigation generated information about clergy sexual abuse, we must better understand the noneconomic motivations of plaintiffs and their attorneys.

We begin first with an analysis of how plaintiffs used discovery to compel information disclosure. Next, we examine briefly what motivated plaintiffs and their attorneys to reject lucrative secret settlements.

We then look beyond discovery to examine how other elements of the litigation process, through framing and agenda setting, encouraged information disclosure.

Plaintiffs' Discovery Techniques

Clergy sexual abuse litigation has posed some novel challenges for plaintiffs seeking to uncover information to support their claims. First, church officials have hidden personnel records relating to clergy sexual abuse in secret archives. Canon 489 of the Code of Canon Law mandates that "[i]n the diocesan curia there is also to be a secret archive, or at least in the common archive there is to be a safe or cabinet, completely closed and locked, which cannot be removed; in it documents to be kept secret are to be protected most securely." Canon 490 states that "[o]nly the bishop is to have the key to the secret archive" and that "documents are not to be removed from the secret archive or safe."

During the first wave of litigation following the Gauthe case, plaintiffs' lawyers gradually discovered that the information they were seeking was contained not in diocesan personnel files but in secret archives. Plaintiffs' attorney Jeff Anderson recalls how, with the help of canon lawyer Thomas Doyle, he learned of the secret archives and began to refer to them specifically in discovery requests and depositions. "I would issue subpoenas for those files in advance of the depositions of the Chancellor, the Vicar General, the Bishop, Auxiliary or the Archbishop . . . and then that subpoena required them to deal specifically with the production of this sub-secretal file."[34] In response, church defendants refused to produce documents from secret archives, arguing that the contents of secret archives were not discoverable based on a common-law privilege protecting the confidentiality of priest-penitent communications. Defendants also argued that canon law forbade the removal of files from the secret archive for the purpose of inspection or copying and that the free exercise clause of the First Amendment prevented courts from requiring the bishop to violate canon law.[35] Courts resolved these discovery disputes sometimes in favor of plaintiffs, sometimes in favor of the Church. Either way, specific requests for documents from the secret archives helped to establish their existence and, in some cases, forced disclosure of their contents.

A second challenge to discovery has been that church officials have often kept incomplete records of allegations or failed to record them at all. According to a 2004 Philadelphia grand jury report, "in their internal files, Archdiocese officials tried to limit evidence of priests' crimes and their own guilty knowledge of them . . . Written records of allegations often left out the names of potential victims, while euphemisms obscured the actual nature of offenses. An attempted anal rape of a 12-year-old boy, for example, was recorded in Archdiocese files as 'touches.' . . . Under Cardinal Bavilaqua's policy, aides would inform him when abuse allegations came into the Archdiocese, but not in writing. His initial response and instructions were not recorded."[36]

In some instances, church officials have even destroyed potentially incriminating documents.[37] Indeed, Canon 489 requires that "[e]ach year documents of criminal cases in matters of morals, in which the accused parties have died or ten years have elapsed from the condemnatory sentence, are to be destroyed. A brief summary of what occurred along with the text of the definitive sentence is to be retained." Canon lawyer and auxiliary bishop of Cleveland James Quinn, in a 1990 address to the Midwest Canon Law Society, advised his audience that prior to discovery, "personnel files should be carefully examined to determine their content. Unsigned letters alleging misconduct should be expunged. Standard personnel files should contain no documentation relating to possible criminal behavior." Once files have been subpoenaed, he counseled, "they cannot be tampered with, destroyed, [or] removed," but "if there's something there you really don't want people to see, you might send it off to the Apostolic Delegate [the Vatican's diplomatic representative in the United States], because they have immunity to protect something that is potentially dangerous."[38]

In the face of incomplete record keeping and document destruction, plaintiffs' lawyers have found other sources of information that have helped them advance their claims. For example, plaintiffs' attorneys have used the *Official Catholic Directory* which provides the complete assignment history of priests in the United States. Plaintiffs' lawyer Steve Rubino recalls his discovery of the *Directory* during the first wave of litigation as a "major breakthrough." Gaps in a particular priest's assignment history or entries indicating that the priest was off duty or on sick leave often supported suspicions that the priest had a history of sexual abuse. Up until the mid-1950s, Rubino explains, there were even explicit entries that mentioned assignment to specific treatment facilities with programs for sexual abusers. Using the *Directory*, plaintiffs' lawyers were able to piece together a priest's history "like a huge jigsaw puzzle," and use it as a guide in deposing accused priests and their superiors.[39]

Third, plaintiffs' attorneys suspect that church officials have provided incomplete or misleading answers in depositions in reliance on the Catholic doctrine of mental reservation. This doctrine permits a person to mislead another by making a statement that, while not strictly untrue in the sense intended by the speaker, is vague or equivocal in order to fulfill one's obligation to keep secrets faithfully. Plaintiffs' lawyer Eric MacLeish offers the following hypothetical example:

> Q. Father, do you recall receiving this letter in 1982, which states that Father Joe Juice sexually molested an altar boy?
> A. I have no *active* memory of receiving that letter.
> Q. Regardless of your *active* memory, do you have any memory of receiving that letter?
> A. Yes.

For evidence that clerics use mental reservation, MacLeish cites a written memorandum from a Father Ryan to then auxiliary bishop of the Boston archdiocese Thomas Daily in which Ryan recounts falsely telling a *New York Times* reporter that Daily was not available for comment because he was at a confirmation, after which Ryan writes "(broad mental reservation, I think you were going to have one this evening . . .)."[40] Plaintiffs' lawyers in Los Angeles report that they have encountered the doctrine during depositions. When pressed as to whether they subscribed to the doctrine, some church officials have responded yes, while others have refused to answer the question.[41]

By being doggedly persistent in discovery, plaintiffs' lawyers have overcome the evasiveness of church defendants. "Be relentless," MacLeish counseled plaintiffs' lawyers at a 2003 conference on clergy sexual abuse, "[p]ropound standard written discovery and push clergy abuse defendants to conduct proper searches for responsive documents by taking depositions to ascertain whether there has been compliance with those discovery requests, i.e., who looked where for what?"[42]

Plaintiffs' lawyers have also used information from other sources to judge the veracity of church officials' statements. Some of these other sources were individuals who contacted the lawyers as a result of publicity surrounding a case. In litigating the Kos case, for example, plaintiffs' attorney Sylvia Demarest recalls,

> we underwent traditional discovery-type techniques, and, with some exception, the Dallas diocese had made a decision to cooperate. They wanted to be able to go into court and act like they were the good guys.

And so, it wasn't that difficult to get information out of them. But getting complete information was another matter. The fact that this was in the newspapers every once in a while was just amazing in terms of what information it produced. People would just call you up. People ask me, "how did you conduct discovery in the Kos case," and I say, "I answered the telephone." People just called me up and said, "we wrote letters to the bishop," or "we had a meeting with the bishop," or "we reported this," or "I'm another victim and this is what happened, and I know so-and-so who ran out of the rectory with only his underwear." People calling me up and giving me information that helps you put things into context and flush out a time line of what happened.

"Publicity is so important," concludes Demarest, "because that's the only way to find out if they're lying to you."[43]

Fourth, some church defendants have vigorously resisted court orders to produce documents either by pursuing interlocutory appeals or by simply refusing to comply. Says L.A. plaintiffs' attorney Ray Boucher "[t]he hardest thing has been getting documents. It's 'Katie bar the door,' scorched earth, 'We're not turning anything over,' and a united front by the Church and by the individual priests to try to impede access to public disclosure and sunshine on the documents that have existed in their files for some years."[44] In an article published in *Catholic Lawyer,* defense lawyer Carl Eck advised diocesan attorneys on how to vigorously resist discovery of records stored in secret archives by raising privileges and, if they were rejected at the trial level, insisting on interlocutory appeals:

> The court must be convinced that you are not trying to defeat discovery. You are trying to protect the secret archives establishment as a canon of the Church. As a right, the Church had to establish rules and regulations and these Canons were set up long before anybody thought of pedophilic lawsuits or sexual molestation cases. If you do not succeed, the plaintiff will try his case in discovery. Also, the bishop and diocese may be very reluctant to try the case on its merits. It really requires a great deal of advocacy to present and protect the documents and it is getting tougher and tougher, but there is no alternative. The alternative is to give up the documents or not to give them up and be saddled with a default judgment.[45]

This kind of aggressive litigation in order to avoid document production has characterized clergy sexual abuse litigation in Los Angeles, where diocesan attorneys have unsuccessfully attempted to have their interlocutory appeals on claims of privilege heard by the U.S. Supreme Court.[46]

In some instances, church defendants have simply refused to comply with court orders. David France recounts how diocesan attorney Wilson Rodgers, Jr.—after swearing in court that he had complied with an order to release every record of every priest in Boston accused of molesting children—insisted to plaintiffs' attorney Eric MacLeish that the only records of sexual misconduct not turned over involved personnel records related to sexual misconduct with adults which were irrelevant to the litigation. Rodgers declared that MacLeish was welcome to review the files in Rodgers's office. When MacLeish and several colleagues accepted the offer, they found that two dozen of the files contained allegations of child sexual abuse. "Apparently," concludes France, they had been classified as adult-victim files because "these guys *also* fornicated with adults."[47]

Again, plaintiffs' attorneys have met this challenge by being persistent. Many plaintiffs' attorneys are repeat players, who have a long-term perspective on discovery. Jeff Anderson describes the gradual advances in obtaining information from case to case as "a kind of a base of knowledge that is cumulatively obtained that is still progressing in some ways."[48] In addition, as we saw in the previous chapter, many plaintiffs' lawyers pool their resources by sharing information and strategy.

In addressing these challenges to discovery, plaintiffs lawyers have benefited from knowledge of the inner workings of the Church—for example, the maintenance of secret archives, the existence of the *Official Catholic Directory,* and reliance on the doctrine of mental reservation. They have been helped in this regard by experts like Thomas Doyle and former priest and psychotherapist Richard Sipe. L.A. plaintiffs' attorney John Manly explains that "a number of years ago, I hired a former priest and canon lawyer to help me because basically if you don't use the right word—and frequently the key documents are in Latin—they won't produce it."[49]

Some plaintiffs' lawyers bring to the litigation their own Catholic expertise. It may be no coincidence that many of the leading plaintiffs' lawyers are Catholics, including J. Minos Simon, Steve Rubino, Sylvia Demarest, John Manly, and Ray Boucher. When asked what might explain the prominence of Catholics among successful plaintiffs' lawyers in clergy sexual abuse litigation, Sylvia Demarest, "born and raised Catholic in south Louisiana," suggested, "I think we understand the institution better than most. And let me tell you, in this litigation against the Dallas Diocese [i.e., the Kos case], if you didn't understand the language you wouldn't have gotten anywhere. It was possible to ask a question and not get an answer unless you asked the question absolutely correctly. I noted that with my co-counsel who wasn't familiar with the issues. He could ask a question, not get an answer. I could ask the question, and they were forced to answer because I knew the language."[50] Steve Rubino, educated within "the warm embrace" of Catholic schools and the recipient of an undergraduate degree from Mount St. Mary's College and a law degree from Catholic University, ventured that Catholic lawyers better understand the vulnerability of victims and their families to priests, who are viewed as "God's earthly representative."[51]

Plaintiffs' attorneys have also benefited from judges becoming more liberal on discovery. Attorneys on both sides of the litigation suggest that in early cases, judges restricted discovery to files concerning the priest named in the complaint. Over time, discovery rules "opened up," and judges allowed discovery of files related to other priests that might help plaintiffs establish a pattern of wrongdoing by diocesan officials in handling clergy sexual abuse allegations.[52] According to Rubino, "There has been a sea change in the way the judiciary understands this now."[53] Explains one attorney involved in the Boston litigation, this shift "followed on the heels of enormous pressure—constant tales in the newspapers of victims saying how they'd been abused and by whom and how nothing had been done about it and how efforts had been made to obtain records and how the counsel for the Church was unwilling to produce these records and how there were cover-ups. Judges were not deaf or blind to that drum beat, and they were influenced by this notion that there was an enormous cover-up going on . . . And, as a consequence, certain judges to whom these cases were assigned took a very lenient position with respect to discovery."[54]

Non-Economic Motivations

The success of discovery in forcing disclosure of stubborn information about clergy sexual abuse was made possible only by plaintiffs' rejection of lucrative secret settlements. In order to explain plaintiffs' rejection of secret settlements and their lawyers' persistence in pursuing discovery, we should look at non-economic motivations for suing the Church. To be sure, some plaintiffs and their lawyers aggressively pursued litigation simply because they believed that they could secure verdicts more lucrative than defendants' settlement offers. But this was not always the case. In many instances, victims wanted most of all to have their claims aired publicly and vindicated by a court and to hold church officials accountable for their role in facilitating and covering up abuse.[55] Many plaintiffs' attorneys shared this desire to hold church officials accountable.

For some attorneys, personal experience with child sexual abuse may help to explain their persistence in pursuing discovery. David France reports that Eric MacLeish harbored anger against a boarding school French instructor who attempted several times to molest him. In a 2002 interview with *People* magazine, Jeff Anderson disclosed that his daughter Amy had been molested at age eight by a therapist who was a former priest. "It was very painful," Anderson explains, "I came to feel like I didn't protect her, and to this day I understand how parents of victims blame themselves." The article quotes Amy as saying that "[m]y pain is what makes him keep going."[56]

For Catholic attorneys, however, there is sometimes a different type of personal motivation. For those whose Catholic experience was a positive one, there may be a desire to redeem the Church. "When I realized the level of corruption in the Church," recalls Rubino, "it made me angry. I felt that something personal was being taken away from me. I wanted to effect change on a practical level, to reform the institution for the future."[57] John Manly, the product of "a Dominican military school and Jesuit training," shared this sense that something precious was being taken from him:

> I went to Catholic schools my whole life . . . And I think that you look at what you were taught as a young person, which is you follow Christ's example. You do the right thing . . . And if you're engaged in evil or sin, you stop. And no one's suggesting that priests should be perfect. They're human beings . . . But the notion that the people who on Sunday would tell you you're going to hell because you didn't go to Mass, something so trivial and so venial, would engage in the kind of behavior these people engage in, it makes you fucking mad. Yeah, I'm pissed! Sorry, there's no other word for it. I'm fucking pissed that they've taken—they basically are no better than the lowest scum bag televangelist . . . The reality is that none of the people in charge of the Church really believe it. They completely walked away from—when you walk away from protecting kids, you're capable of any act of evil, in my opinion . . . They just don't care . . . [I]t's the hypocrisy that drives a lot of us to go after these guys.[58]

Sylvia Demarest, who, unlike Rubino and Manly, feels alienated from her Catholic upbringing, is motivated not by a desire to redeem the Church but rather by a desire to punish it:

[T]he fact of the matter is that this institution is corrupt because of the individuals and their secrets that inhabit the institution. It was very irritating for me, for example, to see that a number of cardinals and bishops had come out with this new thing to prohibit gay marriage when a majority of the bishops, cardinals, and priests in the United States are gay and they are sexually active. In fact that kind of hypocrisy just goes all over me, and so nothing has changed in the Church and nothing will change in the Church unless and until enough pressure is put upon them. Unfortunately, that's money. Until they say uncle and they're absolutely compelled to change ... [F]or those who grew up [in the Catholic Church] and did not have a good experience, being able to deal with some of the issues that that led to that is very gratifying from a personal standpoint.[59]

Thus, outrage and a desire for vindication, accountability, redemption, and perhaps even revenge help explain the persistence of plaintiffs' and their attorneys in pursuing discovery despite the financial incentives to accept secret settlements.

Beyond Discovery

To understand the full extent of information generated by clergy sexual abuse litigation, we must look beyond discovery. We will look first at how the framing and agenda-setting effects of the litigation prompted and shaped investigations by church officials, grand juries, and attorneys general. We will then examine the use of settlement to force disclosure of stubborn information.

As we saw in chapters 4 and 5, litigation framed clergy sexual abuse as an issue of institutional failure and helped to place this issue on the agendas of church and government policymaking institutions. In addressing clergy sexual abuse, many of these institutions conducted investigations and published reports. An account of litigation's role in generating information would not be complete without attention to these sources of information.

The most comprehensive study of clergy sexual abuse is the 2004 John Jay study, *The Nature and Scope of Sexual Abuse of Minors by Catholic Priests and Deacons in the United States 1950–2002*, commissioned by the National Review Board under the terms of the *Charter for the Protection of Children and Young People* adopted by the bishops at the June 2002 USCCB conference in Dallas. The study examines the prevalence of clergy sexual abuse in the Catholic Church, the demographics of perpetrators and victims, the types and circumstances of abuse, responses to the abuse by church and civil authorities, and the financial costs of claims against the Church. The study's findings are based on survey responses from diocesan officials, and they represent a significant disclosure of information contained in diocesan files and secret archives. The report also includes an extensive literature review and annotated bibliography of child sexual abuse. The John Jay research team subsequently published a *Supplementary Data Analysis* in 2006. While this first study focuses on the nature and scope of the problem, the John Jay team is currently conducting a second study called for by the Dallas Charter on the causes and larger context of clergy sexual abuse. The National Review Board itself published in 2004 an extensive *Report on the Crisis in the Catholic Church in the United States* that summarizes what is known about clergy sexual abuse in the Catholic Church, presents findings of fact, and makes policy recommendations. The National Review Board also oversees the annual publication starting in 2004 of reports on the implementation of the Dallas Charter that include new survey information and further recommendations.

In addition, individual bishops around the country have, since 2002, launched internal investigations and issued their own reports with regular updates on clergy sexual abuse within their dioceses. One of the most extensive such reports is Cardinal Mahoney's 2004 *Report to the People of God: Clergy Sexual Abuse, Archdiocese of Los Angeles, 1930–2003*, a thirty-five-page report counting 244 sexual abuse allegations against clergy in the diocese accompanied by a subsequent 155-page addendum with details of the assignment history of over 140 priests accused of abuse. This information was gathered and organized by the archdiocese as part of a mediation process with plaintiffs' attorneys. It is highly unlikely that this information would have been collected, organized, and disclosed in the absence of litigation.[60]

Grand jury investigations have produced extensive local reports on clergy sexual abuse. The Suffolk County grand jury investigated clergy sexual abuse in the Diocese of Rockville Center, New York. The grand jury "heard testimony from 97 witnesses and considered 257 exhibits, many consisting of multiple pages of documents." It had "unprecedented access to thousands of pages of records, memos, notes, and other confidential documents," including materials contained in the diocese's secret archive.[61]

The Suffolk County grand jury's 181-page report details child sexual abuse perpetrated by eighteen priests. Even more shocking, however, are its findings concerning the way abuse allegations were handled by church officials. The grand jury summarized its findings as follows:

> The response of priests in the Diocesan hierarchy to allegations of criminal sexual abuse was not pastoral. In fact, although there was a written policy that set a pastoral tone, it was a sham. The Diocese failed to follow the policy from its inception even at its most rudimentary level. Abusive priests were transferred from parish to parish and between Dioceses. Abusive priests were protected under the guise of confidentiality; their histories mired in secrecy. Professional treatment recommendations were ignored and dangerous priests allowed to minister to children. Diocesan policy was to expend as little financial capital as possible to assist victims but to be well prepared for the possibility of enormous financial and legal liability. Aggressive legal strategies were employed to defeat and discourage lawsuits even though Diocesan officials knew they were meritorious. Victims were deceived; priests who were civil attorneys portrayed themselves as interested in the concerns of victims and pretended to be acting for their benefit while they acted only to protect the Diocese. These officials boldly bragged about their success and arrogantly outlined in writing mechanisms devised to shield them from discovery. These themes framed a system that left thousands of children in the Diocese exposed to predatory, serial, child molesters working as priests.[62]

The report provides specific examples of each of these allegations and includes excerpts from church officials' grand jury testimony admitting that they placed known abusers in parishes despite the clear recommendations of clinical psychologists and requirements of their own policies.[63]

An 800-page Philadelphia grand jury report provided even greater detail on twenty-eight priests accused of abuse and identified them by name. (The Suffolk County grand jury report referred to priest-perpetrators as "Priest A" through "Priest R.") The Philadelphia grand jury report also offered extensive support for its finding of a concerted effort to conceal abuse allegations.[64] Additional grand jury investigations have taken place in Long Island, Cleveland, Cincinnati, Dayton, Phoenix, and Los Angeles.

In addition to grand juries, state attorneys general have also conducted investigations and published reports on clergy sexual abuse. Massachusetts attorney general Thomas Reilly issued a report on the Boston archdiocese in order to "create an official public record of what occurred."[65] Reilly's investigative team "reviewed personnel files of at least 102 priests alleged to have sexually abused children . . . and . . . more than 30,000 pages of documents obtained from the Archdiocese."[66] The report's findings include that church officials of the Boston archdiocese "knew the extent of the clergy abuse problem for many years before it became known to the public," "did not notify law enforcement authorities of clergy sexual abuse allegations," "did not provide all relevant information to law enforcement authorities during criminal investigations," "failed to conduct thorough investigations of clergy sexual abuse allegations," "placed children at risk by transferring abusive priests to other parishes," "placed children at risk by accepting abusive priests from other dioceses," and "failed to adequately supervise priests known to have sexually abused children."[67] Attorneys general in New Hampshire and Maine issued similar reports on the dioceses of Manchester and Portland respectively. New Hampshire attorney general Peter Heed agreed not to press charges against officials in the Manchester diocese on the condition that the diocese report all allegations of clergy sexual abuse to law enforcement and submit to an annual audit by the attorney general's office.

Litigation promoted the generation of information not only among bishops and government officials but also by victims, lawyers, and activists who were mobilized by the litigation. These groups have collected and organized vast amounts of existing information and made it publicly accessible on the web. For example, the BishopAccountability.org website contains over 25,000 news articles, thousands of documents from diocesan archives, and twenty-five reports. BishopAccountability.org has posted 9,000 pages of documents from the Manchester diocese and is currently in the process of uploading 45,000 pages of documents filed in the Boston litigation. In addition to collecting and organizing this information, the organization has also generated its own database of over 3,000 accused priests and other church personnel, searchable by name, diocese, and state. Other groups such as SNAP, Voice of the Faithful, and Survivor Connections maintain less extensive websites.[68]

In some cases, litigation encouraged whistleblowers to come forward. For example, Jason Berry recounts how an anonymous church insider was prompted by news coverage of the Gauthe case to provide plaintiffs' lawyer J. Minos Simon and Berry himself information about clergy sexual abuse within the Lafayette diocese.[69] The Gauthe case also led Thomas Doyle, perhaps the most well-known whistleblower, to begin a long-running personal campaign to expose the role of church officials in facilitating clergy sexual abuse.[70]

Settlement has also been a means of generating information about clergy sexual abuse. In a $100 million settlement with ninety clergy sexual abuse victims in 2005, the Diocese of Orange in California agreed to the release of 10,000 pages of documents from diocesan files, which the plaintiffs' attorneys made available to the press and many of which are currently posted on the BishopAccountability.org website.[71] Subsequent settlements in Los Angeles, San Diego, and Portland, Oregon, in 2007 similarly required the release of diocesan personnel files.[72]

What Have We Learned from Litigation?

It seems fitting at this point to take stock of what litigation has revealed about clergy sexual abuse. While it is not possible to catalogue everything that has been disclosed or to quantify it, we can survey the types of information generated by the litigation. This will give us a sense of the value of litigation as a means of generating information.

First, litigation has generated information about abusers and victims. It has revealed publicly the identities of individual abusers. SNAP national director David Clohessy contends that "in the overwhelming majority of cases, we would not even know who the perpetrators are, much less be able to get them out of ministry, without the civil justice system."[73] Litigation has also encouraged victims to disclose their abuse. Albany bishop Howard Hubbard suggests that "the litigation has served to bring people forward that maybe previously wouldn't have come forward because of shame or because of fear of not being believed."[74] Indeed, Hubbard himself implemented an outreach effort using radio and newspaper advertisements to encourage clergy sexual abuse victims to come forward so that the diocese can offer them services and investigate allegations.[75]

Second, litigation has generated aggregate information about the nature and scope of clergy sexual abuse within the Catholic Church. The John Jay study, individual diocesan reports, grand jury reports, attorney general reports, and online data bases are examples of aggregate information generated as a result of the framing and agenda-setting effects of litigation. Litigation has also shown some of the Church's self-reporting to be incomplete. For example, litigation documents obtained in October 2005 by plaintiffs suing the L.A. archdiocese showed the archdiocese's February 2004 *Report to the People of God* to be incomplete, and this prompted the archdiocese to publish a detailed addendum disclosing additional information.[76]

Third, litigation has educated church leaders and the public about child sexual abuse. Church leaders have a better understanding of the effects of abuse on victims as a result of litigation. Explains Bishop Hubbard, "it has given us a greater appreciation for the harm that was inflicted on victims and the lifelong consequences of that trauma, which cannot be addressed through therapy." Litigation has also helped educate the public about the risk of child sexual abuse. "When I was a kid," says attorney for the L.A. archdiocese J. Michael Hennigan, "we never heard anything about pedophilia. There were people whom we thought lurked in public restrooms and in parks who might jump out and grab us, but that's not the image at all of the pedophile that we've come to know through this process. The pedophile that we've come to know is a family friend, maybe a relative, certainly someone who's trusted and who develops relationships over a long period of time with the children that ultimately become intimate and sometimes sexual. Nobody was aware of that at all before about 1985."[77] We have learned from the litigation, echoes plaintiffs' attorney Sylvia Demarest, that "[t]he problem isn't stranger danger. You're much more likely to be abused by someone that you know and trust than you are to be picked up by some pervert on the street."[78]

Fourth, and finally, the litigation has revealed institutional dimensions of clergy sexual abuse. We now know that the Catholic Church as an institution has been struggling with the problem of child sexual abuse by clergy for decades. As the John Jay study reveals, diocesan officials dealt with dozens of allegations in the 1950s and 1960s, hundreds in the 1970s and 1980s, and thousands in the 1990s and the early 2000s. We also know that the bishops addressed the problem collectively as far back as the early 1970s, when the NCCB contributed funds to support a program run by the Servants of the Paraclete specifically aimed at the treatment of priests with psychosexual disorders, including sex with minors. Indeed, this program was built on decades of prior experience treating priests with psychosexual disorders in Catholic treatment centers for addiction and mental illness dating back to 1924. "By the late 1970s," explain coauthors Thomas Doyle, Richard Sipe, and Patrick Wall, "Catholic treatment centers were using cutting-edge psychological and psychiatric modalities to treat priests and religious who had abused minors."[79] The list of Catholic institutions that treated abusers includes The Institute of Living in Connecticut, the St. Luke Institute in Maryland, the Seton Institute also in Maryland, the House of Affirmation in Massachusetts, and retreat centers operated by the Servants of the Paraclete in New Mexico and Minnesota. These institutions have treated thousands of priests accused of sexually abusing children, including Gilbert Gauthe, James Porter, and John Geoghan. Doyle and his coauthors have recently published a history of institutional responses to clergy sexual misconduct within the Catholic Church dating back to the beginning of the Church's formal legal system in the early fourth century.[80]

Litigation exposed the failure of the Church's institutional response to clergy sexual abuse. Take, for example, litigation against the L.A. archdiocese. Referring to materials obtained through discovery, plaintiffs' attorney Ray Boucher relates that:

> We've got the documents from the 1950s from the Servants of the Paraclete and they mirror some of the documents that came out of Orange County in 1960. The documents show that they knew in 1950 that you couldn't treat pedophile priests. You couldn't put them back into the community. You couldn't let them be exposed to children without warning people who would come into contact with them. And the most important thing that you should do is to segregate them in a way where they don't run the risk of molesting another child, because they will. And the documents are very clear and precise on that idea. That comes from their own treating doctors in their own treating facilities that are solely for priests. And it's unheard of in the world. There's no other institution, there's no other government, there's no other entity in the world that has set up this kind of an intricate treatment facility program and have it solely treat these priests. It tells you just how large a problem this was.[81]

Discovery documents from litigation against dioceses across the country tell the same story.

By shining a spotlight on the institutional failure of the Catholic Church, litigation has also sparked interest in addressing sexual abuse within other institutions, religious and secular, throughout U.S. society and in other countries. Litigation has already exposed sexual abuse perpetrated by protestant and Jewish clergy and covered up by their religious superiors.[82] Moreover, lawyers on both sides of the litigation have suggested that, as a society, it is now time to turn our attention to child sexual abuse within secular institutions such as schools and youth programs.[83] The John Jay research team has already launched an extensive study of child sexual abuse in other countries.[84] Thus, it appears that litigation has begun a slow and painful process of revealing the pervasiveness of child sexual abuse and the role of institutions in facilitating it.

PART THREE

Tort Litigation as a Policy Venue

At this point in our examination of clergy sexual abuse litigation, two important questions remain. Chapter 7 addresses whether the policy-making benefits of the litigation are worth its costs. Chapter 8 explores whether the policymaking benefits of clergy sexual abuse litigation are applicable to other forms of litigation. It also considers more generally the policymaking role of tort litigation and addresses objections that lawsuits are an ineffective, inefficient, and illegitimate way to promote social change.

CHAPTER SEVEN

Assessing the Results of Clergy Sexual Abuse Litigation

These cases . . . drove the Church, as an institution, to
be very serious about reforming itself, so that these
kinds of accusations could never be made with the
same facility again—of cover-up, protecting the priest,
ignoring the pain of the victims, things like that. That
is pretty clearly now part of the Church's past.

—J. MICHAEL HENNIGAN, ATTORNEY FOR THE
L.A. ARCHDIOCESE

No one denies that terrible offenses occurred, but
this does not justify . . . transferring hundreds of
millions of dollars away from inner-city schools, from
ministries to families and their children, from soup
kitchens and immigration services and from ministries
to the grieving—all of which constitute the good work
of a church humbled by its sins and resolved not to
repeat them.

—L. MARTIN NUSSBAUM, "CHANGING THE RULES:
SELECTIVE JUSTICE FOR CATHOLIC INSTITUTIONS,"
AMERICA, MAY 15, 2006

So far, we have seen that clergy sexual abuse litigation has had a significant impact on church and government policymaking. The chapters in
Part II demonstrated how litigation framed clergy sexual abuse as an issue of institutional failure, placed this issue on the agendas of church
and government policymakers, and uncovered information essential to
understanding the problem. We turn now to the question of whether the
litigation's impact has been beneficial and, if so, whether its benefits
outweigh its costs.

Clergy sexual abuse litigation has yielded a number of significant benefits. They include victim compensation, church policies designed to prevent future abuse, greater willingness among law enforcement officials to
investigate allegations and prosecute where appropriate, and the thera-

peutic value of public disclosure. These benefits flow from the framing, agenda-setting, and information-generating effects of litigation.

A complete accounting of clergy sexual abuse litigation, however, requires more than merely attention to its benefits. We must know whether, in the end, if those benefits are worth the costs. These costs are not trivial, and we should be careful not to gloss over or discount them. The Church has paid out over $2.6 billion in settlements, adverse judgments, legal fees, treatment, and prevention. It has been forced to curtail the educational and antipoverty services that it offers. And it has suffered a loss of prestige that has diminished the capacity of the clergy to carry out its pastoral mission and the bishops to play a significant role in public life.

It should be noted at the outset that any attempt to weigh the costs and benefits of clergy sexual abuse litigation must proceed with caution. To begin with, we do not have full information. The litigation includes thousands of claims in jurisdictions across the country, many of which are unreported. Secret settlements render a great deal of relevant information unobtainable. There is a dearth of quantitative data. But where quantitative data do exist, they are incomplete. And qualitative data, while more prevalent, are anecdotal. Moreover, many of the most significant costs and benefits are intangible and impossible to measure. How, for example, would one measure the value of greater transparency in the handling of abuse allegations or the loss of institutional prestige suffered by the Church? To complicate matters even further, categorizing the results of the litigation as costs or benefits requires making value choices that may be highly controversial. For example, the weakening of clerical authority within the Church is a cost to those who support traditional notions of hierarchy and a benefit to those who do not. Thus, in assessing the results of clergy sexual abuse litigation, precise and value-neutral calculations are not possible. Any conclusions will be unavoidably a matter of impression.

In addition to these difficulties, there is a question of perspective: costs and benefits *to whom?* It is important to distinguish costs or benefits to a particular party from costs and benefits to society as a whole. For example, compensation payments are a cost to the Church but a benefit to victims. From the point of view of society, it is not clear whether they are a cost or a benefit. This depends upon whether the loss to the Church is greater or less than the gain to the victims, and such comparisons are impossible to make with any precision. We would need to know not only on how much each party values money but also what they would have or have done, or might do with it. Indeed, from society's point of view, compensation payments may simply be neutral wealth transfers from one group to another that do not leave society as a whole better or worse off. In assessing the costs and benefits of clergy sexual abuse, I do not adopt any one perspective. Instead, I will shift back and forth between them because I wish to make the case that the litigation has, in the end, done more good than harm from the perspective of victims, the Church, and society as a whole.

I do not purport to offer a rigorous cost-benefit analysis of clergy sexual abuse litigation. My aim is, instead, to survey the litigation's consequences and to assess their impact on victims of clergy sexual abuse, the Catholic Church, and society as a whole. In the analysis that follows, I will often use the terms cost and benefit loosely to denote a positive or negative consequence.

The chapter begins with a survey of the litigation's consequences. Next, I argue that, on balance, the litigation has been socially beneficial. I then turn to a concern expressed by many commentators that most of the policymaking benefits of the litigation occurred in the late 1980s and early 1990s and since that time, the litigation has produced few benefits while imposing increased costs. In response, I point to a number of benefits of the third wave of lawsuits and suggest that the litigation has not yet outlived its usefulness.

Payments by the Church

The John Jay study contains estimates of how much dioceses, religious communities, and their insurers have paid out in response to clergy sexual abuse claims between 1950 and 2002. Payments for victim compensation were roughly $476 million, victim treatment $25 million, priest treatment $33 million, and legal fees $38 million, for a total of $572 million. The authors of the study point out that the total may be low since the estimate is based on survey responses submitted by dioceses and religious orders, and not all dioceses and religious orders responded to the survey. Moreover, of those that did respond, not all provided answers to questions regarding payments. In addition, the estimate of compensation may be inflated because some dioceses and religious orders included victim treatment costs in their calculation of compensation.[1] Subsequent USCCB audits of dioceses in 2004, 2005, and 2006 provide payment figures for 2004–2006: settlements $782 million, victim therapy $26 million, support for offenders $47 million, legal fees $152 million, and other costs related to addressing allegations $13 million, for a total of just over one billion dollars. According to these audits, the Church has spent an additional $67 million on abuse prevention programs.[2] To all this should be added $85 million for the 2003 Boston settlement, $660 million for the 2007 L.A. settlement, and $198 million for the 2007 San Diego settlement.[3] These figures make it clear that the Church and its insurers have paid out over $2.6 billion dollars.

The amount of these payments covered by insurance varies from diocese to diocese and year to year. The John Jay study estimates that 38 percent of these costs to dioceses and 32 percent to religious communities were covered by insurance in the 1950–2002 period. Subsequent USCCB audits found that 32 percent in 2004, 49 percent in 2005, and 27 percent in 2006 of costs to dioceses were covered by insurance. The audits found that 12 percent in 2004, 13 percent in 2005, and 23 percent in 2006 of costs to religious communities were covered by insurance.[4] The *Los Angeles Times* reported that 34 percent of the 2007 L.A. settlement and 38 percent of the San Diego settlement would be paid by insurance.[5] These limits on insurance coverage have meant that dioceses themselves have had to shoulder a heavy financial burden.

Victim Compensation

In light of these figures, one might argue that victim compensation has been a significant benefit of the litigation. The figures suggest that between 1950 and 2007, victims received over $2.2 billion in compensation and $51 million treatment assistance. Some of the $2.2 billion in compensation—as much as 40 percent in some cases—went to plaintiffs' lawyers based on contingent fee arrangements.[6] Reported damage awards and settlement payments to individual victims after legal fees range from thousands of dollars to just over $3 million.[7] Victim advocates assert that compensation in many cases has been inadequate, while defenders of the Church suggest that awards and settlements are too high. One thing that both sides agree upon is that there is a great deal of inconsistency in the amounts paid to individual victims.[8]

Cutbacks in Programs and Services

Critics of the litigation assert that payments in response to clergy sexual abuse claims have resulted in significant cutbacks in church programs and services. Former defense attorney (now federal judge) Patrick Schiltz suggests that "[a] large and growing percentage of the clergy sexual misconduct litigation brought against churches is not covered by insurance. Churches have only two ways to pay the costs of such litigation—churches can ask the people in the pews to donate more money, or churches can reduce the services that they provide . . . Because it is not realistic to expect donations to increase, churches have no alternative but to pay for the litigation by cutting back on the services they provide."[9] Such cutbacks, asserts Schiltz, come at the expense of those who rely on the educational, healthcare, and antipoverty services provided by church organizations. Clergy sexual abuse litigation, he concludes, "has the potential to create a new class of victims, much larger than those now suing churches."[10] There are fears that this drain on funding for programs and services has been exacerbated by reduced giving in response to the scandal. Existing empirical data, however, offer a more nuanced picture.

By way of background, it is important to note that within the Catholic Church many different organizations receive donations and provide services. These include individual parishes, dioceses, religious orders, the Catholic Charities network, lay societies, and individual service organizations. The Catholic Charities network alone has over 170 local agencies, each of which is independently incorporated, raises its own funds, and supports services provided at numerous branches and affiliates. Funding for programs and services provided by Catholic organizations comes from a variety of sources, including not only individual giving and diocesan support but also government grants, program fees, investments, and in-kind contributions. In 2006, roughly 65 percent of Catholic Charities' $3.6 billion annual income came from government grants and contracts. Another 11 percent came from fees, while only 11 percent came from community support, and a mere 4 percent from diocesan and church support. In annual reports dating back to 1991, these percentages have been more or less consistent.[11]

Litigation has had the clearest impact on donations to dioceses hard hit by clergy sexual abuse claims and services that rely heavily on funding from them. The Boston archdiocese is a case in point. The *Boston Globe* reported that "[a]fter the clergy abuse crisis unfolded, giving [to the Boston archdiocese's Annual Catholic Appeal] dropped from $15.6 million in 2001 to $8.8 million in 2002."[12] Diocesan programs and services in Boston are heavily dependent on the Annual Catholic Appeal. As an attorney involved in the Boston litigation explains:

[The Church] has enormous obligations under the priest retirement program which are unfunded. It has enormous obligations under its cemetery maintenance programs which are under funded. It has the operation of churches and schools that lose money. But for the annual collection—in which everybody ponies up to the extent they are willing or able and comes up with money once a year—the Church would just sink right under the waves. So it was an institution which was totally dependent on the largesse of its parishioners, particularly the wealthy ones. This [litigation] comes along and the Church is spending millions of dollars to settle priests abuse cases. Well, immediately people would say, "I'm not giving any money to the Church to settle priests abuse cases. I give money to the Church to run schools and take care of poor parishes and orphanages and this, that, and the other thing, not to pay blood money for sinning, vile priests." So, all of the collections went down. Now the Church is in a serious situation as it tries to settle this. And it has to sell its property and mortgage the institution. So the financial stability of the archdiocese was crippled.[13]

The $85 million settlement in September 2003 appears to have set off a major financial reorganization of the archdiocese. In 2004, the archdiocese sold the cardinal's residence for $99 million and, by the end of 2005, the archdiocese had sold or reached agreements to sell another $90 million in real estate. "There's very definitely a massive liquidation going on with regard to the archdiocese," commented Massachusetts secretary of state William F. Gavin. Church officials insisted that the archdiocese was merely selling properties that it no longer needs.[14] The archdiocese also laid off dozens of staff people and closed 59 of its 357 parishes.[15]

We should be careful, however, before we extrapolate too much from the situation in Boston. Given the scope of the scandal in Boston and the intense media focus on it, Boston may represent an extreme case. According to the *New York Times,* the Boston archdiocese's $46 million operating deficit "is the largest any diocese has ever had."[16] Unfortunately, a lack of available financial data makes it difficult to compare the magnitude of the Boston archdiocese's losses to those of other dioceses.

Not all dioceses have suffered revenue losses or cutbacks in programs and services as a result of the litigation. Notably, the *Los Angeles Times* reported that "less than a year after a landmark payout of $100 million to settle sex-abuse claims against priests, the Roman Catholic Diocese of Orange has repaid most of the money it borrowed and expects to be debt-free by July . . . Church officials stressed that no parish or school funds were spent on the settlement." After insurance paid for half of the settlement, the diocese reportedly laid off eleven individuals, engaged in "belt-tightening," and secured a one-year bank loan. The diocese paid the loan by liquidating part of its $200 million investment portfolio, using profits from diocesan businesses, and securing additional loans. Church officials insist that they paid off the loan without cutting programs or selling properties and without using any funds from parish collections.[17] In Los Angeles, the archdiocese insists that it will finance its share of the $660 million 2007 settlement by liquidating investments, selling properties, and seeking loans. While this is likely to create budgetary problems, officials insist that the archdiocese has no plans to sell any parish or school properties and that "there will be no impact on essential ministries."[18]

Moving beyond individual dioceses, aggregate data on Catholic giving nationally paints a more complicated picture. A 2002 survey of Catholic parishioners conducted by Foundations and Donors Interested in Catholic Activities (FADICA) found that 12 percent of respondents gave less or stopped giving to their local parish as a result of the clergy sexual abuse scandal, and 19 percent gave less or stopped giving to diocesan appeals. At the same time, some respondents reported increasing their contributions as a show of support for the Church—3 percent gave more to their local parish and 2 percent to diocesan appeals. These figures reveal that more parishioners directed their anger at bishops than at their parish priests. They also show that increased contributions by some partly offset the decrease in contributions by others. A follow-up 2004 survey found that the percentage of those who increased their contributions in response to the scandal more than doubled.[19]

While the clergy sexual abuse scandal may have caused some Catholics to contribute less to their parishes and dioceses, the impact on organizations such as Catholic Charities is less clear. Figure 10 charts the total annual income and expenditures nationally for the Catholic Charities network based on reports from member agencies. (Reports for 1998 and 2001 are not available. The Catholic Charities USA press office has no copy of the 1998 report on file and no report was issued in 2001 due to serious flaws in the survey instrument.) The data reflect increases in income every year since 1991 with two exceptions: a decrease of $3 million (less than two-tenths of a percent) between 1993 and 1994 and of $500,000 (less than two-hundredths of a percent) between 2002 and 2003.[20] Shelley Borysiewicz, the manager of media relations for Catholic Charities, suggests that the very small decrease in income between 2002 and 2003 does not reflect a widespread reduction in contributions due to the clergy sexual abuse scandal. She opined in late 2002:

> Our information is anecdotal. From what we are hearing, we have a mixed bag out there in terms of how Catholic Charities agencies are faring with donations and other funding sources. Some agencies are up, setting records in fundraising events; others are down. It is difficult for the agencies to tease out what may be causing a decline in donations: the scandal, the economy, 9/11, the war on terrorism. If pressed, most of the agencies would say it is the economy that is having the most significant impact. With the stock market down, foundations may have less to give. With state and federal budgets running deficits, government contracts that pay for vital services are also in peril. Only Boston is directly attributing the scandal to a decline in donations.[21]

In some instances, organizations like Catholic Charities may have benefited from anger over the scandal directed against dioceses. A 2002 Beliefnet.com poll of Catholics found that 12 percent of respondents reported diverting contributions from diocesan appeals to "another Catholic charity."[22]

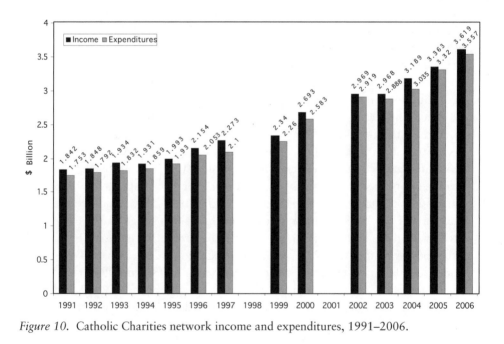

Figure 10. Catholic Charities network income and expenditures, 1991–2006.

To further complicate the picture, the duration of reduced giving to parishes and dioceses appears to be temporary. In the Boston archdiocese, some parishes have recently been experiencing an increase in donations. The annual appeal, which fell to $8.8 million in 2002, reported totals of $11 million in 2004 and 2005 and $13.8 million in 2006.[23] Other dioceses hard hit by the scandal, such as Tucson, Portland, and Spokane—all of which declared bankruptcy in response to litigation—reported successful annual appeals in 2006. The Tucson diocese received record donations, and its 35 percent participation rate exceeded the national average.[24] A 2006 study by the Center for Applied Research in the Apostolate (CARA) at Georgetown University suggests that, nationwide, the percentage of Catholics contributing to parish collections fell slightly in 2002 and 2003 and then began to rebound in 2004 and 2005.[25] As Figure 10 reflects, the small decrease in income experienced by the Catholic Charities network in 2003 was followed by increases in 2004, 2005, and 2006.

Another measure of the level of programs and services is expenditures. Figure 10 also charts the total annual expenditures nationally for the Catholic Charities network based on reports from member agencies. As was the case with income, there is a small, temporary decrease of $31 million (1 percent) between 2002 and 2003. Figure 11 charts the total annual number of people served nationally by Catholic Charities affiliates. This is an even more direct measure of programs and services provided. The data are based on reports from member agencies, and they begin in 2000, the first year in which individuals who received multiple services were counted only once. (As already mentioned, no report was issued in 2001 due to flaws in the survey instrument.) The data reflect a decrease of 537,000 people served (7.5 percent) between 2002 and 2003, and then an increase above the 2002 level in 2004, followed by additional increases in 2005 and 2006.

We should be careful not to make too much of all this aggregate data. The FADICA and CARA surveys measure only self-reported decreases or increases in individual contributions to parishes and dioceses. They do not tell us whether the total amount of contributions nationwide to parishes and dioceses decreased or increased, by how much, or for how long. The Catholic Charities network data are based on reports by member agencies. Not all member agencies submitted reports each year, so the data for each year are incomplete. Variations in the data could, to some degree, represent changes in reporting rates rather than changes in contribution and service levels.

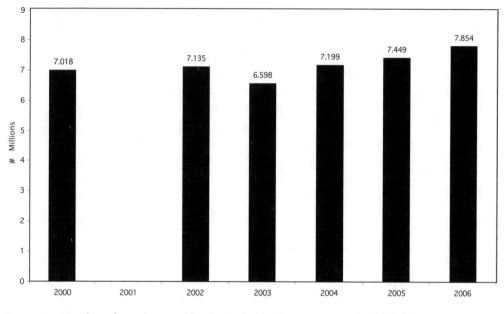

Figure 11. Number of people served by the Catholic Charities network, 2000–2006.

It may simply be safest to conclude that existing data do not support, as some have suggested, a significant and widespread cutback in Catholic programs and services with long-term implications. More likely, the impact has been greatest on programs and services sponsored by parishes and dioceses—such as churches and schools—and even this may prove to be localized in dioceses especially hard hit by the scandal. It may also prove to be merely temporary.

Preventing Future Abuse

Both sides in the controversy over clergy sexual abuse litigation share a desire to prevent abuse in the future. When plaintiffs' lawyer Eric Mac-Leish asked a group of Boston victims what they hoped to accomplish by suing, they replied that they wanted to make sure nothing like what happened to them happened to others. "We want systemic change," explained one victim. "We want fundamental change in the way these perps do business. We want to get rid of this special dispensation priests have been getting for years."[26] SNAP national director David Clohessy relates that "almost every survivor says, 'I just want to make sure he's not doing it to somebody else. I just want to warn people about him.'"[27] Declared USCCB president bishop Wilton Gregory at the 2002 Dallas conference: "The failures of the past must not be repeated."[28]

The most straightforward measure of deterrence is the number of priests with a history of child sexual abuse removed from ministry. Plaintiffs' lawyer John Manly asserts that "priests have been removed in the United States who have been credibly accused of molesting children . . . And if these cases accomplish nothing else other than to take those men out of a position of trust where they can use their collar as the vehicle to molest, that's a huge victory. By any measure, that's a huge success."[29] The USCCB has counted over 1,000 priests permanently removed from ministry as a result of sexual abuse allegations since 2002.[30] Even when priests are not removed from ministry, filing lawsuits has alerted potential victims about priests against whom allegations have been made. The National Review Board, however, in its 2004 report on the scandal, has suggested that litigation may have impeded the Church's efforts to discipline priests internally. It found that "some diocesan lawyers advised their bishop clients not to invoke a full penal process in those cases where civil litigation was pending or likely because the record of the testimony that was required to be kept in the canonical proceeding would be subject to discovery by a civil plaintiff. Thus, some bishops may have refrained from enforcing canon law to remove predator priests out of concern that victims and their lawyers would gain access to additional information about the priests."[31]

Civil lawsuits have also facilitated criminal prosecution. By raising public awareness and concern about the problem of clergy sexual abuse, civil suits have made it more politically acceptable for law enforcement to go after abusers and church officials who harbored them.[32] Civil discovery has uncovered information about clergy sexual abuse that has sometimes been passed along to law enforcement and used as the basis for criminal investigation and prosecution. Observes SNAP national director David Clohessy, "We're now starting to see cases where the civil process has led to the criminal process. In the last six weeks, I heard of four cases where civil lawyers took everything they got by way of deposition and interrogatory and all the rest and turned it over to D.A.s, and the D.A.s have since issued charges against abusive priests."[33] Another way in which civil lawsuits have facilitated criminal prosecution is by prompting church policies that require dioceses to report allegations to law enforcement authorities.[34]

In addition to removal from ministry and criminal prosecution, litigation has led to long-term monitoring of abusers. For example, the New York archdiocese requires known abusers to live in a supervised residential program as a condition of remaining in the priesthood and receiving housing, healthcare, and pension benefits to which priests are entitled. Priests in the program receive therapy, may not dress as a priest or celebrate Mass in public, are forbidden to be alone with children, and must fill out a log book each day to account for their whereabouts and activities.[35] No data are available on how many such programs exist or how many priests are enrolled in them.

Perhaps most significant for our purposes, litigation has prompted church officials to institute new policies aimed at preventing abuse before it occurs and reporting it after it happens. As we have seen, these policies have been developing over time, starting with responses to the Gauthe case in 1985 and culminating in the 2002 Dallas Charter. The charter requires all dioceses to establish "safe environment" programs designed to educate children, parents, clergy, educators, and volunteers about child sexual abuse. Help in designing and implementing safe environment programs has been provided by the National Catholic Risk Retention Group, a major provider of liability insurance for clergy sexual misconduct, through a program called VIRTUS. Conceived in 1997 in response to the Kos case in Dallas, VIRTUS today provides information, training materials, expert consulting, and web-based educational resources to 103 dioceses around the country. VIRTUS's safe environment program, called Protecting God's Children, offers training for adults in how to prevent abuse before it happens, detect abuse when it occurs, investigate allegations, and support victims. Training for children teaches them how to distinguish appropriate from inappropriate contact and to alert adults when abuse occurs. The VIRTUS website receives 75 million hits a year from all over the world.[36]

The effectiveness of safe environment programs instituted by dioceses is unclear. To be sure, they are prevalent. A 2005 USCCB audit found that 90 percent of dioceses had established safe environment programs and had trained over 7 million people, including 5.7 million children.[37] Some are skeptical of these efforts. "The Church reforms have been largely smoke and mirrors," suggests David Clohessy. "The bishops have hired these so-called audit teams. So it's like the bishops have basically drawn up the rules for the ball game, they've decided who gets to play, they've hired the umpires and—lo and behold, surprise, surprise—they say that they're winning."[38] But even if one has confidence in the USCCB audit, the figures for the number of individuals trained by safe environment programs do not tell us whether they have been successful in reducing clergy sexual abuse. According to former USCCB general counsel Mark Chopko, the National Review Board is currently studying this question.[39]

In addition to safe environment programs, litigation has prompted the bishops and the Vatican to exclude candidates for the priesthood whom they believe pose a high risk of committing child sexual abuse. In June 2005, the bishops adopted revised guidelines on priestly formation that exclude seminary applicants with any history of sexual abuse of minors, require close attention to a candidate's past, and emphasize the need to foster a strong commitment to celibacy.[40] Information generated by litigation may prove crucial to the success of such screening efforts. By exposing large numbers of abusers and their treatment records, litigation has generated data that can enhance the Church's ability to isolate risk factors for abuse. Psychotherapist and former priest Richard Sipe suggests that Catholic priests in the United States comprise a sizeable and relatively homogeneous population, at least in terms of educational background, professional training, and spiritual formation. Analysis of characteristics that distinguish priests who have committed child sexual abuse from the larger population of priests may help to isolate risk factors that make it more likely that a particular individual will engage in child sexual abuse.[41]

In some cases, policy reforms have been proposed by plaintiffs and included in the terms of settlements. For example, in 2001, plaintiff Ryan DiMaria settled a lawsuit against the Archdiocese of Los Angeles and the Diocese of Orange for sexual abuse that he suffered at the hands of Father Michael Harris, his high school principal. In addition to a payment of $5.2 million, the settlement required the Church to institute a list of reforms, which included monitoring schools, establishing a toll-free phone number and a website for anonymous complaints, providing counseling for victims, instituting guidelines for appropriate teacher-student relationships, conducting annual awareness trainings for students and school staff, maintaining complete personnel records on those accused of abuse, and issuing written apologies to victims.[42] Again, no data exist on whether these policies have reduced clergy sexual abuse in the diocese.

Clergy sexual abuse litigation has had beneficial spillover effects, heightening sensitivity to child sexual abuse in other contexts and framing it as an issue of institutional failure. There is, perhaps, no better example of this than the congressional page scandal in the fall of 2006. On September 30, the *New York Times* ran a front-page story below the fold entitled "Lawmaker Quits Over E-Mail Sent to Teenage Pages," that reported Florida congressman Mark Foley's resignation in the face of reports that he had sent sexually explicit email messages to congressional pages in 2005. Four days later, the story made it to the top of the front page and was now about the failure of speaker of the house Dennis Hastert to take action against Foley earlier. The headline, "Hastert Fights to Save His Job in Page Scandal," reflects how easily a story that prior to clergy sexual abuse litigation would have been confined to the misconduct of a single congressman was cast in the now familiar frame of institutional failure and managerial responsibility. The story continued inside the A-section with a large chart detailing what Hastert knew and when he knew it. The Op-Ed page ran an essay by a former page, now a law professor, outlining institutional reforms to improve oversight of the page program. For those who missed the obvious influence of the clergy sexual abuse scandal on the framing of the congressional page scandal, the Sunday Week in Review section printed a cartoon depicting Hastert dressed as a bishop whispering to an aide wearing a Roman collar, "We should've just moved Foley to another Parish." Two days after that, on October 10, the *Times* ran another front-page story, "A History of Sex With Students, Unchallenged Over the Years," about a New Jersey school teacher who sexually abused male students for decades without reprimand. The story highlighted the lawsuit brought by one of her victims against school officials who failed to stop her or report her to law enforcement. The focus in both of these news stories on the institutional failures that facilitate child sexual abuse is undoubtedly one of the most important legacies of clergy sexual abuse litigation. As lawyer for the L.A. archdiocese J. Michael Hennigan put it, "now, of course, it's widely understood that organizations do bear responsibility for the criminal misbehavior of members to the extent that it is foreseeable. That's probably a positive thing that came out of all this. That the law, in its wisdom and experience, examined this phenomenon and decided that we need deeper levels of accountability."[43]

Therapeutic Implications for Victims and Perpetrators

Clergy sexual abuse litigation has had a significant impact on therapy for both victims and perpetrators. Public disclosure of abuse claims through litigation has improved treatment for victims. Revelations and publicity about the nature and scope of clergy sexual abuse has made it easier for victims to seek out treatment and, once in therapy, more readily make the connection between past abuse and current difficulties. As Richard Sipe puts it, "As a result of the litigation and the publicity, I have seen great shifts in terms of patients' ability to sort out their lives in therapy." Moreover, reports Sipe, patients are less apt to blame themselves, and they are more likely to receive support from family and friends.[44]

To be sure, litigation also takes a heavy toll on many victims. Suing the Church, "can be emotionally traumatizing," explains plaintiffs' attorney Jeff Anderson. "When they engage in very hardball kinds of tactics, it becomes a war of attrition, and many survivors get worn down and worn out and re-victimized by the process."[45] Plaintiffs' lawyers, suggests St. Luke Institute president and CEO Stephen Rossetti, may play up the magnitude of the damage suffered by victims, and "victims may end up feeling like permanently damaged goods."[46] Former doctoral student Jennifer Balboni interviewed many Boston victims who found accepting money damages as compensation for sexual abuse demeaning. They related how aggregate settlement led them to compete against each other for shares of a fixed compensation fund. This undermined the group solidarity that had built up in the earlier stages of the litigation, which was one of the most significant therapeutic benefits of suing.[47]

Nevertheless, explains David Clohessy, merely filing a lawsuit, regardless of the outcome, can have therapeutic value to victims. "If you want to relieve yourself of some of the shame. If you want people to know that Father Mike is dangerous. If you want parents to not let their kids go to the movies with him. If you want to hold church leaders accountable. If you want to expose the truth. All that happens the day that your lawsuit is filed . . . For many victims, [filing suit is] the first step toward taking action and putting the blame where it belongs and reclaiming your life."[48] Balboni explains that many victims found therapeutic value even prior to filing, in initial client interviews with attorneys who were willing to listen to them and believe their allegations. Balboni suggests that other parts of the litigation process as well, such as arbitration, can give victims a chance to tell their story at length and be heard.[49] Confronting the Church through litigation is transformative, says plaintiffs' lawyer John Manly. "[F]or a lot of survivors, this process is profoundly healing because it allows them to get their power back . . . [F]or a survivor, it's a huge thing to be able to sit across the table from their perpetrator or sit across from the people who aided their perpetrator and confront them and walk out and be okay. And I've seen that process, along with a lot of therapy, change people's lives."[50]

Settlement negotiations between clergy sexual abuse victims and the diocese of Spokane attest to the desire of many victims to publicly disclose their abuse. In addition to monetary compensation, victims demanded that the diocese agree to publish their accounts of abuse in the diocesan newspaper on a full page dedicated to that purpose each month for a year. They also demanded that the bishop visit every parish where abuse occurred and disclose to parishioners that an abusive priest had served there.[51]

Litigation may also fuel research aimed at addressing the needs of victims in the future. Plaintiffs' attorney Ray Boucher suggests that "the most important thing that's come about as a result of all these cases being filed is the medical profession's exposure to and understanding of this problem and how, hopefully, to develop treatments that will help the victims."[52] The large number of victims coming forward as a result of litigation may also provide useful data.

In addition to its therapeutic benefits for victims, litigation has contributed to advances in the treatment of perpetrators. According to Dr. Leslie Lothstein of The Institute of Living, litigation has helped therapists "get behind offenders' lies and denials" which are barriers to successful therapy. Litigation has also broken down the "structure of denial within the Church" and thereby made it more likely that church officials who refer perpetrators to treatment will be more forthcoming with medical records and other information that can make therapy more effective.[53] In addition, clinical psychologists Donna J. Markham and Samuel Mikail suggest that the hundreds of priests recently removed from ministry and referred to treatment since 2002 have provided to clinicians a significant cohort of cases from which to draw generalizations about treatment outcomes.[54] Litigation has also exposed decades of past clinical experience within Catholic treatment programs, from which important lessons may be learned.

But not everyone agrees that litigation has been beneficial for treating perpetrators. According to Dr. Fred Berlin of Johns Hopkins University, who specializes in the treatment of sexual disorders, while lawsuits have "called attention to the seriousness of the problem and the need to address it, litigation has also swung the pendulum in a punitive direction" away from treatment. Lothstein shares this view, and laments a recent shift away from psychotherapy toward residential confinement programs that instead rely on prayer and pastoral counseling. Berlin suggests that litigation and media coverage have "demonized" offenders in a way that "discourages them from coming forward" to receive treatment. Moreover, he contends, information generated by the litigation has been mostly aggregate and "not terribly useful" for treating individual cases.[55]

Demoralization and Division within the Church

An important cost of the litigation is what former USCCB general counsel Mark Chopko calls the "wear and tear on the psyche of the community."[56] Litigation and the press coverage it has generated have taken a toll on Catholic morale. Stephen Rossetti conducted surveys showing that clergy sexual abuse has fed dissatisfaction with the priesthood and the Church. Rossetti found that among Catholics in dioceses where there had been no accusations of clergy sexual abuse, 69 percent of respondents agreed with the statement "Overall, I am satisfied with the priests we have in the Church today" and 63 percent with the statement "Overall, I am satisfied with the Catholic Church today." But among Catholics in dioceses where one or more priests had been accused, whose own parish priest had not been accused, these numbers fell to 50 percent and 47 percent respectively. And among Catholics whose parish priest had been accused, the numbers fell even further to 34 percent for each statement.[57]

Internal division is also part of the fallout of the litigation. Parishes, suggests Rossetti, are "victims" of clergy sexual abuse: "[a] parish whose pastor has been charged with child sexual abuse is almost always divided" between those who side with the accuser and those who defend the pastor.[58] Public airing of the scandal has also exacerbated tensions between traditionalist and reform factions within the Church. For example, Voice of the Faithful has openly criticized the bishops for their handling of clergy sexual abuse and called for structural change in the way the Church is governed. In response, some bishops around the country have accused the group of exploiting the clergy sexual abuse scandal to promote a liberal reform agenda, and some have even banned the group from meeting on church property.[59]

Low morale among priests is another cost of the litigation. In 1993, the NCCB charged its Ad Hoc Committee on Sexual Abuse with, among other things, "rais[ing] the morale of bishops and priests whose lives and ministry have been burdened with these terrible offenses of the few."[60] Even more so today, priests feel ashamed and embarrassed by the scandal, believing that they are viewed with suspicion and stereotyped as pedophiles.[61]

Priests have also expressed anger at what they perceive as the bishops' aloofness and failure to take responsibility for the scandal. "As a priest," explains one clergy member, "I can tell you the morale has never been lower—at least in this diocese of Phoenix. The bishops just won't talk to the priests and really find out what is happening in the trenches. It would help if they would start taking some responsibility for their actions and stop blaming the priests or the times."[62] Sixty-nine priests of the New York archdiocese wrote Cardinal Edward Egan in December of 2003 that "We need not tell you again what you already know; the morale of the New York presbyterate is at an all-time low."[63]

In addition, many priests feel sold out by the bishops. They believe that the bishops, in order to bolster their own public image, instituted harsh procedures in Dallas that did not properly protect the rights of the accused. Some priests formed organizations, such as the Boston Priests Forum and the Voice of the Ordained in New York, to make known their concerns and shore up morale. These organizations are independent of diocesan priest councils, the traditional route through which priests' concerns were addressed. Cardinal Law denounced the independence of the Boston Priests Forum as "unpriestly," and he threatened that involvement with it could damage one's career. This threat merely angered the priests more, and they eventually called for Law's resignation.[64]

The impact of clergy sexual abuse litigation on priestly morale should not, however, be overstated. Survey data suggests that, aside from their anger at the bishops, morale among priests is high in terms of job satisfaction. A *Los Angeles Times* survey of 1,854 priests conducted between June and October 2002, found that 91 percent of respondents were satisfied with the "way your life as a priest is going these days" and 90 percent said that, given the opportunity to make the choice over again, they would choose to be a priest.[65] In a survey of priests conducted between September 2003 and January 2004 to assess the effects of the abuse scandal on priestly morale, Rossetti found that 92 percent of respondents agreed with the statement, "Overall, I am happy as a priest," 83 percent agreed with the statement, "My morale is good," and 84 percent with the statement, "I am proud to be a priest today."[66] Rossetti found similar results from additional surveys through April 2005. Interestingly, while Rossetti found priestly morale high, he also found that most priests believe that, as a whole, priestly morale is low.[67] "The overall morale of priests in this country is high," concludes Rossetti. "Priests themselves say that their own morale is good. And these high rates of satisfaction have been consistent over several years and different surveys."[68]

Impaired Pastoral Capacity Due to Loss of Trust in the Clergy

By publicizing clergy sexual abuse, litigation has undermined confidence in the clergy. As one loyal Catholic who regularly attends Mass and sends her children to parochial school put it, "I always said going to church was setting the right example for my kids. Now I am just so glad my son has never been an altar boy."[69] For their part, priests are wary of intimacy with parishioners for fear that their conduct might be misconstrued as a sexual advance that could subject them to allegations in a climate where priests no longer enjoy a presumption of innocence. Explained one young Massachusetts priest, "[j]ust the possibility of being accused scares the hell out of me and makes me colder in my relationships with children."[70]

This mutual mistrust has serious implications for priests' capacity to carry out their pastoral mission. Without emotional intimacy and appropriate physical contact, clergy cannot provide vital pastoral services. These include caring for children, comforting mourners, and helping people deal with personal crises.

Damage to the Institutional Prestige of the Church

By framing clergy sexual abuse as a failure on the part of bishops and by focusing public attention on the issue, litigation has damaged the institutional prestige of the Church. Albany Bishop Howard Hubbard believes that "the greatest costs [of the litigation] have been the lack of trust in the leadership of the Church and the diminishment of our moral voice in the public forum."[71] The scandal has seriously eroded the bishops' credibility among both Catholics and the general public. The bishops' statements on the most salient policy issues throughout the 1980s and 1990s—nuclear arms, healthcare, welfare reform, immigration, abortion, end of life

issues—were widely reported by the media and taken seriously both inside and outside of the Church. By contrast, the bishops' collective statement against a preemptive war against Iraq in November 2002 attracted
little press attention and drew little if any notice from the public and policymakers.[72] "[W]hile we did take a position on the war," recalls Hubbard, "our leaders and public opinion makers were less likely to weigh
our position that seriously because our ability to be a moral voice had
been severely compromised by the sexual abuse crisis."[73]

Survey data complicate this picture somewhat. CARA surveys of
Catholics in the fall of 2003, 2004, and 2005 asked, "How much, if at
all, has the issue of sexual abuse of young people by priests hurt the
credibility of church leaders who speak out on social issues?" Three-
quarters of respondents in each poll responded either "a great deal" or
"somewhat." CARA surveys between 2000 and 2005 reflect an increase
in dissatisfaction with "the leadership of the Catholic Church" following widespread media coverage of the scandal in early 2002, but this
trend was short lived. By September 2004, satisfaction with the leadership of the Church was back to its pre-2002 levels and climbing. Satisfaction with "the leadership of the bishops" also fell in the wake of the
2002 press coverage and similarly rebounded by late 2004. Interestingly,
satisfaction with the leadership of respondents' "local bishop or cardinal" remained high—around 80 percent—throughout the scandal.[74]
Thus, damage to the Church's institutional prestige, at least among
Catholics, seems to be temporary, and the prestige of bishops within
their own dioceses seems relatively high despite the scandal.

There is also concern that the scandal will damage the credibility of
religious leaders' defense of religious liberty and the freedom of religious entities from government regulation. "Scandal causes merited and
principled arguments about the autonomy of religious institutions to
sound hollow and empty," laments Mark Chopko. "It causes legislators
and judges to give less credence to those arguments in particular cases.
It incites those who have policy agendas that run counter to religious institutions to take new interest in commencing campaigns that limit the
reach and impact of religion."[75]

Apology, Atonement, and Reconciliation

Litigation has played a role in repairing the damage done to the Church
by clergy sexual abuse. By exposing the scandal, litigation has opened

up opportunities for apology, atonement, and reconciliation. Church leaders throughout the United States have issued public apologies. Cardinal Law declared on January 9, 2002: "These days are particularly painful for the victims of John Geoghan. My apology to them and their families, and particularly to those who were abused in assignments which I made, comes from a grieving heart. I am indeed profoundly sorry."[76] Cardinal Mahony wrote in the cover letter to his February 2004 report on clergy sexual abuse in the L.A. archdiocese, "I sincerely apologize to anyone who has suffered from sexual misconduct or abuse by a priest, deacon, lay minister, employee or volunteer of the Archdiocese. I acknowledge my own mistakes during my eighteen years as your Archbishop."[77] Said USCCB president Bishop Wilton Gregory in his address at the June 2002 Dallas conference, "in my own name and in the name of all of the bishops, I express the most profound apology to each of you who have suffered sexual abuse by a priest or another official of the Church. I am deeply and will be forever sorry for the harm you have suffered. We ask your forgiveness."[78] Bishops or their representatives have, in some cases, offered private apologies to victims, sometimes as a condition of settlement.[79]

Some church leaders have come to view the litigation and its fallout as an opportunity for atonement. As St. Paul and Minneapolis Archbishop Harry Flynn put it, speaking on *Nightline* in 2002, "I feel tremendously strong about the fact that out of this the Church will be stronger, more purified, certainly more humiliated, and will be able to bring forth the kingdom of God in a much better way because of what we are going through."[80] In the words of Spokane Bishop William Skylstad, when serving as USCCB vice president, "a boil has been lanced, and I do feel strongly that this is a time of grace for us, as painful and difficult as this moment is. The fact is that the pain and the hurt were there, under the surface, for those who have been carrying this around for years, and opening this up helps us minister to that situation as best we can, and begin the process of healing and reconciliation."[81]

In some instances, there appears to be a measure of reconciliation between church officials and victims. Boston's Cardinal Sean O'Malley, who succeeded Cardinal Law, embarked in 2006 on a nine-day "pilgrimage of repentance and hope," during which he offered special Masses at churches that had been served by priests accused of sexual abuse. In the spirit of reconciliation, he invited victims to address each service. Said one such victim, an outspoken advocate for reform, "[w]e need to promote a dialogue of understanding." A parishioner at one of the churches visited by the cardinal suggested that "[i]t's been a very painful time, and now it's time to heal."[82] Michael Burnett, a consultant on clergy sexual abuse claims resolution, recalls how one victim who had left the Church as a result of his abuse "underwent a conversion experience" after receiving an apology from the diocese's vicar general. Following the apology, the victim requested that the vicar general hear his confession, after which the victim went to Mass for the first time in many years.[83]

We should be careful, however, not to overstate the extent to which the litigation facilitated apology, atonement, and reconciliation. In some instances, litigation did just the opposite. According to journalists Frank Bruni and Elinor Burkett, church officials often "immediately distanced themselves from children and families claiming abuse, fearful that any apology or offer of help might seem an admission of guilt for which they would pay in court."[84] Balboni relates that

> after the [2003] Boston global settlement had been completed, Arch-bishop Sean O'Malley wrote a letter to each of the litigants apologizing for the harm that had happened to each of them. However, because the Church was never privy to the litigants' personal information (address and phone), and because as part of the settlement they were barred from contacting the plaintiffs about this matter, the letters were sent in care of the corresponding attorneys in hopes that each would forward the letters to their clients. It is my understanding that two of the three main firms did not forward the correspondence, leaving at least one third of the "global settlement" clients without any idea that such a letter ex-isted. Tragically, this is precisely what many clients had wanted out of litigation.

When she asked one firm why they had failed to forward the letters, they replied that they did not want to intrude or interrupt their clients' lives with a reminder of the past.[85]

Some are skeptical of the sincerity of church officials' apologies. Thomas Doyle asserts that public apologies by bishops are little more than a public relations strategy.[86] Michael Burnett has observed that apologies offered as a condition of settlement often sound more like carefully crafted explanations than apologies.[87] Finally, while public apologies by church officials have been widely reported in the media, personal apologies by abusers are rare.[88]

The Bottom Line

As I cautioned at the outset, any attempt to weigh the benefits and costs of clergy sexual abuse litigation is, ultimately, a matter of impression. With this caveat in mind, it is my sense that the benefits have outweighed the costs. Let me briefly explain why.

First of all, some costs to the Church have turned out to be lower than initially expected, and they appear to be merely temporary. Decreases in contributions beginning in 2002 were largely limited to dioceses hard hit by the litigation, and contributions to even these dioceses have been recovering since 2004. Some have even surpassed their pre-2002 levels. Aside from dioceses, Catholic Charities USA reports that its income was unaffected by the scandal. Similarly, cutbacks in programs and services have been limited to dioceses hard hit by the litigation. Yet even some of the hardest hit dioceses, such as Orange, report no significant cutbacks. And, again, Catholic Charities USA reports no cutbacks in programs and services. Survey data suggest that satisfaction with the Church's national leadership dropped temporarily in 2002 and 2003 but then rebounded starting in 2004.

Second, some costs suggested by anecdotal evidence are not borne out by aggregate empirical data. While there is a widespread perception of low morale among the priesthood, survey data reflect a consistently high level of job satisfaction (over 90 percent) among priests. Similarly, while many insist that Catholics have lost faith in their leaders, survey data suggest that satisfaction among Catholics with their local bishop or cardinal has remained high (about 80 percent) throughout the scandal.

Third, some costs to the Church have provided substantial benefits to victims and society at large. Payments by the Church for victim treatment, perpetrator treatment, and abuse prevention programs are socially beneficial. One could also argue that they are beneficial to the Church insofar as they further its pastoral mission. Of the $2.6 billion in payments by the Church, $197 million (8 percent) were for treatment and prevention. Most would agree that, given the circumstances, it is a good thing for the Church to fund treatment and prevention within the Catholic community. In addition, payment of whatever one considers to be fair compensation for victims is also a benefit. Payments to compensate victims were $2.2 billion. Subtracting 40 percent for contingency fees (in reality, they were often lower), leaves $1.3 billion for victims—

roughly half of the $2.6 billion paid by the Church. Just how much of that should be counted as fair compensation is a highly subjective and controversial question. The remaining payments were $880 million (34 percent) for contingency fees for plaintiffs' attorneys and $190 million (7 percent) paid to defense counsel. We should be careful not to dismiss these legal costs out of hand as a waste of resources that might be better used in other ways. Plaintiffs' contingent fees provide the necessary incentive for lawyers to pursue litigation. Insofar as litigation yields social benefits unobtainable by less expensive means, contingency payments to plaintiffs' lawyers are not a waste. They are the price we pay for desirable social goods.

Fourth, some losses to the Church may be viewed as either social costs or social benefits depending upon one's perspective. Loss of trust in clergy is a social cost insofar as it reduces the capacity of individual clergy members to provide pastoral care, not only to their coreligionists but also throughout society. At the same time, greater wariness of people with authority over children is a social benefit insofar as it is an effective means of reducing child sexual abuse. Loss of reverence for bishops as moral authorities is a social cost insofar as the U.S. bishops have for many decades played an important role in the nation's political life, offering well-thought-out positions on issues of national importance such as nuclear arms, welfare reform, abortion, immigration, civil rights, and foreign policy. For dissidents in the Church and critics on the outside, diminished reverence for and obedience to the Catholic hierarchy is a social benefit. Finally, the weakening of religious autonomy—of legal protections for religious institutions from government regulation—is a dangerous development to some and a welcome change to others.

Fifth, there are several clear and substantial benefits of the litigation. More than 1,000 child abusers have been removed from ministry. Law enforcement is finally taking allegations of clergy sexual abuse seriously, investigating them, and prosecuting where appropriate. Church leaders nationwide have made child abuse prevention a top priority and have instituted concrete reforms to investigate allegations, remove perpetrators from ministry, and report crimes to civil authorities. Seminaries are now more attentive to psychosexual development in priestly formation and are better equipped to address problems of emotional immaturity and isolation that give rise to sexual pathology. There is a heightened sensitivity among the general public to the institutional dimensions of child sexual abuse and the need for institutional reforms not only in religious organizations but also in secular institutions such as schools, recreation programs, and even government. The claims of thousands of victims have been publicly vindicated and church officials have been forced to provide a specific accounting of their handling of clergy sexual abuse.[89]

To be sure, there may still be known perpetrators in ministry. Law enforcement efforts may fall short in many cases. The effectiveness of church reforms may vary widely from diocese to diocese and may not be ascertainable given the lack of oversight aside from USCCB-sponsored audits. Seminaries may be excluding celibate homosexuals from the priesthood in the name of risk reduction. Our efforts as a society to address abuse in other institutional contexts may be proceeding at a slow pace. And the bishops' accounting of the scandal to date may yet be incomplete. But to acknowledge the limits of the litigation's benefits is not to negate them.

And what did they cost? At most, overcompensation of victims and legal fees, temporary declines in revenue and services in some of the dioceses especially hard hit by the scandal, a measure of internal division among Catholics, mistrust of clergy, and a loss of institutional prestige. Overcompensation, legal fees, and temporary declines in revenue are finite costs that are hardly likely to seriously damage the Church in the long run. Internal division among Catholics, mistrust of clergy, and the loss of institutional prestige, however, may have more serious, long-term negative implications for the Church and, given the productive role it plays in the larger society, for the nation. Nevertheless, in time, the faith and commitment of Catholics and the goodwill of the rest of the nation may enable the Church eventually to heal even these wounds.

Was This Much Litigation Really Necessary?

Some commentators have argued that the primary benefits of clergy sexual abuse litigation were achieved in the early 1990s and that subsequent litigation has been of little value in terms of promoting policy reforms. For example, Mark Chopko asserts that the third wave of litigation beginning in 2002 has uncovered little new information that was not already revealed during the second wave of litigation in the 1990s. Moreover, he asserts, the Dallas Charter is merely a modest revision of the Five Principles adopted by the bishops in 1992 and elaborated in the 1996 report of the Bishops' Ad Hoc Committee on Sexual

Abuse, *Restoring Trust*. By the mid-1990s, he suggests, "there were a lot of dioceses in the United States that were handling this quite openly, quite consistently, quite correctly."[90] From this point of view, the Gauthe and Porter cases may have played a role in uncovering new information and promoting policy reforms, but litigation since the mid-1990s has not yielded similar benefits. The primary function of litigation since that time, according to this view, has been to punish the Church for past wrongs that have already been addressed.

The third wave of litigation, however, has not merely rehashed the disclosures and reforms of the first two waves, as Chopko contends. Rather, it has added something new. The third wave of litigation, more than any other, has placed clergy sexual abuse on the agendas of the general public and the Catholic laity and created the pressure necessary to make it a top priority on the institutional agendas of the Church, law enforcement, and state legislatures. The information generated as a result— the John Jay study, subsequent USCCB audits, attorney general reports, and grand jury investigations—has provided a better picture of the scope and nature of the problem than anything prior to 2002.[91] Litigation continues to uncover abuse allegations and perpetrators not disclosed by dioceses—as recently as 2005 in the Archdiocese of Chicago and 2006 in the Archdiocese of Los Angeles.[92] Deposition testimony in 2007 revealed that Orange County Bishop Tod Brown had himself been the subject of child sexual abuse allegations ten years earlier.[93] Litigation has also begun to expose the international dimensions of the problem in terms of the transfer of priests across national borders. A 2006 lawsuit alleges that the Archbishop of Mexico City, Cardinal Noberto Rivera, when serving as bishop of Tehuacan, transferred a priest accused of sexual abuse to Los Angeles, where he was assigned to parish work and subsequently allowed to escape back to Mexico by Cardinal Mahony following fresh allegations of abuse in his new assignment.[94]

Litigation has exposed noncompliance with the Dallas Charter policies by certain dioceses. For example, in 2006, investigators found that the Archdiocese of Chicago had failed to investigate abuse allegations against a priest dating back to 1992 or to adequately monitor the priest, who was arrested in 2005 for molesting a child.[95] Litigation has also maintained clergy sexual abuse on the Church's agenda and provided external pressure that supports ongoing USCCB compliance audits. These audits promise to provide useful policy information—not only for the Church but also for other institutions—concerning the effectiveness of the Church's policies in reducing child sexual abuse.[96] This kind of feedback on implementation is essential to good policymaking.[97] And finally, ongoing litigation has maintained the issue of clergy sexual abuse on the agendas of public officials, some of whom have provided external oversight of dioceses within their jurisdiction.[98]

Aside from its policy benefits, the third wave of litigation has held bishops publicly accountable for their role in clergy sexual abuse. While the third wave of litigation has often involved abuse for which priests had already been removed from ministry, as some critics point out, it has served to chasten church officials who, until 2002, remained largely untouched and unmoved by the scandal.[99] To be sure, church officials who concealed abuse have escaped criminal liability and have remained in office. Moreover, civil settlements often include language in which church defendants deny liability.[100] Nevertheless, like truth commissions established to expose governmental abuses, the litigation has established an historical record, offered victims a measure of justice, opened up possibilities for forgiveness and reconciliation, and provided a powerful deterrent against future attempts to shield abusers from civil authorities.[101]

Finally, it should be mentioned that the third-wave litigation has and continues to provide victims with compensation for the wrongs done to them by abusers and church officials. Thus, the third wave of clergy sexual abuse litigation has uncovered new information; bolstered enforcement, oversight, and feedback; held church officials publicly accountable; and provided compensation to victims. Of course, some day, the litigation may outlive its usefulness. But that day has not yet arrived.

CHAPTER EIGHT

The Complementary Policymaking Role of Tort Litigation

The law is filling a void, a vacuum of leadership caused
by the religious community's failure to act promptly
and adequately.

—DONALD CLARK, JR., "SEXUAL ABUSE IN THE CHURCH:
THE LAW STEPS IN," *CHRISTIAN CENTURY*, APRIL 14, 1993

The sexual abuse of over 13,000 children and adolescents by Catholic priests in the United States since 1950 is an astonishing fact. Even more astonishing is that church officials knew of these crimes and, for the most part, failed to report them to civil authorities or remove the perpetrators from ministry. Law enforcement authorities, even when notified, often failed to investigate or prosecute. Legislators were either unaware of the problem or unwilling to address it for fear of political repercussions. The clergy sexual abuse scandal is a story of multiple institutional failures.

Tort litigation has played an essential role in correcting these failures. Litigation uncovered the widespread scope of clergy sexual abuse and its mismanagement by church officials. It framed the issue as one of institutional failure requiring institutional reform. And it prompted church and government policymakers to take action. Clergy sexual abuse litigation is a remarkable institutional success for the tort system.

In this final chapter, I examine the implications of clergy sexual abuse litigation for our understanding of the tort system and its role in the policymaking process. Tort litigation has traditionally been understood as a means of dispute resolution and risk regulation. Clergy sexual abuse litigation illustrates how tort litigation can also function as what political scientists call a policy venue—an institutional setting where policymaking takes place.

Tort litigation can contribute to policymaking in a number of ways. In clergy sexual abuse litigation we have seen how lawsuits framed issues, placed them on institutional policy agendas, and generated information essential to understanding them. Addressing complex social problems usually requires the cooperation of many different public and private policymaking institutions, and tort litigation, depending upon the circumstances, may be one of them. Clergy sexual abuse litigation not only contributed to policymaking, it also enhanced the performance of other policymaking institutions.

Clergy sexual abuse litigation is part of a larger class of lawsuits known as social policy tort litigation. Other examples are pharmaceutical, tobacco, and gun litigation. The extent to which these other examples have enhanced policymaking—in the areas of drug safety, tobacco-related illness, and gun violence—varies widely. By locating clergy sexual abuse litigation within this larger class, we can identify certain conditions under which tort litigation enhances policymaking.

I begin with a brief review of my central claims regarding the impact of clergy sexual abuse litigation on policymaking. I offer a few important clarifications and qualifications as well as comparisons with responses to clergy sexual abuse in Ireland and Canada. Next, I specify in greater detail what it means to view tort litigation as a policy venue. Finally, I place clergy sexual abuse within the larger context of social policy tort litigation. I argue that tort litigation is most effective as a policy venue when it plays a complementary role supporting the efforts of other policymaking institutions. I also address some common concerns about using litigation to make policy.

Causal Claims, Qualifications, and Feedback Effects

My central thesis—that clergy sexual abuse litigation has enhanced policymaking—rests on three causal claims. First, I argue that litigation led the news media to report clergy sexual abuse and to frame it as an issue of institutional failure. Second, I suggest that litigation and the news media coverage it generated placed this issue on public and institutional agendas and put pressure on policymakers to address it. Third, I contend that litigation generated previously undisclosed information about clergy sexual abuse that informed policy responses to it. Thus, the "impact" of private lawsuits on policymaking consists of framing issues in terms of institutional responsibility, achieving agenda access, and generating new information.

I do not mean to suggest that litigation is always necessary to these aspects of policymaking or that litigation always advances them. Under different conditions, other institutions perform these functions. In the Watergate scandal, for example, policymaking was shaped by a bold press, an aggressive special prosecutor, and an outraged Congress. More recently, in the Enron scandal, policy responses to corporate misconduct were heavily influenced by criminal prosecutions. In each case, institutions other than the tort system framed issues in terms of institutional failure, placed them on institutional policy agendas, and uncovered new information.

In the case of the clergy sexual abuse scandal, however, it appears unlikely that either church or government officials would have implemented policy reforms in the absence of tort litigation. A steadfast desire among church officials to prevent public disclosure of the problem and to protect offenders from prosecution, combined with deference to the Church on the part of law enforcement and legislators, facilitated decades of child sexual abuse by priests. All this, as we have seen, began to change with the Gauthe litigation in 1984.

This is not to say that clergy sexual abuse litigation was by itself sufficient to bring about church and government policy responses. A number of factors contributed to the efficacy of litigation in framing issues, achieving agenda access, and generating information. First, popular culture in the mid-1980s was highly receptive to the litigation's story about child sexual abuse, clerical misconduct, and institutional responsibility. Public awareness of child sexual abuse was fueled throughout the 1970s and 1980s by child-welfare advocates and feminist activists.[1] Concurrent with the Gauthe case, a series of high profile prosecutions for ritual child sexual abuse in daycare centers swept the nation from California to Florida to Massachusetts.[2] The late 1980s saw a series of popular televangelists taken down by sexual and financial scandals.[3] Government and corporate corruption have been recurring popular concerns throughout American history, and the post-Watergate 1980s were no exception. These cultural factors made the frame of institutional responsibility for clergy sexual abuse culturally resonant and, therefore, highly persuasive.[4] Media coverage enhanced the frame's persuasiveness by giving it prominence and repeating it frequently.

Second, activists pursued policy reforms outside the context of litigation. Advocacy organizations such as SNAP and Voice of the Faithful mobilized members to publicize and lobby for their reform agendas. Church insiders—some with close ties to the church hierarchy, such as former USCCB general counsel Mark Chopko, and others viewed as dissidents, such as canon lawyer Thomas Doyle—worked actively to develop detailed reforms and seek their adoption.

Third, church and government policymakers initially failed to address the problem proactively despite their knowledge of it. This institutional failure constituted the legal basis for lawsuits against the Church and a political opportunity that allowed plaintiffs' lawyers to drive the policymaking process. To be sure, as the scandal progressed, church leaders did develop new policies, law enforcement officials became more aggressive, and legislatures passed reforms. But at the outset of the litigation in 1984, there was a policy vacuum waiting to be filled.[5]

The causal relationships that I have asserted between litigation, on the one hand, and news coverage, policy agendas, and information, on the other hand, are not unidirectional. For example, there was feedback between litigation and news coverage. Litigation generated and shaped news coverage which in turn fueled more litigation by emboldening more victims to file lawsuits. News coverage also made plaintiffs' frames more culturally resonant among judges and potential jurors in subsequent cases. Moreover, news coverage of ritual child sexual abuse and corporate scandals prior to clergy sexual abuse litigation accounted for much of the persuasive power of the plaintiffs' frames in the first place. (Of course, the theme of corporate wrongdoing was itself culturally familiar, in part, due to tort litigation dating back to the 1950s holding corporate entities liable for employee misconduct and product defects.) Similarly, in terms of agenda setting, litigation helped to mobilize elites—victims, lawyers, and activists—who, in turn, pursued further litigation as part of their strategy to achieve reform. Finally, feedback effects also occurred with regard to information generation. Litigation uncovered new information through discovery and by encouraging church and government investigations that produced information subsequently used by plaintiffs in later lawsuits to support their claims.

By making causal claims, I do not mean to suggest a straightforward chain of causation between litigation and policy outcomes. Rather, we should view litigation as one causal factor—within a complex interplay of causal factors and feedback effects—that prompted and shaped policy responses to clergy sexual abuse.

Comparisons to Ireland and Canada

Comparison with responses to clergy sexual abuse in other countries supports the view that litigation played a significant role in bringing about church and government policy reforms in the United States. International comparisons also suggest that, under different cultural and

institutional conditions, civil litigation may play a smaller role in policymaking. Let us look briefly at events in Ireland and Canada.

Ireland

Public concern over clergy sexual abuse in Ireland began in 1994 with
media coverage of a landmark case involving Father Brendan Smyth
who molested hundreds of children over forty years in Belfast, Dublin,
and the United States. Smyth pled guilty to seventy-four charges of sexual assault and was sentenced to twelve years in prison in his native Ireland. News media reports revealed that church officials repeatedly
reassigned Smyth despite knowledge of abuse allegations against him.
The case became even more notorious when Irish attorney general
Harry Whelehan refused to comply with an extradition warrant by authorities in Northern Ireland to make Smyth face similar charges there,
leading to the collapse of Prime Minister Albert Reynolds's coalition
government. The Smyth case exposed not only the failure of church officials to protect Smyth's victims but also the efforts of government officials to protect the Church from further scandal.[6]

Following the Smyth case, increasing numbers of victims began to
come forward publicly with allegations of abuse. These allegations included physical abuse and sexual abuse by clergy in state-funded residential facilities for children operated by religious orders. Law enforcement
launched investigations and victims filed civil suits in increasing numbers,
although the great majority of potential claims were barred by the statute
of limitations.[7] Public outrage against church and government officials
was fueled by a steady stream of books, television documentaries, newspapers articles, and radio talk shows that gradually exposed the broad
scope of abuse in both dioceses and residential institutions.[8]

The Irish Bishops' Conference and the Conference of Religious of Ireland (CORI) responded to the growing scandal by promulgating new
policies for responding to abuse allegations. These policies, set forth in a
document entitled *Child Sexual Abuse: Framework for a Church Response* (known as the Framework Document), were voluntarily adopted
by all dioceses in 1996. The bishops' conference and CORI subsequently
established a telephone counseling service for church-related abuse, set
up an office to develop training programs and advise dioceses, commissioned a study on clergy sexual abuse in Ireland and, in 2005, launched
a new child-protection policy, *Our Children, Our Church.*[9]

The government responded to growing public concern over abuse in residential institutions with a speech by Prime Minister Bertie Ahern in 1999 offering "a sincere and long overdue apology to the victims of childhood abuse for our collective failure to intervene, detect their pain, to come to their rescue" and establishing a commission to investigate child sexual abuse in residential institutions, chaired by High Court judge Mary Laffoy and known as the Laffoy Commission. In response to pressure from an ad hoc committee of plaintiffs' attorneys representing 1,200 abuse victims, the government also enacted a one-year suspension of the statute of limitations for clergy sexual abuse and established a compensation scheme for victims abused in residential institutions. Under the scheme, the religious orders contributed 128 million Euros (roughly $120 million at the time) in exchange for government indemnification of any additional liability. The Residential Institutions Redress Board, set up to administer the scheme, received over 14,000 applications for compensation between 2002 and 2005 and has so far issued over 8,300 awards of up to 300,000 Euros (roughly $390,000) based on a matrix of factors. Compensation by the board is limited to victims of residential abuse, and the final deadline for applications was December 15, 2005. As for victims of diocesan priests, suspension of the statute of limitations unleashed an unexpected flood of civil claims in the courts. With a few notable exceptions, most have been settled.[10]

Public outrage over abuse by diocesan priests led to an official government investigation of the Diocese of Ferns, which resulted in a 2005 report detailing 100 allegations of abuse between 1962 and 2002 against twenty-one priests, their repeated reassignment to ministry by diocesan officials, and frequent refusals of law enforcement and child protection authorities to investigate complaints. Following publication of the Ferns Report, the government launched an inquiry into clergy sexual abuse in the Archdiocese of Dublin, and it left open the possibility of similar investigations into other dioceses.[11]

Civil lawsuits appear to have played a less significant role in Ireland's clergy sexual abuse scandal than they did in the United States. The Irish scandal was initially fueled by media coverage of criminal prosecutions, starting with the Smyth case in 1994. Aside from criminal proceedings, the primary sources for early news coverage of clergy sexual abuse, according to former *Irish Times* religious affairs correspondent Andy Pollack, were church contacts and victims' family members.[12] It was only in the wake of the early press coverage in 1994–1995 that the number of civil claims began to grow. News coverage appears to have engendered litigation more than litigation shaped news coverage. While the news media did, in turn, report on the growing number of civil claims, later coverage relied primarily on government documents from official investigations and interviews with victims.[13] By stoking a level of public outrage far beyond anything experienced in the United States—perhaps due to the extraordinary presence of the Catholic Church in Irish culture and politics—news coverage ultimately forced one prime minister to step down and another to publicly apologize. "It is the media," concludes Irish sociologist Tom Inglis, "that have shattered the myth that it is bad luck to criticize the priest. It is the media that have broken the tradition of not criticizing the Church and its teachings in public. It is the media that have forced the Church into giving a public account of itself."[14]

We should be careful, however, not to overlook the role of civil litigation in the Irish context. News of the Gauthe and Porter cases and the growth of clergy sexual abuse litigation in the United States was reported in the Irish press in the years preceding the Smyth case. In conjunction with growing public awareness of intrafamilial child abuse and a gradual erosion of church influence, media coverage of U.S. clergy sexual abuse litigation helped make later coverage of the scandal culturally familiar and, therefore, more newsworthy and credible to the general public. A 2003 study of clergy sexual abuse commissioned by the Irish Bishops' Conference and the government's 2005 Ferns Report both agreed that the general public and the clergy became aware of the problem "through media reports, in particular media reports from America . . . in the late 1980s or early 1990s."[15] Litigation in the United States also appears to have placed the issue on the institutional agenda of the Irish bishops, most of whom purchased liability insurance against clergy sexual abuse claims between 1987 and 1990, years before the Smyth scandal.[16] "We are aware of the cases in the U.S.," Ossory Bishop Laurence Forristal, chairman of the Bishops' Advisory Committee on Child Sexual Abuse, told the *Irish Times* in 1994, "and the fact that they happened is a warning to us of what could happen here."[17] Litigation and insurance coverage may also have played a role in the timing of the Framework Document in 1996 when, according to victims' advocate Deirdre Fitzpatrick, dioceses were negotiating new liability insurance contracts.[18] Civil suits continue to attract press coverage and make headlines, keeping the issue on public and institutional agendas.[19]

Civil litigation was also instrumental in suspending the statute of limitations and establishing the government's compensation scheme. It was pressure from the plaintiffs' attorneys' ad hoc committee representing 1,200 victims that led the government to open the window to civil claims and religious orders and to seek the indemnification deal that laid the groundwork for the Residential Institutions Redress Board.

Moreover, it would be a mistake to assume that government-sponsored investigations in Ireland have eliminated the need for civil suits. Justice Laffoy resigned from the Laffoy Commission in protest in the fall of 2003, "alleging that the government and the church had failed to cooperate with investigators."[20] Victim advocates have also complained that police investigations of clergy sexual abuse have produced only a handful of prosecutions and no charges against senior church officials.[21] By contrast, civil suits may provide an alternative strategy by which to hold church officials publicly accountable. For example, as part of the 2003 settlement of a lawsuit brought by leading victim advocate Colm O'Gormann, Bishop Eamonn Walsh read an admission of negligence into the Irish High Court record.[22] And, as the government's compensation scheme covers only those abused in residential institutions, civil lawsuits remain the only way for victims of diocesan priests to obtain compensation. High profile civil suits continue to generate sustained press coverage and keep attention focused on the issue.[23]

Canada

In Canada, public concern over clergy sexual abuse was ignited in 1988 and 1989 by a series of criminal convictions of parish priests in Newfoundland for child sexual abuse. Concern intensified with explosive revelations in 1989 of sexual abuse at the Mount Cashel orphanage operated by the Christian Brothers' religious order in St. John's, Newfoundland. Concurrent church and government investigative commissions heard testimony from dozens of victims who described physical and sexual abuse at the hands of the superintendent, staff, and other residents over the course of more than two decades. The commissions also found evidence of collusion among church officials, law enforcement, and the press to cover-up abuse allegations in the late 1970s and 1980s. Subsequent government inquiries, criminal investigations, and civil lawsuits in the 1990s and 2000s uncovered similar abuse and cover-up at dozens of residential institutions for children throughout Canada. Canada also experienced a rising number of sexual abuse allegations against parish priests during this time. The overwhelming majority of civil claims against both residential institutions and dioceses have been settled. Large aggregate settlements in cases against residential institutions have been common.[24]

The Canadian Conference of Catholic Bishops (CCCB) responded to the scandal by creating an Ad Hoc Committee on Child Sexual Abuse which, in 1992, produced a report entitled *From Pain to Hope*. The report included fifty recommendations covering pastoral care for victims, diocesan response policies, media strategy, confidentiality of personnel files, adequate liability insurance coverage, and treatment for perpetrators.[25] In 2005, the CCCB established a special task force to review the 1992 policy recommendations, which resulted in a proposal currently under consideration to adopt a new mandatory national policy.[26]

The government responded to growing public concern about residential institution abuse with a series of investigations at the provincial, territorial, and national levels. A 1998 government report, *Institutional Child Abuse in Canada,* offers an inventory of what was known at the time about physical and sexual abuse in residential institutions, an overview of different strategies for addressing the problem, and a review of existing reform proposals.[27] A subsequent 1999 government study counted 1,643 civil claims for physical and sexual abuse by Catholic victims involving forty-six Catholic schools nationwide. The report counted 2,671 cases involving seventy-two schools for all religious denominations.[28] Many of these cases name the government as a defendant alongside church defendants. A companion study on criminal cases counted over 100 criminal prosecutions against individual perpetrators.[29] These reports dealt exclusively with residential institution abuse and did not include abuse by diocesan priests. Plaintiffs' attorney Paul Ledroit estimates that the number of civil claims against Canadian dioceses is in the hundreds.[30]

There are many similarities between the clergy sexual abuse scandals in Canada and Ireland. In Canada, as in Ireland, widespread public concern was originally sparked by criminal investigations and government inquiries. Civil claims, for the most part, followed in the wake of these. Also, the prominence of abuse in state-funded residential institutions made the government's institutional failures more prominent than they have been in the United States.

At the same time, civil litigation played a significant role in Canada as it did in Ireland. The Canadian news media carried stories of U.S. litigation prior to the outbreak of scandal in Newfoundland in 1988. News coverage of U.S. litigation may explain why the CCCB first adopted guidelines for responding to abuse allegations in 1987.[31] More-over, civil claims generated press coverage throughout the 1990s and 2000s, contributing to the presence of the issue on public and institutional agendas.

Civil litigation may yet be the most effective way to make the Canadian bishops publicly accountable for diocesan abuse not addressed by government investigations focused on abuse in residential institutions. The bishops' 1992 report *From Pain to Hope* falls far short of a full acceptance of institutional responsibility like that eventually offered by the U.S. bishops. "We acknowledge," begins the report, "that media headlines, incriminating priests or religious as the actual or presumed perpetrators of sexual offenses against children, have been the source of very real suffering. In our opinion, the Catholic Church in Canada has lived through truly difficult times as we confronted the numerous accusations of reprehensible conduct on the part of some of its ministers. In the eyes of a good number of our fellow citizens, the Church has lost a great deal of credibility over the past few years due to these scandals and the suspicion that there were attempts to conceal these intolerable acts."[32] By this account, the *media* have inflicted "very real suffering" on the Church based on its incrimination of "actual or presumed" clerical sex offenders, who, even if guilty, amount to no more than a few bad apples. This acknowledgment further suggests that damage to the Church's good name resulted from mere "suspicions" that there were "attempts" to cover-up abuse. The document provides no accounting of the number of abuse allegations or any discussion of the scope of the problem. While Irish bishops have provided some figures on the scope of abuse within their dioceses, Canadian bishops have not. A recent public inquiry into abuse allegations and cover-up in Cornwall, Ontario, may be the first step toward the kind of public accounting provided by grand jury and attorney general reports in the United States and the Ferns and Dublin inquiries in Ireland.

This brief comparison of the United States, Ireland, and Canada supports three conclusions concerning the impact of civil litigation on policy responses to clergy sexual abuse. First, media coverage of the Gauthe case and the first wave of clergy sexual abuse litigation initially raised public awareness and prompted policymaking among church officials not only in the United States but also in other countries as well. It might be overstating the case to say that the first wave of litigation played an *essential* role in Canada and Ireland as it did in the United

States, but it certainly contributed to the newsworthiness of clergy sexual abuse, public openness to suggestions of institutional responsibility, and a fear of liability that prompted bishops' initial policy responses.

Second, once public and official awareness was raised, civil litigation generated media coverage that helped maintain clergy sexual abuse on public and institutional agendas. The extent to which civil litigation, as opposed to criminal prosecution or government inquiries, gave the media story legs, varied from country to country. Nevertheless, civil litigation made headlines, stoked public outrage, and prompted official responses in all three countries.

Third, civil litigation in the United States—with its doctrinal expansiveness, large awards, high level of organization among plaintiffs' attorneys, large pool of available plaintiffs, and experience with mass tort litigation—appears to have generated more information about church officials' mismanagement of clergy sexual abuse in the diocesan context than is currently available in either Ireland or Canada. Civil lawsuits in the United States have also been more successful in holding bishops publicly accountable. In Ireland and Canada, government and to a lesser extent, church inquiries have uncovered extensive information about residential abuse, and they have placed the blame for it squarely on the institutional failures of church and government officials. This has not, however, been the case with clergy sexual abuse in the diocesan context. In Canada, the bishops have not been forthcoming with aggregate information about clergy sexual abuse and their handling of it. Without more civil litigation, it seems unlikely that they ever will. In Ireland, government inquiries like those in Ferns and Dublin may prove an alternative way to generate such information and hold church officials accountable. But even if this is the case, civil litigation has still played a role in generating press coverage, emboldening victims to come forward, stoking public outrage, and mobilizing activists—all of which help to make such government inquiries successful. In terms of what is known in the aggregate about the role of church officials in facilitating clergy sexual abuse, the United States is still far ahead of other countries, and it seems fair to say that civil litigation is one reason.

Tort Litigation as a Policy Venue

Clergy sexual abuse litigation illustrates how private lawsuits can sometimes function as what political scientists Frank Baumgartner and

Bryan Jones call a *policy venue*.[33] Baumgartner and Jones suggest that policymaking with regard to any particular issue may experience periods of "equilibrium," characterized by public apathy and institutional stasis, and periods of "instability," characterized by heightened concern and policy innovation. Equilibrium often occurs after an organization or a government agency establishes jurisdiction over an issue and a policy is put in place. Public attention dies down and vested interests both inside and outside the institution protect the status quo from challenges. By contrast, instability results when existing policy is altered.

Policy change, according to Baumgartner and Jones, is a function of two factors: framing and venue. When an issue is reframed, it may excite public interest and engender pressure for policy reform. When an issue falls under a different institutional jurisdiction, the change in venue may bring with it new ways of approaching the problem and different tools for responding to it. Moreover, reframing and venue change reinforce each other. Reframing leads other institutions to exercise jurisdiction over an issue, often resulting in venue change, and venue change often results in reframing an issue to conform to the particular institutional perspectives and expertise of the new venue. For example, "[t]obacco policy in the agriculture arena is seen as an important source of jobs; in health policy circles it evokes images of disease; in insurance and business cost-containment circles it is seen as a source of increased health insurance premiums; in foreign trade circles it is seen as an important source of U.S. export earnings. Each institutional venue is home to a different image of the same question."[34] Just as framing and venue are mutually reinforcing, so too are the mobilization of public opinion on the one hand and framing and venue on the other. Shifts in public opinion influence the institutional framing and venue of an issue, while official frames and venues influence public opinion.[35] All of this mutual reinforcement, or "positive feedback," accelerates change during periods of instability. It also strengthens entrenchment during periods of equilibrium.

Prior to 1984, the Catholic Church exercised almost exclusive jurisdiction over clergy sexual misconduct with little, if any, interference from public authorities. The problem was framed as an issue of moral failing on the part of the offending priest to be addressed through confession, forgiveness of sins, a resolution not to repeat the offense and, in some cases, psychotherapy. The Church was able to maintain its exclusive jurisdiction over clergy sexual abuse and to avoid scrutiny of its response to the problem because of the great respect and reverence for clergy and church officials among the general public and, to an even greater extent, the Catholic laity. The Church also exerted significant political influence that protected it from interference by government officials.

Litigation was a new institutional venue for addressing clergy sexual abuse in which plaintiffs' attorneys reframed the issue in terms of institutional failure and, by generating press coverage, changed public opinion. This prompted policy reforms by both church and government officials. Litigation functioned as a policy venue that jump-started reform efforts within other policy venues. Note that clergy sexual abuse litigation did not by itself formulate, implement, and review policy. Instead, it reframed the problem, placed it on the agendas of other policymaking institutions, and generated new information for addressing it. As a policy venue, tort litigation played a complementary role, stirring up policy instability and influencing policy reforms carried out in other policy venues.

Social Policy Tort Litigation

Clergy sexual abuse litigation is part of a larger class of mass tort litigation that seeks not only redress for past injuries but also prospective changes in regulatory policy. Scholars refer to this class of lawsuits as "regulation through litigation" or "social policy tort litigation."[36] Two prominent examples are lawsuits against tobacco companies aimed at smoking reduction and litigation against gun makers designed to produce new gun controls. In addition to the standard features of mass tort litigation—such as aggregation of claims, coordination among lawyers on both sides, and collective settlements—social policy tort litigation is further characterized by especially vulnerable victims; powerful institutional leaders accused of egregious misconduct; titillating themes such as sex, drugs, and violence; morally shocking revelations; and the reduction of complex social problems to simple, nontechnical narratives. Thus, tobacco litigation plaintiffs tell a story about mendacious tobacco executives who market cigarettes to children and turn them into addicts by secretly manipulating the nicotine levels of cigarettes to make them more addictive. Tobacco executives are, on this account, responsible for 400,000 U.S. cancer deaths a year. Along similar lines, gun litigation plaintiffs tell a story about greedy and callous gun makers who knowingly profit from the illegal diversion of their weapons into black markets where they fuel urban youth gang violence and are used in suburban school shootings. Plaintiffs have asserted an easily traceable link between the failure of gun makers to stem the illegal flow of guns into the black market and thousands of gun violence deaths per year. Social policy tort litigation is also normally linked to preexisting reform movements mobilized by interest groups such as antismoking and gun-control organizations, and the litigation is often justified as part of a larger strategy to overcome the influence of opposing interest groups such as the tobacco lobby and the National Rifle Association (NRA).

My analysis of clergy sexual abuse litigation as a policy venue builds on earlier studies of social policy tort litigation. In particular, scholars such as Lynn Mather, Peter Jacobson, Kenneth Warner, and Wendy Wagner have developed detailed accounts of the framing, agenda-setting, and information-generating functions of tobacco litigation and the ways in which it complemented the policymaking efforts of legislatures, agencies, and private industry to affect tobacco-control policy.[37] My own earlier work focuses on the policymaking impact of gun litigation.[38]

When compared to these other forms of social policy tort litigation, clergy sexual abuse litigation has had an especially powerful impact on policymaking. Tobacco and gun litigation played significant but relatively small roles in larger antismoking and gun-control movements that preceded them by decades. And while litigation did focus attention on the role of the tobacco and gun industries in facilitating smoking addiction and gun violence, the results in terms of industry reform and government regulation have been modest.[39] By contrast, clergy sexual abuse litigation initiated widespread public concern and began the mobilization of interest groups such as SNAP and Voice of the Faithful. Not only did the litigation draw attention to the role of church officials in facilitating child sexual abuse, it also placed the issue on the agendas of church and government policymakers for the first time and generated pressure on them to address the problem. Most of what is publicly known about clergy sexual abuse was discovered by lawyers or comes from studies and investigations that, but for the litigation, would likely never have been undertaken. The results of the litigation include new, mandatory, nationwide church policies, a public accounting of the role of church officials in facilitating decades of child sexual abuse, and a heightened public sensitivity to the institutional dimensions of child sexual abuse. Clergy sexual abuse litigation is, in short, a poster child for the policymaking benefits of tort litigation.

Three aspects of clergy sexual abuse litigation help explain why it has had such a powerful impact compared to other forms of social policy tort litigation. First, allegations of widespread child sexual molestation by compulsive pedophile priests covered up at the highest levels of the Catholic Church made for an especially scandalous narrative that fueled an unusual level of moral outrage. Second, clergy sexual abuse litigation shattered decades of near universal silence about a social problem of shocking depravity and scope. Prior to the Gauthe case in 1984, what little knowledge there was of clergy sexual abuse was not openly discussed or addressed by victims, their families, fellow parishioners, clergy, church officials, therapists, the press, lawyers, law enforcement, or legislators. Third, clergy sexual abuse litigation enhanced the performance of other policymaking institutions, including the USCCB, the criminal justice system, and legislatures. By framing the problem, putting it on the agenda, and providing essential information, litigation enabled these other institutions to address it more effectively.

The Complementary Policymaking Role of Tort Litigation

All institutions are well suited to perform certain tasks and poorly suited to perform others. By analyzing the relative strengths and weaknesses of tort litigation in comparison to other policymaking institutions, scholars have identified the ways in which litigation can complement the efforts of other policymaking institutions. Peter Schuck has proposed a number of criteria by which the policymaking capacities of different institutions can be compared.[40] These include the ability to acquire and evaluate technical information, weigh political support for different policy options, implement regulations using a variety of incentives and sanctions, monitor results and make adjustments, and promulgate predictable rules that are easy to follow. Under all of these criteria, argues Schuck, courts are usually less well suited to design and implement complex policy than are legislative committees and regulatory agencies. Moreover, he suggests, the high level of public respect accorded to courts would be eroded were they to function too much like legislatures and agencies, which are frequently the object of public disappointment when policies fail. Schuck's comparative institutional analysis thus identifies some of the limits of regulation through litigation.

Under Schuck's rubric, courts are, on the whole, institutionally less well equipped to design and implement policy than are agencies and legislatures. Nevertheless, he does suggest a few comparative advantages of regulation through litigation. First, the decentralized nature of litigation may stimulate innovation, allowing judges in different cases to try novel approaches to problem solving. Second, popular reverence for the jury system and suspicion of government bureaucracy and the political process may give regulation through litigation a higher level of popular support in some cases than policy solutions crafted by agencies and legislatures. Third, litigation that involves a large volume of claims generates, over time, information about the value of claims for the purposes of compensation and often leads to administrative schemes for efficient claims resolution.

Schuck's comparative institutional analysis focuses on the policy-making capacities of courts in adjudicating disputes and imposing remedies. It is this focus on adjudication and remedies that has led many scholarly commentators to view social policy tort litigation as, ultimately, disappointing. And from this perspective, it is. Neither tobacco nor gun litigation, for example, produced many courtroom victories or remedies that significantly reduced smoking-related illness or gun violence.[41]

The case of clergy sexual abuse litigation, however, suggests that we look elsewhere for the most significant policymaking capacities of tort litigation. Schuck's analysis focuses on adjudication and remedies, which are activities of judges and juries during and after trial. By contrast, clergy sexual abuse litigation's most significant policymaking impacts—framing, agenda access, and information generation—were carried out by lawyers in the pretrial stages of pleading and discovery. By shifting our focus to these aspects of the litigation process, we see that under certain circumstances—for example, where litigation frames have a high degree of cultural resonance, other policymaking institutions are inactive, and there are strong incentives to conceal policy-relevant information from government regulators—litigation has comparative advantages over other policymaking institutions in framing issues, placing them on public and institutional agendas, and generating useful information.

Previous scholarship has done much to elucidate how the litigation process complements the policymaking efforts of agencies, legislatures, and private organizations. Schuck, himself, has described how mass tort lawyers are often the first group to take up and grapple with the problems created by widespread risks that are unaddressed by other policymaking institutions.[42] Political scientist Lynn Mather and public health scholars Peter Jacobson and Kenneth Warner have documented how tobacco litigation performed framing, agenda-setting, and information-generating functions.[43] Tort scholars Robert Rabin and Wendy Wagner have offered more general accounts of how tort litigation has a unique capacity for uncovering policy-relevant information that regulated parties seek to conceal.[44] My analysis of clergy sexual abuse litigation adds to this robust literature an especially clear example and detailed account of tort litigation's complementary policymaking role.

Tort Reformers and Litigation Skeptics

A variety of commentators have raised concerns about using tort litigation to make policy. First, litigation skeptics question the *effectiveness* of lawsuits in promoting policy change. Gerald Rosenberg argues forcefully in his careful study of constitutional litigation, *The Hollow Hope*, that "U.S. courts can *almost never* be effective producers of significant social reform," and that litigation is a drain on the scarce resources of reform advocates who could achieve more through the political process.[45] Second, tort-reform advocates question the *efficiency* of tort litigation as a means of compensation, risk regulation, and policy change. Peter Huber and Walter Olson contend that whatever benefits tort litigation might have are insignificant when compared to the costs of frivolous claims and inflated jury awards, which have caused widespread fear of liability, the withdrawal of essential products and services, and the stifling of safety innovation.[46] Third, tort-reform advocates also challenge the *legitimacy* of using tort litigation as a means of promoting policy change. They argue that the job of courts is to resolve disputes and to enforce legislative mandates, not to make public policy.[47] Clergy sexual abuse litigation provides a counterexample to each of these objections.

Litigation skeptics argue that litigation is ineffective as a means of achieving social change.[48] Adherents to what Gerald Rosenberg terms the "Constrained Court" view suggest that among the reasons litigation is ineffective at producing social change is that "framing issues in legally sound ways robs them of 'political and purposive appeal.'"[49] Rosenberg himself suggests that "courts are in a weak position to produce change [since] . . . [o]nly a minority of Americans know what the courts have done on important issues."[50] Moreover, quoting another scholar, he adds, "litigation, by its complexity and technical nature and its lack of dramatic moments, furnishes an ineffective peg around which to build a mass movement." "Rally round the flag is one thing," Rosenberg concludes, "but rally round the brief (or opinion) is quite another!"[51]

Rosenberg's contention that "U.S. courts can *almost never* be effective producers of significant social reform" is built on careful empirical and historical analysis of U.S. Supreme Court decisions regarding racial segregation, abortion, environmental protection, electoral reapportionment, and criminal procedure reforms.[52] When we shift our attention to the work of plaintiffs' lawyers in tort litigation against the Catholic Church, we see a very different picture.

As we have seen, framing claims in "legally sound ways" enhances their appeal. Good litigation strategy demands that plaintiffs' frame their claims in terms of compelling narrative drama. For this very reason, they are newsworthy, and news coverage generates widespread public awareness of them. Even if Rosenberg is right that the public are largely unaware of what *courts* do in these cases, they are very aware—as the case of clergy sexual abuse litigation shows—of the claims made and the frames generated by the *litigants*. Clergy sexual abuse litigation was neither complex nor technical, and it provided a highly effective "peg" on which to base news stories and around which to organize and energize groups such as Voice of the Faithful, SNAP, and VOCAL. Neither the public nor policymakers rallied round briefs or opinions in clergy abuse litigation. They did, however, rally round the frames promulgated by the litigation.[53]

In contrast to Rosenberg's sweeping claim that "U.S. courts can *almost never* be effective producers of significant social reform," litigants in clergy sexual abuse litigation *were* effective in producing major policy changes within the Catholic Church and among law enforcement, and smaller but still significant policy changes within state legislatures across the country. The extent to which this is also true of other examples of social policy tort litigation varies. I would suggest—and Rosenberg's work provides an excellent model—that we examine each individual case based on empirical facts rather than on generalized claims.

Rosenberg criticizes defenders of the "Dynamic Court" view—that court decisions do effect significant social change—for their failure to spell out the precise mechanisms and causal connections by which this purported change occurs. My account of clergy sexual abuse litigation does just that. It describes in detail how litigation framed the problem of clergy sexual abuse as an issue of institutional failure, placed that issue on public and institutional agendas, and generated information essential to addressing it.

Tort-reform advocates regularly cite social policy tort litigation as evidence that tort litigation is largely frivolous and wasteful. They allege that rampant litigation and inflated jury awards constitute a major drain on society's resources. They argue that widespread fear of liability created by the tort system leads to the withdrawal of essential products and services and stifles safety innovation.[54] Defenders of the current tort regime have responded by pointing to the benefits of this litigation for regulatory policymaking in terms of framing, agenda setting, and generating policy-relevant information. The debate to date has been largely anecdotal, with tort-reform advocates citing horror stories and defenders offering counterexamples.[55] Unfortunately, this book does not advance the debate beyond the battle of examples. It does, however, provide a clear example of the benefits of tort litigation for policymaking. Even if one does not agree with my conclusion in chapter 7 that the litigation's benefits outweigh its costs, I have shown that the benefits are significant—so significant, I would argue, that they should cause tort reform advocates to take another, more careful look at the benefits of tort litigation for policymaking.

This is not to say that social policy tort litigation is always beneficial or that its benefits are always worth its costs. There is ongoing debate about the value of litigation for the regulation of consumer products, pharmaceuticals, public health, and the environment. One should be careful about making general claims about the policymaking benefits of tort litigation solely on the basis of clergy sexual abuse litigation. Assessing the contribution of litigation to policymaking requires case-by-case analysis. At the very least, however, the lessons of clergy sexual abuse litigation give us reason to revisit the case for tort reform and to reconsider broad generalizations regarding the usefulness of litigation in addressing social problems.

Finally, tort-reform advocates challenge the legitimacy of using litigation to make policy. They argue that the traditional role of courts in our constitutional system is to resolve disputes and enforce legislative mandates, leaving policymaking to the legislative and executive branches of government. Using courts to make public policy will, in the end, they assert, politicize the judiciary, undermine the integrity of the litigation process, and erode public confidence in the courts.[56]

As applied to tobacco and gun litigation, this challenge raises a number of questions. First, it is not clear what, exactly, tort reform advocates mean by legitimacy. Does legitimacy derive from adherence to tradition, grounding in some historically significant agreement, widespread public acceptance, or some other source? And what gives any one of these possible sources of legitimacy moral significance? One suspects that such underdeveloped challenges that are based on legitimacy are employed more for their rhetorical power than for their normative force.[57] Second, it is unclear how the idea that courts have no business making law applies to tort law, which is, for the most part, common law made by judges. Do the critics mean to suggest that common law lacks legitimacy, or that judges ought not to adapt it to new circumstances? Third, tort-reform advocates offer little in the way of empirical evidence for their claims that regulation through litigation will politicize the judiciary, undermine the integrity of the litigation process, and erode public confidence in the courts. Elsewhere, I have offered reasons to doubt these predictions.[58]

As applied to clergy sexual abuse litigation, this legitimacy challenge seems largely irrelevant. To begin with, clergy sexual abuse litigation has involved little judicial innovation. Novel theories like clergy malpractice have been rejected universally by courts, and the most prevalent theories of recovery—respondeat superior and negligent supervision—have long been recognized and applied by courts. The most significant changes in the law—extension and suspension of statutes of limitation, removal of charitable immunity and damage caps, and elimination of clergy exclusions in mandatory reporting laws—have all been legislative and are, therefore, hardly subject to challenges based on judicial policymaking.

Moreover, the legitimacy challenge is based on the view that social policy tort litigation is a kind of end-run around legislative politics. Even if this were true for tobacco and gun litigation, clergy sexual abuse is different. Both tobacco and gun regulation were the subject of ongoing legislative battles that preceded litigation by decades, and there were specific federal and state agencies charged with regulating key aspects of those industries under complex statutory frameworks. By contrast, clergy sexual abuse litigation filled a regulatory void created by legislative and law enforcement ignorance and quiescence. There was, unfortunately, no robust national legislative debate or agency regulation around which to run.

Finally, the policy impacts of clergy sexual abuse litigation, rather than undermining the legitimacy of the civil justice system, arise out of an essential element of the system's legitimacy: transparency. With few exceptions, we expect legal proceedings to be open to the public. Public access to legal proceedings, facilitated by uncensored press coverage, is considered an essential safeguard against abuses of government power.[59] This aspect of civil litigation means that private claims submitted to a court are thereby placed in the public domain. In controversial cases, these claims will attract media coverage and public attention, and this has implications for policymaking. Transparency gives private tort claims the potential to frame issues, gain agenda access, and disseminate information.

The alternative is to conceal private litigation from public view. In clergy sexual abuse litigation, prior to 2002, courts routinely did just that by sealing case files. Parties themselves did the same by making confidential settlements. This secrecy hardly strengthened public confidence in the civil justice system. To the contrary, it created an impression that courts and litigants on both sides were protecting the Church from scandal. Clergy sexual abuse litigation highlights that, insofar as transparency is a valued aspect of our legal system, tort litigation cannot help but have potential policy implications.

Coda

Gilbert Gauthe was released from prison in 1995 for "good behavior" after serving only half of his twenty-year sentence. He moved to Texas where, shortly after his arrival, he was charged with sexually molesting a three-year-old boy. He pled guilty, and the judge, unaware of his prior record, sentenced him to probation. A year later, he was charged in Lafayette with raping a twelve-year-old girl in 1982 and imprisoned pending trial. The case against him was dismissed in 2000 as violating the terms of his 1985 plea bargain. (In exchange for his guilty plea, he had been granted immunity from any other child molestation charges for crimes prior to 1985.) He was released, after which he returned to Texas, where he is presumably living today.[60]

Clergy sexual abuse litigation did not put an end to child sexual abuse. It did, however, lead to institutional reforms that make it less likely that the Catholic Church in the United States will ever again facilitate or conceal the crimes of serial pedophiles like Gilbert Gauthe, James Porter, or John Geoghan. Church leaders have publicly committed themselves to preventing abuse before it occurs and reporting it when it does. Moreover, the impact of the litigation goes beyond the Catholic Church. Child sexual abuse claims, according to insurance counsel Catalina Sugayan, "are increasingly being brought against churches of all denominations, social service providers in the business of residential and foster home placements, schools, camps and scouting organizations."[61] Throughout the country—indeed throughout the world—institutions charged with the care of children have provided safe havens for perpetrators of child sexual abuse. While it will take a lot more than lawsuits to fix this problem, litigation has been a good start.

Newspaper and Magazine Articles (Table 1)

News outlets searched in the Lexis/Nexis electronic database were the *New York Times, Chicago Tribune, Los Angeles Times, Washington Post, Christian Science Monitor, Time* magazine, *Newsweek* magazine, *The Nation, Forbes* magazine, *U.S. News & World Report,* and *People* magazine. News outlets searched in the Westlaw electronic database were the *Boston Globe, Miami Herald, Philadelphia Inquirer, San Francisco Chronicle, Seattle Times, St. Louis Post Dispatch, San Jose Mercury News, Wall St. Journal Abstracts, Cosmopolitan,* and *Esquire.* The search terms on Lexis/Nexis were "date is [YEAR] and (priest or clergy w/15 abus! or moles!) and not substance or alcohol or drug or military or "human rights" or spouse or husband or army or guerillas or labor." The search terms for Westlaw were "da([YEAR]) & (priest clergy w/15 abus! moles!) % substance alcohol drug military "human rights" spouse husband army guerillas labor."

Search results were reviewed in accordance with the following guidelines. Articles that are the same or nearly the same, and appear on the same day in separate editions of the same newspaper, were counted once. Nearly the same was defined as most of the words in the article being identical. Many times a later edition contained an abbreviated version of an article printed in the morning edition. It was very clear when an article had been shortened or slightly modified and included in a later edition. Tangentially related articles were included in the count.

For example, articles about non-Catholic clergy sexual abuse, financial or ethical issues related to clergy sexual abuse, international cases, etc., were all counted. Articles that merely mentioned or alluded to the clergy abuse scandal were not counted. This was common in the *Boston Globe,* for example. Completely off-topic articles often included allusions to clergy sexual abuse.

Letters to the Editor (Table 2)

Search terms in the Lexis/Nexis search were "date is [YEAR] and section (letter) or headline (letter edit!) or (section (editorial) and body (to the editor)) or terms (letters) and (priest or clergy w/15 abus! or moles!) and not substance or alcohol or drug or military or "human rights" or spouse or husband or army or guerillas or labor." Search terms in the Westlaw search were "oi(letter editor) & da([YEAR]) & (priest clergy w/15 abus! moles!) % substance alcohol drug military "human rights" spouse husband army guerillas labor." Search results were reviewed and duplicates and off-topic letters were not counted.

Articles in Catholic Periodicals (Methodology and Raw Data for Figure 9)

This search was conducted in the Catholic Periodical and Literature Index database using the following search terms: "sex* misconduct", "sex* abus*", "sex* crim*", "child* abus*", "child* molest*", and "pedophile*". Search results were reviewed and articles were included if (1) the title of article indicated that subject matter was sexual abuse of minors by clergy or other church personnel (e.g., nuns, brothers . . .); (2) the article was listed under relevant subject indexing such as "child sexual abuse by clergy," "child sexual abuse by religious," "victims of sex crimes," and "sexual misconduct by clergy," (3) the title of the article referred to a nationwide (or worldwide) sex abuse scandal; (4) a review of the text of the article revealed relevance to clergy sexual abuse; (5) subject indexing or the title referred to names of individuals or events strongly connected with clergy sexual abuse; and (6) the title of the article used phrasing frequently used in connection with clergy sexual abuse. Discretion was used where subject indexing or the title of article was ambiguous. Articles were considered duplicates, and therefore not counted, if they had the same title, author, and subject.

Table A3.1. Raw data for Figure 9: Number of articles in Catholic periodicals

	1984	1985	1986	1987	1988	1989	1990	1991	1992
Acta Apostilicae Sedis			0	0	0	0	0	0	0
America	0	0	0	0	0	0	1	0	4
Amer. Catholic Studies		0	0	0	0	0	0	0	0
Amer. Cath. Stud. Newsletter			0	0	0	0	0	0	0
Canadian Catholic Review			0	0	0	0	0	0	1
CARA Report	0	0	0	0	0	0	0	0	0
Catholic Digest	0	0	0	0	0	0	0	0	0
Catholic Education	0	0	0	0	0	0	0	0	0
Catholic Lawyer	0	0	0	0	0	0	0	0	0
Cath Theo. Soc. of Amer. Proc.			0	0	0	0	0	0	0
Christ to the World		0	0	0	0	0	0	0	0
Church	0	0	0	0	0	0	0	0	0
Columbia	0	0	0	0	0	0	0	0	0
Commonweal	0	0	0	0	0	0	0	0	1
Crisis	0	0	0	0	1	0	0	0	1
Critic	0	0	0	0	0	0	0	0	1
Cross Currents	0	0	0	0	0	0	0	0	0
Doctrine and Life	0	0	0	0	0	0	0	0	0
Ethics and Medics	0	0	0	0	0	0	0	0	0
Etudes	0	0	0	0	0	0	0	0	0
Furrow	0	0	0	0	0	0	0	0	0
Health Progress	0	0	0	0	0	0	0	0	0
Heythrop Journal	0	0	0	0	0	0	0	0	0
Homiletic and Pastoral Rev.			0	0	0	0	0	0	0

1993	1994	1995	1996	1997	1998	1999	2000	2001	2002	2003	2004
0	0	0	0	0	0	0	0	0	1	0	0
5	3	0	0	0	0	2	2	1	47	7	5
0	0	0	0	0	0	0	0	0	1	0	0
0	0	0	0	0	0	0	0	0	0	1	1
0	0	0	0	0	0	0	0	0	0	0	0
0	0	0	0	0	0	0	0	0	1	0	0
0	0	0	0	0	0	0	0	0	8	1	0
0	0	0	0	0	0	0	0	0	1	0	0
1	0	1	0	0	0	0	0	0	0	0	0
0	0	0	0	0	0	0	0	0	1	2	0
0	0	0	1	0	0	0	0	0	0	1	0
1	0	0	0	0	0	0	0	0	5	3	1
0	0	0	0	0	0	0	0	0	0	1	0
1	1	1	0	0	0	0	1	0	22	7	0
0	0	0	0	0	0	0	0	1	2	1	0
0	0	0	0	0	0	0	0	0	0	0	0
0	0	0	0	0	0	0	0	0	1	0	0
0	0	0	0	0	0	0	0	0	4	0	0
0	0	0	0	0	0	0	0	0	1	0	0
0	0	0	0	0	0	0	0	0	1	1	0
1	0	1	2	0	1	2	0	1	11	6	0
0	0	0	0	0	0	0	0	0	1	0	0
0	0	0	0	0	0	0	0	0	1	0	0
0	0	0	0	0	0	0	0	0	3	2	0

(cont.)

Table A3.1. Raw data for Figure 9: Number of articles in Catholic periodicals *(cont.)*

	1984	1985	1986	1987	1988	1989	1990	1991	1992
Human Development		0	0	0	0	0	0	0	0
Inside the Vatican	0	0	0	0	0	0	0	0	0
Irish Theo. Quarterly		0	0	0	0	0	0	0	0
Jurist	0	0	0	0	0	0	0	1	0
La Civilta Cattolica	0	0	0	0	0	0	0	0	0
Liguorian	0	0	0	0	0	0	0	0	0
Louvain Studies	0	0	0	0	0	0	0	0	0
Momentum	0	0	0	0	0	0	0	0	0
Month	0	0	0	0	0	0	0	0	0
National Catholic Register		0	3	0	1	0	0	0	1
National Catholic Reporter		3	2	0	2	1	5	0	6
New Blackfriars	0	0	0	0	0	0	0	0	0
New Convenant	0	0	0	0	0	0	0	0	0
New Oxford Review	0	0	0	0	0	0	0	0	0
New Theo. Review	0	0	0	0	0	0	0	0	0
Origins	0	0	0	0	1	1	1	0	4
Osservatore Romano		0	0	0	0	1	0	0	0
Osservatore Romano (wkly)			0	0	0	0	0	0	0
Our Sunday Visitor	0	0	0	0	0	0	0	0	0
Pastoral Life	0	0	0	0	0	0	0	0	0

1993	1994	1995	1996	1997	1998	1999	2000	2001	2002	2003	2004
0	0	0	0	0	0	0	1	0	0	3	12
0	0	0	0	1	0	0	0	0	13	2	1
0	0	0	0	0	0	0	0	0	0	2	1
0	0	0	0	0	0	0	0	0	0	1	0
0	0	0	0	0	0	0	0	0	2	1	0
0	1	0	0	0	0	0	0	0	4	0	0
0	0	0	0	0	0	0	1	0	0	0	0
0	0	0	0	0	0	0	0	0	2	0	0
0	0	1	0	0	0	0	0	0	0	0	0
2	3	1	2	2	11	4	1	3	55	12	5
13	10	6	5	18	21	34	14	5	137	60	22
0	0	0	0	0	0	0	1	0	0	0	0
0	1	0	0	0	0	0	0	0	0	0	0
0	0	0	0	0	0	0	0	0	3	1	0
0	1	0	0	0	0	0	0	0	0	0	0
9	3	0	0	0	0	0	1	0	53	10	13
0	0	0	0	0	3	0	0	0	0	0	0
0	0	0	0	0	0	0	0	0	5	0	3
4	1	0	3	2	4	0	0	1	58	23	3
0	0	0	0	0	0	0	0	0	2	0	1

(cont.)

Table A3.1. Raw data for Figure 9: Number of articles in Catholic periodicals *(cont.)*

	1984	1985	1986	1987	1988	1989	1990	1991	1992
Periodeica de Re Canonica		0	0	0	0	0	0	0	0
The Pope Speaks	0	0	0	0	0	0	0	0	0
Priest	0	0	0	0	0	1	1	0	0
Priests and People		0	0	0	0	0	0	0	0
Review for Religious		0	0	0	0	0	0	0	0
Rite	0	0	0	0	0	0	0	0	0
Seminarium	0	0	0	0	0	0	0	0	0
Social Justice Review		0	0	0	0	0	0	0	1
St. Anthony Messenger		0	0	0	0	0	0	0	0
Stimmen der Zeit	0	0	0	0	0	0	0	0	0
Studia Canonica	0	0	0	0	1	0	1	0	2
Studies	0	0	0	0	0	0	0	0	0
Tablet	0	0	0	0	0	0	0	1	1
Theological Studies	0	0	0	0	0	0	0	0	0
Today's Catholic Teacher		0	0	0	0	0	0	0	0
Today's Parish	0	0	0	0	0	0	0	0	1
U.S. Catholic	0	0	0	0	0	0	0	0	0
The Way	0	0	0	0	0	0	0	0	0
TOTAL FOR YEAR:	0	3	5	0	6	4	9	2	24

1993	1994	1995	1996	1997	1998	1999	2000	2001	2002	2003	2004
0	0	0	0	0	0	0	0	0	1	0	1
0	0	0	0	0	0	0	0	0	1	0	0
1	1	0	0	0	0	0	1	0	8	2	1
1	0	0	0	0	0	0	0	1	0	3	1
0	0	0	0	0	0	0	0	0	1	0	0
0	0	0	0	0	0	0	0	0	1	0	0
0	0	0	0	0	0	0	0	0	1	0	0
0	0	0	0	0	1	0	0	0	2	1	1
0	0	0	0	0	2	0	0	0	9	9	2
0	0	0	0	0	0	0	0	0	1	0	0
1	0	0	0	0	0	0	0	1	0	0	0
0	0	0	0	0	0	0	5	0	0	0	0
4	1	1	1	4	6	24	18	6	28	8	4
0	1	0	0	0	0	0	0	0	1	0	0
0	0	0	0	0	0	0	0	0	1	0	0
0	0	0	0	0	0	0	0	0	2	0	0
5	0	0	0	0	0	0	0	0	9	0	0
5	0	0	0	0	0	0	0	0	0	1	0
54	27	12	14	27	49	66	46	20	512	172	78

Notes

Introduction

1. My discussion of the Gauthe affair relies extensively on Jason Berry, *Lead Us Not Into Temptation: Catholic Priests and the Sexual Abuse of Children* (1992; reprint, Urbana: University of Illinois Press, 2000); Frank Bruni and Elinor Burkett, *A Gospel of Shame: Children, Sexual Abuse, and the Catholic Church* (1993; reprint, New York: Perennial-HarperCollins, 2002); J. Minos Simon and David Leon Chandler, *Law in the Cajun Nation* (Lafayette, La.: Prescott Press, 1993), chap. 8.

2. Arthur Jones, "Legal Actions Against Pedophile Priests Grow as Frustrated and Angry Parents Seek Remedies," *National Catholic Reporter,* June 7, 1985, 4.

3. See Dan Dobbs, *Dobbs's Hornbook on the Law of Torts* (St. Paul, Minn.: West, 2000), §§9–11, 13–21; Kenneth Abraham, *The Forms and Functions of Tort Law: An Analytic Primer on Cases and Concepts,* 2nd ed. (New York: Foundation Press, 2002), 14–17.

4. See, e.g., Lynn Mather, "Theorizing About Trial Courts: Lawyers, Policymaking, and Tobacco Litigation," 23 *Law & Social Inquiry* 897 (1998); Peter Jacobson and Kenneth Warner, "Litigation and Public Health Policy Making: The Case of Tobacco Control," 24 *Journal of Health Politics, Policy & Law* 769 (1999); Robert L. Rabin, "The Third Wave of Tobacco Tort Litigation," in Robert L. Rabin and Stephen D. Sugarman, eds., *Regulating Tobacco* (Oxford: Oxford University Press, 2001), chap. 7; Deborah Hensler, "The New Social Policy Torts: Litigation as a Legislative Strategy—Preliminary Thoughts on a New Research Project," 51 *DePaul Law Review* 498 (2001); Timothy D. Lytton, ed., *Suing the Gun Industry: A Battle at the Crossroads of Gun Control and Mass Torts* (Ann Arbor: University of Michigan Press, 2005). For a more general discussion of the complementary regulatory role of tort law, see Susan Rose-Ackerman, "Tort

Law in the Regulatory State," in Peter H. Schuck, ed., *Tort Law and the Public Interest: Competition, Innovation, and Consumer Welfare* (New York: Norton, 1991), chap. 3.

5. Gerald Rosenberg, *The Hollow Hope: Can Courts Bring About Social Change?* (Chicago: University of Chicago Press, 1991), 338–342.

6. Peter Huber, *Liability: The Legal Revolution and Its Consequences* (New York: Basic Books, 1988); Walter Olson, *The Rule of Lawyers: How the New Litigation Elite Threatens America's Rule of Law* (New York: St. Martin's Press, 2003). For a more nuanced critique of tort litigation, see Robert A. Kagan, *Adversarial Legalism: The American Way of Law* (Cambridge, Mass.: Harvard University Press, 2001).

7. See, e.g., Olson, *Rule of Lawyers*; Catherine Crier, *The Case Against Lawyers* (New York: Broadway Books, 2002); Peter Schuck, "The New Judicial Ideology of Tort Law," in *New Directions in Liability Law*, Walter Olson, ed. (Montpelier, Vt.: Capital City Press, 1988), 4–17.

1. A Short History

1. Mark E. Chopko, "Restoring Trust and Faith," 9 *Human Rights: Journal of the Section of Individual Rights & Responsibilities* 22 (1992); Mark Chopko, interview by the author, March 22, 2006.

2. Arthur Jones, "Legal Actions Against Pedophile Priests Grow as Frustrated and Angry Parents Seek Remedies," *National Catholic Reporter*, June 7, 1985, 4.

3. Chopko, interview.

4. A. W. Richard Sipe, "Sipe Report," www.bishopaccountability.org (accessed 12/12/06), 48–53.

5. "Priest Child Abuse Cases Victimizing Families; Bishops Lack Policy Response," *National Catholic Reporter*, June 7, 1985, 1.

6. Chopko, interview.

7. Margaret Leland Smith, email message to author, July 21, 2006.

8. Jeffrey R. Anderson, interview by the author, March 10, 2006.

9. Stephen C. Rubino, interview by the author, April 5, 2006; David Clohessy, national director of the Survivors Network of Those Abused by Priests (SNAP) also suggested that there was an increase in the number of victims seeking legal advice following the Geothe case. David Clohessy, interview by the author, March 13, 2006.

10. This paragraph and the next rely extensively on Mark E. Chopko, "USCCB Efforts to Combat Clergy Sexual Abuse Against Minors: A Chronology 1982–2006," www.usccb.org (accessed 12/12/06). For details and a copy of the Mouton, Doyle, Peterson Report, see Thomas P. Doyle, A. W. R. Sipe, and Patrick J. Wall, *Sex, Priests, and Secret Codes* (Los Angeles: Volt, 2006), chaps. 3–4.

11. Howard Hubbard, interview by the author, March 29, 2006.

12. Sylvia Demarest, interview by the author, April 25, 2006.

13. *Code of Canon Law*, Can. 489–490, www.vatican.va (accessed 12/12/06).

14. Anderson, interview.

15. Rubino, interview.
16. Ibid.
17. Anderson, interview.
18. My discussion of the Porter affair relies heavily on Frank Bruni and Elinor Burkett, *A Gospel of Shame: Children, Sexual Abuse, and the Catholic Church* (1993; reprint, New York: Perennial-HarperCollins, 2002); the investigative staff of the *Boston Globe, Betrayal: The Crisis in the Catholic Church* (2002; reprint, Boston: Back Bay-Little, Brown and Company, 2003); David France, *Our Fathers: The Secret Life of the Catholic Church in an Age of Scandal* (New York: Broadway Books-Random House, 2004); Frank Fitzpatrick, *Where It All Began: Bringing Father Porter to Justice* (unpublished manuscript, 2004); Michael Newton, "Father James Porter," www.crimelibrary.com (accessed 12/12/06).
19. Fitzpatrick, *Where It All Began,* appendix B.
20. Stephen Kurkjian, "68 Victims Settle Porter Case with Catholic Church," *Boston Globe,* December 4, 1992, 1.
21. Bruni and Burkett, *Gospel of Shame,* 20.
22. Hubbard, interview.
23. Chopko, interview.
24. Ibid.; USCCB chronology.
25. Demarest, interview.
26. Stephen C. Rubino, "Pedophilia: Organized Religion's Watergate," *Trial Lawyer* (April 1990): 17. See also *Holy Watergate: Abuse Cover-up in the Catholic Church,* directed by Mary Healey-Conlon (Videofilms, 2004), film. Transcript available at: "Transcript of the Film," www.holywatergate.com (accessed 12/12/06).
27. Clohessy, interview.
28. My account of the Bernardin affair relies extensively on Jason Berry and Gerald Renner, *Vows of Silence: The Abuse of Power in the Papacy of John Paul II* (New York: Free Press-Simon & Schuster, 2004), 110–121; Thomas Fox, "Bernardin: 'I Have Never Abused Anyone.'—Cardinal Joseph Bernardin; Sex Abuse Accusations," *National Catholic Reporter,* December 3, 1993, 1; "Panel One: Coverage of the Cardinal Joseph Bernardin Case," www.annenberg.northwestern.edu (accessed 12/12/06).
29. Thomas P. Doyle, interview by the author, March 8, 2006; Thomas P. Doyle, email message to author, October 31, 2006; "Current List of Bishops with Abuse Allegations," www.sandiegosnap.org (accessed 12/12/06).
30. Anderson, interview.
31. Rubino, interview.
32. My discussion of the Kos affair relies extensively on Berry and Renner, *Vows of Silence,* 236–242; investigative staff, *Betrayal,* 43; Anne Belli Gesalman, "Priest Facing Allegations of Sex Abuse Invokes Fifth," *Dallas Morning News,* July 17, 1993, A33; Ed Housewright, "Diocese Should Have Acted Earlier on Kos, Expert Says," *Dallas Morning News,* June 4, 1997, 29A; Ed Housewright, "Ex-Official Says He Never Questioned Kos," *Dallas Morning News,* June 6, 1997, 35A; Ed Housewright, "Kos Abuse Blamed in Suicide," *Dallas Morning News,* June 19, 1997, 25A.

33. Anderson, interview.
34. Rubino, interview.
35. Chopko, interview.
36. Anderson, interview.
37. Demarest, interview.
38. Chopko, interview.
39. My discussion of the Geoghan affair relies extensively on investigative staff, *Betrayal*; France, *Our Fathers*; "Geoghan's Troubled History," www.bishop accountability.org (accessed 12/12/06).
40. Hubbard, interview.
41. Investigative staff, *Betrayal*, 21.
42. France, *Our Fathers*, 137.
43. Investigative staff, *Betrayal*, 228–229.
44. "Geoghan's Troubled History."
45. France, *Our Fathers*, 302.
46. Walter Robinson, "Diocese, Plaintiffs Settle Suit," *Boston Globe*, March 12, 2002, A1; Walter Robinson and Michael Rezendez, "Geoghan Victims Agree to $10m Settlement," *Boston Globe*, September 19, 2002, A1.
47. Michael Rezendez, "Loyal Bishops Seen Drawing New Focus," *Boston Globe*, December 14, 2002, A20.
48. Denise Noe, "Pedophile Priests: The Crimes of Father Geoghan," *Crime Magazine* (December 1, 2003), www.bishopaccountability.org (accessed 12/12/06); Fox Butterfield, "Church in Boston to Pay $85 Million in Abuse Lawsuits," *New York Times*, September 10, 2003, A1.
49. Michael Levenson, "88 Victims Accept Offer from Church," *Boston Globe*, March 10, 2006, A1.
50. Demarest, interview.
51. Interview with anonymous attorney involved in the Boston litigation.
52. Hubbard, interview.
53. My discussion of the Los Angeles litigation relies extensively on investigative staff, *Betrayal*; France, *Our Fathers*; "An Explanation of the Clergy Abuse Litigation in California," *Associated Press*, October 9, 2004, www.snapnet work.org (accessed 12/12/06); Arthur Jones, "Church in Crisis—A Chronology of Sex Abuse in Southern California," www.natcath.com (accessed 12/ 12/06).
54. My discussion of the O'Grady affair relies extensively on Ron Russell, "Mouth Wide Shut: Cardinal Roger Mahony's Harboring of Pedo-Priests Didn't Just Start with the Current Roman Catholic Sex Scandal," *New Times* (Los Angeles), April 18, 2002; "Archbishop of Los Angeles Implicated in Priest Sex Scandal," *CNN NewsNight with Aaron Brown*, December 9, 2004, transcripts.cnn.com (accessed 12/12/06); Anderson, interview.
55. Russell, "Mouth Wide Shut"; James Sterngold, "4 Sue Cardinal Mahony, Using Racketeering Laws," *New York Times*, April 30, 2002, 24; "A Choice for the Bishops," *Los Angeles Times*, June 17, 2003, A14.
56. "An Explanation of the Clergy Abuse Litigation in California"; Drew Griffin, "California Diocese Settles Clergy Sexual Abuse Cases," cnn.com (ac-

cessed 12/12/06); Jean Guccione and Glenn F. Bunting, "Talks on Sex Abuse by Priests Restarted," *Los Angeles Times,* January 6, 2006, 1; Brian Baxter, "Doe et al. v. L.A. Archdiocese," *The American Lawyer,* February 2007, 55; Rebecca Trounson and John Spano, "Abuse Payout is Taking Shape," *Los Angeles Times,* July 19, 2007, B1.

57. France, *Our Fathers,* 338.
58. Demarest, interview.
59. J. Michael Hennigan, interview by the author, March 29, 2006.
60. Hubbard, interview.

2. Statistics

1. The information in this paragraph and the next is drawn from an extensive literature review in Karen Terry et al., *The Nature and Scope of Sexual Abuse of Minors by Catholic Priests and Deacons in the United States 1950–2002* (Washington, D.C.: United States Conference of Catholic Bishops, 2004), 153–162. For recent data concerning clergy sexual abuse in Protestant congregations, see *Associated Press,* "Data Shed Light on Child Sexual Abuse by Protestant Clergy," *New York Times,* June 16, 2007, A11.

2. Dioceses are administrative divisions of the Catholic Church that each cover a geographical area comprised of parishes and presided over by a bishop. Religious orders are groups of clerics and/or nonordained individuals who submit to a common set of rules and are governed by religious superiors. For a discussion of sexual abuse by lay Catholics, see Bruce Lambert, "Case Highlights Sex Abuse at Church, Beyong Priests," *New York Times,* May 15, 2007, B1.

3. Terry et al., *Nature and Scope,* 3–4. The term "priest" here includes sixty-one deacons. Karen Terry and Margaret Leland Smith, *The Nature and Scope of Sexual Abuse of Minors by Catholic Priests and Deacons in the United States 1950–2002, Supplementary Data Analysis* (Washington, D.C.: United States Conference of Catholic Bishops, 2006), 22.

4. *2006 Annual Report: Findings and Recommendations, Report on the Implementation of the Charter for the Protection of Children and Young People* (Washington, D.C.: United States Conference of Catholic Bishops, 2007), 28. Many of the allegations counted in the USCCB audits were made against priests who had already been identified by previous allegations. For this reason, the 1,736 accused priests in the audits do not represent an additional 1,736 priests accused of child sexual abuse. In each audit, between 35 percent and 66 percent of allegations were against priests already identified by previous allegations, and the audit figures suggest approximately 778 additional priests subject to allegations beyond those identified by the John Jay study, for an approximate total of 5,170 priests. Since few victims made more than one allegation, the 2,570 victims reported by the audits most likely means that—according to the Church—between 1950 and 2006, 13,237 children were victims of clergy sexual abuse. *2004 Annual Report: Findings and Recommendations, Report on the Implementation of the*

Charter for the Protection of Children and Young People (Washington, D.C.: United States Conference of Catholic Bishops, 2005), 19–20; *2005 Annual Report: Findings and Recommendations, Report on the Implementation of the Charter for the Protection of Children and Young People* (Washington, D.C.: United States Conference of Catholic Bishops, 2006), 33, 40; *2006 Annual Report,* 12, 22, 25. Margaret Leland Smith, telephone conversation with the author, January 8, 2007.

5. Margaret Leland Smith, interview by the author, January 26, 2006.

6. Barbara Blaine, *Snap Press Statements: Statement Regarding John Jay Self-Study Numbers,* February 27, 2004, www.snapnetwork.org (accessed 1/9/07).

7. Beth Sullivan, "Assume Nothing: A Postscript on the John Jay Report," *America,* September 13, 2004, 22–23; In re County Investigating Grand Jury, Misc. No. 03-00-239 at 4 (Ct. C.P. 1st Jud. Dist. Pa. Sept. 17, 2003) available at "Philadelphia Grand Jury," www.bishopaccountability.org (accessed 12/18/06), 4.

8. "February 26, 2004—Statement of Archbishop Sean P. O'Malley, Regarding Clergy Sexual Abuse in the Archdiocese of Boston from 1950–2003," www.rcab.org (accessed 12/18/06); Att'y Gen., The Sexual Abuse of Children in the Roman Catholic Archdiocese of Boston 13 (July 23, 2003), available at "Reilly Report," www.bishopaccountability.org (accessed 12/18/06).

9. David Briggs and James McCarty, "Diocese's Clerics List Questioned: Prosecutor Didn't Get Names of Four Who Faced Allegations," *Plain Dealer,* April 11, 2002, A1; Laurie Goodstein, "Diocese Resists Releasing Names of Accused Priests," *New York Times,* February 28, 2003, A16; "Bishop Reaffirms Commitment to Protect Children, Ease Suffering," www.diocese ofcleveland.org (accessed 12/18/06).

10. Steven Greenhut, "Bishop Brown Confuses Penance and Public Relations," *Orange County Register,* January 25, 2004, www.bishopaccountability .org (accessed 1/9/07).

11. Jennifer M. Balboni, "'It's Not about the Money': Truth, Consequences, and the Real Meaning of Litigation for Clergy Sexual Abuse Survivors" (Ph.D. diss., Northeastern University 2006), 156.

12. Terry et al., *Nature and Scope,* 6, 72–74.

13. See "Comparative Table of Selected Settlements," bishopaccountability .org (accessed 12/28/06); Steve Rubino, telephone conversation with the author, November 15, 2007.

14. Terry et al., *Nature and Scope,* 52; Karen Terry and Margaret Leland Smith, *Supplementary Data Analysis,* 24.

15. See, e.g., Philip Jenkins, *Pedophiles and Priests: Anatomy of a Contemporary Crisis* (Oxford: Oxford University Press, 1996), 79; John Baker, Jr., "Prosecuting Dioceses and Bishops," 44 *Boston College Law Review* 1084 (2003). See also the discussion of alternative frames in chap. 4.

16. Reproduced by permission of the United States Conference of Catholic Bishops from Terry et al., *Nature and Scope,* 29.

17. Karen Terry and Margaret Leland Smith, *Supplementary Data Analysis,* 13, 53. The supplementary data analysis further shows that this pattern is consistent throughout each of the fourteen geographic regions of the Catholic Church in the United States. Ibid., 4–6. Moreover, the supplementary analysis suggests that the rate of priests alleged to have committed abuse in a single year (that is, the proportion of all priests in service who were alleged to have committed abuse in a given year) follows this same shape. This is because, "[a]lthough the number of men entering the priesthood declined over the period examined in the study, the total number of priests in ministry did not change as significantly." Ibid., 7. According to the supplementary analysis, there were 42,970 priests in service in 1950, 58,908 in 1975, and 45,713 in 2002.
18. Compare Terry and Smith, *Supplementary Data Analysis,* 53.
19. Reproduced by permission of the United States Conference of Catholic Bishops from Terry et al., *Nature and Scope,* 89.
20. Ibid., 91.
21. Terry and Smith, *Supplementary Data Analysis,* 11–12; Margaret Leland Smith, email messages to author, July 21, 2006 and December 5, 2006.
22. Mark E. Chopko, interview by the author, March 22, 2006.
23. Chopko, interview.
24. Margaret Leland Smith, email messages to author, July 21, 2006 and October 24, 2006.
25. See, e.g., Daniel Lyons, "Clergy Sex Scammers?," *Forbes.com,* September 24, 2003, www.forbes.com; L. Martin Nussbaum, "Changing the Rules: Selective Justice for Catholic Institutions," *America,* May 15, 2006, 13–14.
26. Telephone conversation with Margaret Leland Smith, January 8, 2007.
27. Thomas P. Doyle and Stephen C. Rubino, "Catholic Clergy Sexual Abuse Meets the Civil Law," 31 *Fordham Urban Law Journal* 549, 551, fn.11 (2004).
28. Thomas P. Doyle, A. W. R. Sipe, and Patrick J. Wall, *Sex, Priests and Secret Codes: The Catholic Church's 2000-Year Paper Trail of Sexual Abuse* (Los Angeles: Volt, 2006), 177.
29. Terry et al., *Nature and Scope,* 103.

3. Legal Issues

1. For the sake of simplicity, I refer throughout to claims against priests, but my analysis applies equally to claims against nuns and other church personnel.
2. For the sake of simplicity, I refer throughout to claims against dioceses, but my analysis applies, for the most part, also to religious orders.
3. The American Law Institute, *Restatement of the Law, Second, Agency* (The American Law Institute, 1958) §§2, 220, 228, available at LEXIS.
4. Joseph B. Conder, "Liability of Church or Religious Society for Sexual Misconduct of Clergy," 5 *A.L.R. 5th* 530, §§2–3, 2004. See also, Catalina J.

Sugayan, *Coverage and Liability Issues in Sexual Misconduct Claims* (Princeton: American Re-Insurance Co., 2005); Mark C. Chopko, "Stating Claims Against Religious Institutions," 44 *Boston College Law Review* 1113–1114 (2003). For the suggestion that in some circumstances a priest is an independent contractor, see *Brillhart v. Scheier,* 758 P.2d 219 (Kan. 1988). This assertion has been met with considerable skepticism in the context of clergy sexual abuse litigation. Michael Powell and Lois Romano, "Roman Catholic Church Shifts Legal Strategy: Aggressive Litigation Replaces Quiet Settlements," *Washington Post,* May 13, 2002, A1.

5. *Fearing v. Bucher,* 977 P.2d 1163 (Or. 1999).
6. For a state-by-state survey, see Sugayan, *Coverage and Liability Issues.* States where lower courts have refused to dismiss respondeat superior claims for sexual abuse by a priest include California, Iowa, Louisiana, and Pennsylvania.
7. Conder, "Liability of Church," §3 (collecting reported cases); Sugayan, *Coverage and Liability Issues* (providing state-by-state tally).
8. Stephen C. Rubino, telephone conversation with the author, June 15, 2006; interview with anonymous attorney. Former USCCB general counsel Mark Chopko disputes this claim. Mark E. Chopko, email message to the author, June 14, 2006.
9. W. Page Keeton et al., *Prosser and Keeton on the Law of Torts* (St. Paul, Minn.: West Publishing Company, 1984), §56.
10. Marjorie A. Shields, "Liability of Church or Religious Organization for Negligent Hiring, Retention, or Supervision of Priest, Minister, or Other Clergy Based on Sexual Assault," 101 *A.L.R. 5th* 1 (2004).
11. Interview with anonymous attorney.
12. Rubino, telephone conversation.
13. One especially clear example is *J.D.W. v. Ruglovsky,* a 1990 Minnesota case in which a court held that a cleric's sexual misconduct could be considered foreseeable on the basis of newspaper accounts of clergy sexual abuse. Cited in Mark E. Chopko, "Ascending Liability of Religious Entities for the Actions of Others," 17 *American Journal of Trial Advocacy* 319 n. 132 (1993).
14. Conder, "Liability of Church," §6.5.
15. *Sanders v. Casa View Baptist Church,* 134 F.3d 331, 339 (5th Cir. 1998).
16. Jeffrey R. Anderson, Patrick W. Noaker, and Michael G. Finnegan, "When Clergy Fail their Flock: Litigating the Clergy Sexual Abuse Case," 91 *American Jurisprudence, Trials* 151 (2004).
17. 18 U.S.C. §1962(b) (2000).
18. Anderson et al., "When Clergy Fail," §18.
19. Anderson et al., "When Clergy Fail," §§21–22; Russell G. Donaldson, "Running of Limitations Against Action for Civil Damages for Sexual Abuse of Child," 9 ALR 5th 321 (2004); Sugayan, *Coverage and Liability Issues.* Many states also delay the start of the limitations period when the defendant improperly prevents the plaintiff from bringing the claim, for example by fraud or duress.

20. Mark E. Chopko, interview by the author, March 22, 2006.
21. Rubino, telephone conversation.
22. Patrick J. Schiltz, "Defending the Church," 29 *Litigation* 23 (Spring 2003).
23. Howard Hubbard, interview by the author, March 29, 2006.
24. Schiltz, "Defending the Church," 23.
25. Mic Hunter, *Abused Boys: The Neglected Victims of Sexual Abuse* (New York: Ballantine Books-Random House, 1991), 59.
26. Philip Jenkins, *Pedophiles and Priests: Anatomy of a Contemporary Crisis* (Oxford: Oxford University Press, 1996), 142–152.
27. Dorothy Rabinowitz, "A Priest's Story: Not All Accounts of Sex Abuse in the Catholic Church Turn Out to be True," Wall Street Journal Opinion Journal, www.opinionjournal.com (accessed 12/19/06).
28. Alexander Cockburn, "Back to Salem," *The Nation*, March 7, 2005, 12.
29. Martin Gardiner, "The Memory Wars: Parts 2 and 3," *Skeptical Inquirer* 30 (2006): 48.
30. Gardner, "Memory Wars"; Cockburn, "Back to Salem"; Joann Wypijewski, "The Passion of Father Paul Shanley," *Legal Affairs* (September/October 2004): 35.
31. Debbie Nathan and Michael Snedeker, *Satan's Silence: Ritual Abuse and the Making of a Modern American Witch Hunt* (1995; reprint, San Jose, Calif.: Authors Choice Press, 2001).
32. David Hechler, *The Battle and the Backlash: The Child Sexual Abuse War* (Lexington, Mass.: Lexington Books, 1988); the website of the False Memory Syndrome Foundation is www.fmsonline.org (accessed 12/19/06).
33. Sylvia Demarest, interview by the author, April 25, 2006.
34. Margaret Leland Smith, email message to the author, July 21, 2006.
35. Schiltz, "Defending the Church," 22.
36. Gardner, "Memory Wars," 46; Rabinowitz, "A Priest's Story," 2.
37. Susan K. Smith, "State-by-State Survey of Statutes of Limitation Applicable to Civil Claims of Childhood Sexual Abuse," www.smith-lawfirm.com (accessed 12/19/06).
38. Cal. Code Civ. Proc. §340.1(c) (Deering, LEXIS through 2006 ch. 910).
39. Susan Heylman, "As States Suspend Time Limits on Sex Abuse Suits, Clergy Cases Proceed," *Trial* (October 2007): 72.
40. Sugayan, *Coverage and Liability Issues*, i.
41. *Lemon v. Kurtzman,* 403 U.S. 602 (1971).
42. Shields, "Liability of Church," §§3–4; Anderson et al., "When Clergy Fail," §26; John H. Mansfield, "Constitutional Limits on the Liability of Churches for Negligent Supervision and Breach of Fiduciary Duty," 44 *Boston College Law Review* 1167, 1177 (2003). Courts are in agreement, however, that there can be no liability for clergy malpractice. See, Mark A. Weitz, *Clergy Malpractice in America: Nally v. Grace Community Church of the Valley* (Lawrence: University Press of Kansas, 2001).
43. Shields, "Liability of Church," §§3&4; Anderson et al., "When Clergy Fail," §24; Mansfield, "Constitutional Limits," 1173; Sugayan, *Coverage and Liability Issues*.

44. Shields, "Liability of Church," §§3&4; Anderson et al., "When Clergy Fail," §25; Mansfield, "Constitutional Limits," 1167. For an extensive analysis, see Ira C. Lupu and Robert Tuttle, "Sexual Misconduct and Ecclesiastical Immunity," 2004 *BYU Law Review* 1789.

45. Carl E. Eck, "Discovery of Church Records," 35 *Catholic Lawyer,* 231–232 (1994).

46. See Shields, "Liability of Church," §§3&4.

47. Stephen C. Rubino, interview by the author, April 5, 2006.

48. Interview with anonymous attorney.

49. Shields, "Liability of Church," §6.

50. J. Minos Simon, *Law in the Cajun Nation* (Lafayette, La.: Prescott Press 1993), 149–150; Bob Wright, interview by the author, May 25, 2005.

51. Supplemental and Amending Answer at ¶ I.7, No. 84-48175-A (December 13, 1985) (on file with author); David Milner, "Testimony Begins in Suit Against Diocese," *Baton Rouge Morning Advocate,* February 5, 1986, 2B.

52. "Deposition of Cardinal Bernard Law, June 5, 2002, Suffolk County Superior Court," www.boston.com (accessed 12/19/06) (objections and interruptions omitted). For additional examples, see Mary Gail Frawley-O'Dea, *Perversion of Power: Sexual Abuse in the Catholic Church* (Nashville: Vanderbilt University Press, 2007), 134–135.

53. Schiltz, "Defending the Church," 22; see Shields, "Liability of Church," §6 for reported cases.

54. Victor E. Schwartz and Leah Lorber, "Defining the Duty of Religious Institutions to Protect Others: Surgical Instruments, not Machetes, are Required," 74 *University of Cincinnati Law Review* 11, 13–17 (2005); Janet Fairchild, "Tort Immunity of Non-Governmental Charities—Modern Status," 25 A.L.R. 4th 517 (2006); Sugayan, *Coverage and Liability Issues.*

55. Conder, "Liability of Church," §§7, 8; Shields, "Liability of Church," §5.

56. Carol McCormick, "Testimony to Massachusetts Judiciary Committee Regarding Statute of Limitations and Charitable Immunity Legislation," www.snapnetwork.org (accessed 12/19/06); Mary Harter Mitchell, "Must Clergy Tell? Child Abuse Reporting Requirements Versus the Clergy Privilege and the Free Exercise of Religion," 71 *Minnesota Law Review* 723, 737 (1987).

57. Karen L. Ross, "Revealing Confidential Secrets: Will it Save Our Children?," 28 *Seton Hall Law Review* 963, 975 (1998); Claudia G. Catalano, "Subject Matter and Waiver of Privilege Covering Communications to Clergy Member or Spiritual Advisor," 93 A.L.R. 5th 327 (2005); J. Michael Keel, "Law and Religion Collide Again: The Priest-Penitent Privilege in Child Abuse Reporting Cases," 28 *Cumberland Law Review* 681 (1997); Mary Harter Mitchell, "Must Clergy Tell?"; Thomas P. Doyle, A. W. R. Sipe, and Patrick J. Wall, *Sex, Priests, and Secret Codes* (Los Angeles: Volt, 2006), 217–227.

58. Doyle et al., *Sex,* 218; "Article Explains Reasons for Appeal of Documents," la-clergycases.com (accessed 12/19/06).

59. Jean Guccione and William Lobdell, "Mahony Must Give D.A. Files," *Los Angeles Times,* April 18, 2006, 1.

60. Milo Geyelin, "Cross Purposes: The Catholic Church Struggles with Suits Over Sexual Abuse," *Wall Street Journal,* November 24, 1993, A1; Michael Powell and Lois Romano, "Roman Catholic Church Shifts Legal Strategy; Aggressive Litigation Replaces Quiet Settlements," *Washington Post,* May 13, 2002, A1; Jason Berry, *Lead Us Not Into Temptation: Catholic Priests and the Sexual Abuse of Children* (1992; reprint, Urbana: University of Illinois Press, 2000), 326, 340; Frank Bruni and Elinor Burkett, *A Gospel of Shame: Children, Sexual Abuse, and the Catholic Church* (1993; reprint, New York: Perennial-HarperCollins, 2002), 123; Frawley-O'Dea, *Perversion of Power,* 135–137; Leslie M. Lothstein, "The Relationship Between the Treatment Facilities and the Church Hierarchy: Forensic Issues and Future Considerations," in Thomas G. Plante, ed., *Sin Against the Innocents: Sexual Abuse by Priests and the Role of the Catholic Church* (Westport, Conn.: Praeger-Greenwood Publishing Group, 2004), 131; Rubino, interview; Jeffrey R. Anderson, interview by the author, March 10, 2006; Anderson et al., "When Clergy Fail," §31; Thomas P. Doyle, interview by the author, March 8, 2006; David Clohessy, interview by the author, March 13, 2006; John Manly, interview by the author, September 5, 2006; Bonnie Anderson, "Fall From Grace, Part 3—The Conditions of Pedophilia," and "Fall From Grace, Part 4—Alleged Victims Band Together," *CNN Specials,* CNN, November 14, 1993. Transcripts #247-3 and #247-4 available at LEXIS; Ed Bradley, "I Solemnly Swear; Catholic Church Now Countersuing Anyone Who Sues Priests for Sexual Abuse," *60 Minutes,* CBS, May 14, 1994. Transcript available at LEXIS. In response to a defamation suit by an accused priest, two abuse victims recently filed a countersuit for emotional distress. Margaret Ramirez, "It's Suit vs. Suit in Priest Case: Accusers Counter Cleric's Legal Move," *Chicago Tribune,* December 14, 2006, C3.

61. Mark A. Sargent, "Legal Defense: When Sued, How Should the Church Behave?," *Commonweal,* June 14, 2002, 13.

62. Schiltz, "Defending the Church," 24.

63. Rubino, interview; Patrick Schiltz, "Too Much Law, Too Little Justice: How Lawyers Helped to Turn a Clergy Sexual Abuse Problem into a Clergy Sexual Abuse Crisis" (speech, University of Dayton Law School, Dayton, Ohio, January 10, 2005), 4 (on file with author).

64. Chopko, interview.

65. On anger as a motivation for victims, see, e.g., Jennifer M. Balboni, "'It's Not about the Money': Truth, Consequences, and the Real Meaning of Litigation for Clergy Sexual Abuse Survivors" (Ph.D. diss., Northeastern University 2006), 190. On anger as a motivation for plaintiffs' attorneys, see the discussion of noneconomic motivations in chap. 6.

66. "Number of Federal Tort Trials Fell by Almost 80 Percent From 1985 Through 2003," www.ojp.usdoj.gov (accessed 12/19/06).

67. Lewis Kornhauser and Robert Mnookin, "Bargaining in the Shadow of the Law: The Case of Divorce," 88 *Yale Law Journal* 950 (1979).

68. Interview with anonymous attorney.

69. Peter H. Schuck, *The Limits of Law: Essays on Democratic Governance* (Boulder, Colo.: Westview Press, 2000), chap. 11; Howard M. Erichson, "Informal Aggregation: Procedural and Ethical Implications of Coordination Among Counsel in Related Lawsuits," 50 *Duke Law Journal* 381 (2000); Samuel Issacharoff and John Fabian Witt, "The Inevitability of Aggregate Settlement: An Institutional Account of American Tort Law," 57 *Vanderbilt Law Review* 1571 (2004). For an early analysis of clergy sexual abuse as a mass tort, see Marc Stern, "Masses of Torts," www.trincoll.edu (accessed 1/5/07).

70. "An Explanation of the Clergy Abuse Litigation in California," *Associated Press,* October 9, 2004, www.snapnetwork.org (accessed 12/19/06).

71. "Memorandum of Understanding Between the Steering Committee Representing Victims of Abuse and the Roman Catholic Archbishop of Boston, A Corporation Sole," www.bishopaccountability.org (accessed 12/19/06); Jean Guccione and William Lobdell, "2 Lawyers Break Ranks, File New Suits Alleging Sex Abuse by Priests," *Los Angeles Times,* June 4, 2003, Metro, 5.

72. See, e.g., Jean O. Pasco and William Lobdell, "Church Settles Suit, Toughens Policies; Court: Man who says O.C. priest abused him gets $5.2 million; dioceses will create program for victims," *Los Angeles Times,* August 21, 2001, 1; Kristin Gustafson, "To Clergy Victims, Acknowledgement Proves Invaluable," *St. Cloud Times,* October 2, 2002, www.bishopaccountability.org (accessed 1/3/07); "Settlements between Dioceses and Victims of Sexual Abuse," www.bishopaccountability.org (accessed 1/1/07).

73. See, e.g., Supplement to Joint Motion for Preliminary Approval of Class Action Settlement, *John Doe v. Roman Catholic Diocese of Covington,* No. 03-Cl-181 (Boone Cir. Ct., July 19, 2005), available at www.covington kydioceseabuse.com (accessed 12/19/06).

74. Issacharoff and Witt, "Inevitability," 1625–1626.

75. My discussion of bankruptcy in this and the following paragraphs relies on Alan N. Resnick, "Bankruptcy as a Vehicle for Resolving Mass Torts Liability, 148 *University of Pennsylvania Law Review* 2054 (2000); David A. Skeel, Jr., "Avoiding Moral Bankruptcy," 44 *Boston College Law Review* 1181 (2003).

76. Sandi Dolbee, "Tucson Diocese's Filing Seen as Model," at www.signon sandiego (accessed 4/27/07); Ed Langlois and Robert Pfohman, "Portland Archdiocese Ends Bankruptcy with $75 Million Settlement," at www .catholicnews.com (accessed 4/24/07); John Stucke, "Diocese to Exit Bankruptcy," at spokesmanreview.com (accessed 4/30/07); Richard Marosi, "Church Told to Defend Bankruptcy," *Los Angeles Times,* August 11, 2007, B1; Tony Perry, "Abuse Claims are Settled for $198 Million," *Los Angeles Times,* September 8, 2007, B1; Dan Frosch, "Diocese in Iowa Settles," *New York Times,* December 4, 2007, A24. John Manly, telephone conversation with the author, November 20, 2007.

77. Tony Perry, "San Diego Diocese Files for Bankruptcy," *Los Angeles Times,* February 28, 2007, A1.
78. Wendy Davis, "Church and Chapter 11," *ABA Journal* (October 2005): 15.
79. Daniel Marcinak, "Comment: Separation of Church and Estate: On Excluding Parish Assets from the Bankruptcy Estate of a Diocese Organized as a Corporation Sole," 55 *Catholic Law Review* 583 (2006); Skeel, "Avoiding Moral Bankruptcy"; Davis, "Church and Chapter 11," 15. As part of bankruptcy reorganizations, dioceses have incorporated parishes and schools as independent nonprofits and transferred ownership of church property to them. According to church officials, this is merely a clarification of the state of affairs prior to filing for bankruptcy.
80. Michael J. Bemi, interview by the author, June 15, 2006. The rest of this paragraph also relies on this interview.
81. This paragraph and the next rely on Sugayan, *Coverage and Liability Issues,* and Jenkins, *Pedophiles and Priests,* 137.
82. Bemi, interview.
83. Ibid.
84. I examine insurance coverage estimates in greater detail in chapter 7 in my discussion of the costs of the litigation.
85. I develop this theme further in chapter 7 when assessing the results of clergy sexual abuse litigation.

4. Framing Clergy Sexual Abuse as a Problem of Institutional Failure

1. *A Report on the Crisis in the Catholic Church in the United States* (Washington, D.C.: United States Conference of Catholic Bishops, 2004), 5.
2. Frank Bruni and Elinor Burkett, *A Gospel of Shame: Children, Sexual Abuse, and the Catholic Church* (1993; reprint, New York: Perennial-HarperCollins, 2002), 136.
3. Robert Entman, *Projections of Power: Framing News, Public Opinion, and U.S. Foreign Policy* (Chicago: University of Chicago Press, 2004), 5, 23. See also Erving Goffman, *Frame Analysis: An Essay on the Organization of Experience* (1974; reprint, Boston: Northeastern University Press, 1986), 10–11.
4. Todd Gitlin, *The Whole World Is Watching: Mass Media in the Making and Unmaking of the New Left* (Berkeley: University of California Press, 1980), 6.
5. Goffman, *Frame Analysis,* 82.
6. Entman, *Projections of Power,* 5.
7. My analysis in this paragraph relies on Entman, *Projections of Power,* 5–9, 14–17, and Donald Schon and Martin Rein, *Frame Reflection: Toward the Resolution of Intractable Policy Controversies* (New York: Basic Books, 1994), 27–29.
8. Timur Kuran and Cass Sunstein, "Availability Cascades and Risk Regulation," 51 *Stanford Law Review* 683, 685–687 (1999).
9. My analysis in this paragraph relies on Kuran and Sunstein, "Availability

Cascades," Larry M. Bartels, *Presidential Primaries and the Dynamics of Public Choice* (Princeton, N.J.: Princeton University Press, 1988), 108–112; and Bryan D. Jones and Frank R. Baumgartner, *The Politics of Attention: How Government Prioritizes Problems* (Chicago: University of Chicago, 2005), 138–142.

10. For a discussion of the adoption of plaintiffs' frames by the media in tobacco litigation, see Lynn Mather, "Theorizing About Trial Courts: Lawyers, Policymaking, and Tobacco Litigation," 23 *Law and Social Inquiry* 897, 914–919 (1998). Compare William Haltom and Michael McCann, *Distorting the Law: Politics, Media, and the Litigation Crisis* (Chicago: University of Chicago, 2004), 20, 158, 225, 243–245. Haltom and McCann suggest that the news media are generally more likely to adopt defense frames than plaintiff frames, with the notable exception of tobacco litigation. Haltom also asserts that civil cases are less newsworthy than criminal cases and attract little coverage. William Haltom, *Reporting on the Courts: How the Mass Media Cover Judicial Actions* (Chicago: Nelson-Hall Publishers, 1998), 205, 238.

11. Neil Feigenson, *Legal Blame: How Jurors Think and Talk About Accidents* (Washington, D.C.: American Psychological Association, 2000), 92.

12. Feigenson, *Legal Blame*, 97.

13. See Haltom and McCann, *Distorting the Law*, 33–72.

14. For analysis of news as a frame, see Gaye Tuchman, *Making News: A Study in the Construction of News* (New York: Free Press, 1978), 1, 192; Gitlin, *Whole World*, 6–7, 49.

15. Michael Schudson, *The Sociology of News* (New York: W.W. Norton & Co., 2003), 117–133; Graham Murdoch, "Political Deviance: The Press Presentation of a Militant Mass Demonstration," in Stanley Cohen and Jock Young, eds., *The Manufacture of News: Social Problems, Deviance, and the Mass Media*, rev'd. ed. (Beverly Hills, Calif.: Sage Publications, 1981), 214; Haltom, *Reporting*, 19.

16. Herbert Gans, *Deciding What's News: A Study of the CBS Evening News, NBC Nightly News, Newsweek, and Time* (1979; reprint, Evanston, Ill.: Northwestern University Press, 2004), 171; Murdoch, "Political Deviance," 215; Schudson, *Sociology*, 48, 178; Gitlin, *Whole World*, 28; Haltom, *Reporting*, 19.

17. On personal conflict, see Gans, *Deciding What's News*, 22; Gitlin, *Whole World*, 28; Schudson, *Sociology*, 49. On personification, see Gans, *Deciding What's News*, 8, 19; Gitlin, *Whole World*, 28; Johan Galtung and Mari Ruge, "Structuring and Selecting News," in Cohen and Young, *Manufacture of News*, 57.

18. Gans, *Deciding What's News*, 168; Gitlin, *Whole World*, 35.

19. Gans, *Deciding What's News*, 150; Galtung and Ruge, "Structuring and Selecting News," 54.

20. Galtung and Ruge, "Structuring and Selecting News," 54.

21. Galtung and Ruge, "Structuring and Selecting News," 54; Murdoch, "Political Deviance," 214.

22. Stanley Cohen, "Mods and Rockers: The Inventory as Manufactured News," in Cohen and Young, *Manufacture of News,* 276; Galtung and Ruge, "Structuring and Selecting News," 54–55.

23. Galtung and Ruge, "Structuring and Selecting News," 55.

24. Tuchman, *Making News,* 31.

25. Galtung and Ruge, "Structuring and Selecting News," 56.

26. Gans, *Deciding What's News,* 11–14.

27. Galtung and Ruge, "Structuring and Selecting News," 60–61.

28. Petition for Damages, *Gastal v. Hanan,* No. 84-48175 (15th Jud. Dist. Ct., Vermilion Parish, La., June 27, 1984) (on file with author).

29. Petition for Damages at ¶ 10, *Gastal,* No. 84-48175.

30. Philip Jenkins, *Pedophiles and Priests: Anatomy of a Contemporary Crisis* (Oxford: Oxford University Press, 1996), 141–142. On the wave of 1980s' prosecutions for ritual child sexual abuse, see, Debbie Nathan and Michael Snedeker, *Satan's Silence: Ritual Abuse and the Making of a Modern American Witch Hunt* (1995; reprint, San Jose, Calif.: Authors Choice Press, 2001).

31. Petition for Damages at ¶ 23, *Gastal,* No. 84-48175.

32. First Supplemental and Amending Petition at ¶ 5, *Gastal v. Hanan,* No. 84-48175-A (15th Jud. Dist. Ct., Vermilion Parish, La., October 25, 1984) (on file with author).

33. Petition for Damages at ¶ 23 (l), (m), *Gastal,* No. 84-48175.

34. Answer [on behalf of institutional church defendants], Gastal, No. 84-48175 (October 1, 1984); Answer [on behalf of insurance defendants], *Gastal,* No. 84-48175 (October 16, 1984) (both on file with author).

35. Answer on behalf of Gilbert Gauthe, *Gastal,* No. 84-48175 (October 15, 1984) (on file with author).

36. Ibid., ¶¶ 21, 23.

37. Prior to Yeoman's article, print coverage of the Gauthe affair was limited to the criminal proceedings and consisted of an article by Barry Schultz published in the *Baton Rouge Morning Advocate* which was adopted by the *Associated Press.* Jason Berry, email message to author, July 6, 2005.

38. Barry Yeoman, "Is Nothing Sacred," *Times of Acadiana,* November 1, 1984, 17.

39. Yeoman, "Is Nothing Sacred," 21.

40. Ibid.

41. "The Tragedy of Gilbert Gauthe," *Times of Acadiana,* May 23, 1985, 18 (emphasis added).

42. Steve Blow, "Child Abuse Scandal Underscores Homosexual Issue Among Clergy," *Dallas Morning News,* May 26, 1985, 1A.

43. United Press International, "Parents Say Church Knew Priest Was Child Molester," *Houston Post,* May 27, 1985, 18A.

44. "Priest Child Abuse Cases Victimizing Families; Bishops Lack Policy Response," *National Catholic Reporter,* June 7, 1985, 1.

45. "Priest Child Abuse," 4.

46. The first article, to which Berry contributed research, begins with the Gauthe

case and goes on to discuss several other similar cases from around the country. The second article, written by Berry, is exclusively dedicated to the Gauthe case, and is a shorter version of his three-part series for the *Times of Acadiana*. Arthur Jones, "Legal Actions Against Pedophile Priests Grow as Frustrated and Angry Parents Seek Remedies," *National Catholic Reporter*, June 7, 1985, 4; Jason Berry, "Pedophile Priest: Study in Inept Church Response," *National Catholic Reporter*, June 7, 1985, 6.

47. Jenkins, *Pedophiles and Priests*, 65.

48. Kathy Sawyer, "Priest Child-Molestation Case Traumatizes Catholic Community," *Washington Post*, June 9, 1985, A6.

49. Jon Nordheimer, "Sex Charges Against Priest Embroil Louisiana Parents," *New York Times*, June 17, 1985, A24.

50. "Painful Secrets; Priests Accused of Pederasty," *Time*, July 1, 1985, 51.

51. See, e.g., Bruce Nolan, "Bishops to Revise Rules on Sex Abuse; Retroactive '1-Strike' Policy Among Church Proposals," *New Orleans Times Picayune*, June 13, 2002, 1.

52. "Chronology of Church Abuse Crisis," *Associated Press*, December 13, 2002.

53. See, e.g., Alan Cooperman and Rob Stein, "Pedophile Ex-Priest Is Killed in Prison; Fellow Inmate Strangled Geoghan," *Washington Post*, August 24, 2003, A1. A Lexis/Nexis search of print and broadcast news items in 2002 in the "News, All (English, Full Text)" data base produced twenty-five news items that mentioned Gauthe, Porter, and Geoghan in the same story. Search conducted August 9, 2005.

54. Alison Bass, "Some Fault Church on Sex Abuse by Priests," *Boston Globe*, May 11, 1992, 1.

55. Alison Bass, "Law Limits Church Liability to $20,000; Victims of Abuse Criticize Statute," *Boston Globe*, May 5, 1992, 8.

56. "Child Sexual Abuse in the Catholic Church," *Nightline*, ABC, February 24, 1993.

57. *Nightline*, December 6, 1993.

58. "The Archbishop: Cover-up by Roman Catholic Church of Pedophilia by its Priests," *60 Minutes*, CBS, March 21, 1993.

59. *Primetime Live* host Diane Sawyer explained that Catholics in one community were "in a state of outrage . . . not just because of Father Porter and what he did twenty years ago, but [also because] the Church . . . deceived its own diocese." "Secret No More Follow-Up," *Primetime Live*, ABC, July 23, 1992. CNN host Bonnie Anderson introduced the topic by explaining that "[t]he Roman Catholic Church in the United States is in unparalleled turmoil over clergy sexual abuse," and the show included an extensive interview with activist Bonnie Miller who suggested that "the subsequent abuse by the institution was more destructive" than the initial abuse by an individual priest. "Fall From Grace," *CNN Specials*, CNN, November 14, 1993.

60. Michael Rezendes, "Church Allowed Abuse by Priests for Years," *Boston Globe*, January 6, 2002, A1.

61. "Sins of the Fathers," *Nightline*, ABC, January 28, 2002.

62. Ibid.
63. "Sins of the Fathers: Catholic Church Deals with Sexual Abuse of Minors by Priests in Wake of Former Priest, John Geoghan, being Charged with Sexual Abuse and Sentenced to Prison," *Nightline*, ABC, February 21, 2002.
64. "Sins of the Fathers: The Rising Costs of the Scandal," *Nightline*, ABC, March 14, 2002.
65. "Sins of the Fathers: Spiritual Treatment, Secular Justice," *Nightline*, ABC, March 25, 2002.
66. "Sins of the Fathers: Turning a Blind Eye," *Nightline*, ABC, April 9, 2002.
67. "Sins of the Fathers: Trying to Repair the Breach," *Nightline*, ABC, April 24, 2002.
68. "Sins of the Fathers: A National Accounting," *Nightline*, ABC, June 11, 2002.
69. "Cardinal Law Resignation," *Good Morning America*, ABC, December 13, 2002.
70. "Sins of the Fathers: A National Accounting," *Nightline*, ABC, June 11, 2002.
71. "Sins of the Fathers: A Parish Loses Its Priest," *Nightline*, ABC, June 27, 2002.
72. "Sins of the Fathers," *Nightline*, ABC, December 13, 2002.
73. *Good Morning America* host Charles Gibson opened a February 2002 segment on clergy sexual abuse by stating that "All this year, we have been watching the Catholic Church confront disclosures that priests accused of sexual molestation continued to serve, often moved from parish to parish . . . Church officials, including Cardinal Bernard Law, came under fire for allowing Geoghan to continue working for years, despite knowing he was a pedophile." "Father George Spagnolia Discusses Case of Sexual Abuse Brought by Former Parishioner," *Good Morning America*, ABC, February 27, 2002. In March, *Good Morning America* cohost Robin Roberts interviewed a prominent church official in California who was "calling on Church leaders to be accountable and to change everything." "Monsignor Clement Connolly, from Los Angeles, Discusses Needed Changes in Wake of Sexual Abuse Scandal in Catholic Church," *Good Morning America*, ABC, March 19, 2002. In April, *Good Morning America* featured "a group of men as they confront a bishop they say let a predator inflict so much pain on them years ago." "Mark Serrano and Other Victims of Abuse by Priest Talk to Father Frank Roddhammer about What Could Have and Still Should be Done to Stop Abuse by Priests," *Good Morning America*, ABC, April 23, 2002. Two days later, the program described Cardinal Law as "Boston's Bernard Law, whose mismanagement of abusive priests helped create this scandal." "Cardinals Return to U.S. after Meeting with the Pope on Sexual Abuse Scandal," *Good Morning America*, ABC, April 25, 2002. For similar examples from *Good Morning America*, see "Victims of Priest Sexual Abuse Get Chance to Meet with Bishops in Dallas at Catholic Bishops Conference," *Good Morning America*, ABC, June 13, 2002; "Bishop

Wilton Gregory Discusses the New U.S. Catholic Church Policy to Deal with Sexual Abuse," *Good Morning America*, ABC, June 17, 2002. *20/20* host Barbara Walters introduced a segment by suggesting that "the sins of the fathers are rocking the foundations of the church." "Christopher Dixon and Others Claim Sexual Abuse by Pedophile Catholic Priests," *20/20*, ABC, March 22, 2002. *60 Minutes* commentator Andy Rooney concluded that "It seems as though the Catholic Church should change its rules." For a similar example from *60 Minutes*, see "Catholic Church Dealing with Issues of Sex, Priests Abusing Children, and Birth Control," *60 Minutes*, CBS, March 31, 2002. *60 Minutes II* host Ed Bradley opened a story with the question "Why is it taking the Roman Catholic leadership so long to make the church safe for its children?" "The Church on Trial," *60 Minutes II*, CBS, June 12, 2002. An episode of *Sunday Morning* focused on the way the "Church has handled the sexual abuse scandal." "New Priests in Catholic Church Will Have to Earn Trust," *Sunday Morning*, CBS, April 21, 2002.

74. I used the search terms "date is 1993 and (priest or clergy w/15 abus! or moles!) and (bishop or archbishop or cardinal) and not substance or alcohol or drug or military or "human rights" or spouse or husband or army or guerillas or labor" to generate the first figure and "date is 1993 and (priest or clergy w/15 abus! or moles!) and not substance or alcohol or drug or military or "human rights" or spouse or husband or army or guerillas or labor" to generate the second figure. For both, I excluded articles that were not on topic, and I did not count articles that appeared more than once in the search results. Search conducted August 15, 2006.

75. I used the same search methodology but changed the year to 2002.

76. On media templates, see Jenny Kitzinger, *Framing Abuse: Media Influence and Public Understanding of Sexual Violence against Children* (London: Pluto Press, 2004), 54–78.

77. "The Church on Trial," *60 Minutes II*, ABC, June 12, 2002.

78. See, e.g., Richard Ostling, "Sins of the Fathers: A Honolulu Bishop is Accused of Sex Abuse in a Federal Lawsuit As Catholic Scandals Keep Spreading," *Time*, August 19, 1991, 51; Leslie Bennetts, "Unholy Alliances," *Vanity Fair*, December 1991, 224, 227; David Hechler, "Sins of the Father: A Girl's Abuse by Her Priest," *McCall's*, September 1993, 113, 117.

79. I used the search terms "(priest or clergy w/15 abus! or moles!) and "jason berry" and not substance or alcohol or drug or military or "human rights" or spouse or husband or army or guerillas or labor and date (geq (jan. 1, 1990) and leq (dec. 31, 2004))." Search conducted July 18, 2006.

80. Steve Twomey, "For 3 Who Warned Church, Fears Borne Out; Priest, Journalist and Professor Who Foresaw Sex Abuse Scandal Frustrated by Bishops' Response," *Washington Post*, June 13, 2002, A1.

81. "Child Sexual Abuse in the Catholic Church," *Nightline*, ABC, February 24, 1993; "Sins of the Fathers," *Nightline*, ABC, January 28, 2002; "Sins of the Fathers: Catholic Church Deals with Sexual Abuse of Minors by Priests in Wake of Former Priest, John Geoghan, Being Charged with Sexual

Abuse and Sentenced to Prison," *Nightline,* ABC, February 21, 2002; "Sins of the Fathers," *Nightline,* ABC, June 17, 2003.

82. Some of these later claims were modeled explicitly on the Gauthe case. Others were influenced less directly by interest in institutional liability for clergy sexual abuse among a growing circle of plaintiffs' lawyers that was fueled, in part, by the widely publicized success of the Gauthe case as well as other concurrent cases that garnered less publicity. I discuss this mobilizing effect of the Gauthe litigation on plaintiffs' attorneys in chapter 5.

83. Quoted in Tuchman, *Making News,* 83.

84. See Schudson, Sociology of News, 54; Tuchman, *Making News,* 90.

85. Jennifer M. Balboni, telephone conversation with the author, May 25, 2005.

86. Schudson, *Sociology of News,* 54; Tuchman, *Making News,* 90.

87. Tuchman, *Making News,* 92–94.

88. Jason Berry, *Lead Us Not Into Temptation: Catholic Priests and the Sexual Abuse of Children* (1992; reprint, Urbana: University of Illinois Press, 2000), 73.

89. Barry Yeoman, interview by the author, January 12, 2005.

90. See J. Minos Simon and David Leon Chandler, *Law in the Cajun Nation* (Lafayette, La.: Prescott Press, 1993), 146.

91. John Pope, interview by the author, January 6, 2005.

92. See, e.g., *Associated Press,* "Bishop Says He Got Word of Gauthe's Actions 10 Years Ago," *Baton Rouge Morning Advocate,* January 25, 1985, B8; Blow, "Child Abuse Scandal"; Sawyer, "Priest Child-Molestation Case."

93. Arthur Jones, Legal Actions Against Pedophile Priests Grow"; Jason Berry, "Pedophile Priest."

94. Alison Bass, "Nine Allege Priest Abused Them, Threaten to Sue Church," *Boston Globe,* May 8, 1992, 1.

95. See the investigative staff of the *Boston Globe, Betrayal: The Crisis in the Catholic Church* (2002; reprint, Boston: Back Bay-Little, Brown and Company, 2003), viii–xi, 100; Michael Rezendez, "Scandal: *The Boston Globe* and Sexual Abuse in the Catholic Church," in Thomas G. Plante, ed., *Sin Against the Innocents: Sexual Abuse by Priests and the Role of the Catholic Church* (Westport, Conn.: Praeger-Greenwood Publishing Group, 2004) recounts history of coverage in Plante.

96. I used the search terms "date is 1993 and (priest or clergy w/15 abus! or moles!) and (lawsuit! or plaintiff! or court! or pleading! or deposition! or testimon! or discovery or trial!) and not substance or alcohol or drug or military or "human rights" or spouse or husband or army or guerillas or labor" to generate the first figure and "date is 1993 and (priest or clergy w/15 abus! or moles!) and not substance or alcohol or drug or military or "human rights" or spouse or husband or army or guerillas or labor" to generate the second figure. For both, I did not count articles that appeared more than once in the search results. Search conducted August 9, 2005.

97. I used the same search methodology but changed the year to 2002.

98. Berry, *Lead Us Not,* ix, xxii, 47. See also ibid., 82.
99. Bruni and Burkett, *Gospel of Shame,* p. vii.
100. See, e.g., Bruni and Burkett, *Gospel of Shame,* / 269 n.30.
101. Investigative staff, *Betrayal,* 262. The *Globe*'s 2002 coverage was itself sparked by the filing of claims against Fr. Geoghan. See Michael Rezendes, *Scandal: The Boston Globe and Sexual Abuse in the Catholic Church,* in Plante, *Sin Against the Innocents,* 4.
102. David France, *Our Fathers: The Secret Life of the Catholic Church in an Age of Scandal* (New York: Broadway Books-Random House, 2004), 599.
103. See, e.g., Jason Berry, *Lead Us Not,* xxvii; Bruni and Burkett, *Gospel of Shame,* vii.
104. Schudson, Sociology of News, 3, 138.
105. France, 395–401.
106. There are exceptions. For example, attorney for the L.A. archdiocese J. Michael Hennigan is frequently quoted in the media.
107. For a discussion of plaintiffs' lawyers' cultivation of press coverage in to-bacco litigation, see Mather, "Theorizing About Trial Courts," 917. Compare Haltom, *Reporting,* 207–210. Haltom asserts that civil lawyers shun publicity and are not considered as reliable sources by journalists.
108. Berry, *Lead Us Not,* 35.
109. For a lengthy analysis of the church hierarchy's desire to avoid publicity, see Barbara Balboni, "Through the 'Lens' of the Organizational Culture Perspective: A Descriptive Study of American Catholic Bishops' Understanding of Clergy Sexual Molestation and Abuse of Children and Adolescents," (Ph.D. diss., Northeastern University, 1998), chap. 5. The asymmetry between plaintiff and defense attitudes toward media coverage may also be based on differences among lawyers rooted in professional culture and client confidentiality concerns. Plaintiffs' lawyers are storytellers by profession who often like to talk and—as they do not bill by the hour—are freer with their time. By contrast, defense attorneys more regularly play the role of confidential counselors and are less willing to take time to chat about cases. In addition, a plaintiff's lawyer with many clients can talk in general terms without breaching client confidentiality, whereas defense attorneys usually have one large client—such as a diocese—and may find it harder to speak in general terms without breaching client confidentiality. I am grateful to Howard Erichson for these suggestions. For an example of defense counsel's refusal to speak to the press in the Gauthe litigation, see Sawyer, "Priest Child-Molestation Case." For discussion of lawyers' cultivation of the media in tobacco litigation, see Mather, "Theorizing About Trial Courts," 917.
110. Galtung and Ruge, "Structuring and Selecting News," 55.
111. Schudson, *Sociology,* 180.
112. See, e.g., Yeoman, "Is Nothing Sacred" (citing pleadings); Pope, "Church knew of abuses," (citing depositions); Jason Berry, "Church Accepts Liability," *Times of Acadiana,* July 18, 1985, (citing stipulation of church liability); David McCormick, "Church On Trial For Allegedly Harboring

Priest in Sex Abuse Case," *Associated Press*, February 3, 1986 (citing jury selection); David McCormick, "Mother: Faith Shattered After Son Molested by Priest," *Associated Press*, February 4, 1986 (citing trial testimony); Staff, "Sex Abuse Damage Trial Goes to Jury Today," *Daily Advertiser*, February 7, 1986 (citing submission to jury); Dave Miller, "Decision Reached in Priest Sex Suit," *Baton Rouge Morning Advocate*, February 8, 1986, B1 (citing jury verdict).

113. Jason Berry, "The Tragedy of Gilbert Gauthe, Part II," *Times of Acadiana*, May 30, 1985, 16.

114. "Fall From Grace, Part 2 Clergy Protectionism," *CNN Specials*, CNN, November 14, 1993.

115. "Depositions of Cardinal Law," www.boston.com (accessed 12/20/06). For excerpts from the depositions broadcast on television, see, e.g., Byron Pitts, "Videotape Shows Boston's Cardinal Bernard Law Knew of Secretive Church Policy when Dealing with Abusive Priests," *CBS Morning News*, CBS, August 14, 2002, and for excerpts in print media see, e.g., Pam Belluck, "Cardinal Law Said His Policy Shielded Priests," *New York Times*, August 14, 2002, A1.

116. Mark Fishman, "Crime Waves as Ideology," in Cohen and Young, *Manufacture of News*, 102.

117. Gitlin, *Whole World*, 100; Fishman, "Crime Waves," 106.

118. Fishman, "Crime Waves," 107. Fishman illustrates this point by showing how the proliferation of themes accounts for the creation of crime waves by the media even when the crime rate is declining.

119. Fishman, "Crime Waves," 111.

120. Richard Nagareda, *Mass Torts in a World of Settlement* (Chicago: University of Chicago Press, 2007).

121. Ostling, "Sins of the Fathers," 51; Reverend Andrew Greeley, quoted in Richard Ostling, "Sex Abuse Crisis Not New For Church," *Associated Press*, April 8, 2002.

122. See Karen Terry and Margaret Leland Smith, *The Nature and Scope of Sexual Abuse of Minors by Catholic Priests and Deacons in the United States 1950–2002, Supplementary Data Analysis* (Washington, D.C.: United States Conference of Catholic Bishops, 2006), 4–18. For discussion of this data, see chap. 2.

123. Supplemental and Amending Answer at ¶ I.7, No. 84-48175-A (Dec. 13, 1985) (on file with author); David Milner, "Testimony Begins in Suit Against Diocese," *Baton Rouge Morning Advocate*, February 5, 1986, 2B; Simon, *Law in the Cajun Nation*, 149.

124. Milner, "Testimony Begins."

125. *Associated Press*, "Bishop Says He Got Word"; UPI, "Lawyer Wants Bishop to List Likely Victims," *Baton Rouge Morning Advocate*, January 30, 1985, 10B; Berry, "Tragedy, Part II," 27.

126. Milner, "Testimony Begins."

127. Jenkins, *Pedophiles and Priests*, 130. See also, ibid., 125–132. Compare

Jennifer M. Balboni, "'It's Not about the Money:' Truth, Consequences, and the Real Meaning of Litigation for Clergy Sexual Abuse Survivors" (Ph.D. diss., Northeastern University, 2006).

128. Bob Wright, interview by the author, May 25, 2005. See also, Bruni and Burkett, *Gospel of Shame,* 258; "Deposition of Cardinal Bernard Law, June 5, 2002, Suffolk County Superior Court," www.boston.com (accessed 12/19/06).

129. Patrick Schiltz, "Too Much Law, Too Little Justice: How Lawyers Helped to Turn a Clergy Sexual Abuse Problem into a Clergy Sexual Abuse Crisis" (speech, University of Dayton Law School, Dayton, Ohio, January 10, 2005), 4 (on file with author). For a similar analysis, see Eugene Kennedy, "About Those Priests," *Chicago Tribune,* October 14, 2005, C23. L. Martin Nussbaum, "Changing the Rules: Selective Justice for Catholic Institutions, *America,* May 15, 2006, 13–14. This account is disputed by psychiatric professionals who claim bishops ignored their advice; see Leslie M. Lothstein, "The Relationship Between the Treatment Facilities and the Church Hierarchy: Forensic Issues and Future Considerations," in Plante, *Sin Against the Innocents,* 130.

130. Schiltz, "Too Much Law," 1–2, 6.

131. Patrick J. Schiltz, "Defending the Church," *Litigation* 29 (Spring 2003): 25.

132. Barry Yeoman, "How Much Did the Church Know?," *Times of Acadiana,* February 7, 1985. This quote was repeated in other news articles. See, e.g., Blow, "Child Abuse Scandal."

133. Brooks Egerton, "Documents Show Bishops Transferred Known Abuser, Church Officials Say Policies Have Since Changed," *Dallas Morning News,* August 31, 1997, A1.

134. J. Thavis, "Vatican Spokesman Says Abuse Raises Questions About U.S. Morals," *Catholic News Service,* June 23, 1993, quoted in Stephen J. Rossetti, *Tragic Grace: The Catholic Church and Child Sexual Abuse* (Collegeville, Minn.: Liturgical Press, 1996), 17. See also Stephen J. Rossetti, ed., *Slayer of the Soul: Child Sexual Abuse and the Catholic Church* (Mystic, Conn.: Twenty-Third Publications, 1990), 189.

135. Kay Longcope, "Sexual Abuse by Priests is a 'Betrayal,' 'Rare,' Law Says," *Boston Globe,* May 14, 1992, 29.

136. "Sins of the Fathers: Catholic Church Deals with Sexual Abuse of Minors by Priests in Wake of Former Priest, John Geoghan, being Charged with Sexual Abuse and Sentenced to Prison," *Nightline,* ABC, February 21, 2002.

137. "The Catholic Church is Not on Trial!," *Daily Advertiser,* June 16, 1985.

138. James Franklin, "Catholics Struggle with Delay," *Boston Globe,* November 22, 1992, 1. For a similar sentiment expressed by a Honduran cardinal, see Peter Steinfels, *A People Adrift: The Crisis of the Roman Catholic Church in America* (New York: Simon & Schuster, 2003), 63.

139. France, *Our Fathers,* 213.

140. Jenkins, *Pedophiles and Priests,* 19–32.

141. Steinfels, *People Adrift,* 65. For other examples of this frame, see, e.g.,

Nussbaum, "Changing the Rules," 13. Nussbaum alleges that press coverage has created the false impression that child sexual abuse is a Catholic problem. See also "Sins of the Fathers: Catholic Church Deals with Sexual Abuse of Minors by Priests in Wake of Former Priest, John Geoghan, being Charged with Sexual Abuse and Sentenced to Prison," *Nightline*, ABC, February 21, 2002. Former Boston mayor and U.S. ambassador to the Vatican Ray Flynn suggested that press attention to clergy sexual abuse in the Boston archdiocese is disproportionate.

142. "Scandal in the Church: Four Years Later," *New York Times*, July 7, 2006, A23.

143. Simon, *Law in the Cajun Nation*, 146–148.

144. *Associated Press*, "Bishop Says He Got Word"; Blow, "Child Abuse Scandal"; Sawyer, "Priest Child-Molestation Case."

145. Berry, *Lead Us Not*, 243–258. See also Jenkins, *Pedophiles and Priests*, 103–104.

146. France, *Our Fathers*, 357.

147. Ian Fisher, "In Strong Terms, Rome is to Ban Gays as Priests," *New York Times*, November 23, 2005, A1.

148. Balboni, "Through the 'Lens,'" chap. 5.

149. Pope, "Church knew of abuses."

150. Franklin, "Catholics Struggle with Delay." Jenkins suggests that the rejection of sin as a frame for clergy sexual abuse reflects a more general trend of rejecting religious authority and outlook in favor of secular ideas and state power: "Whereas once the religious institutions would have been thought worthy of enforcing internal standards of behavior and morality, the current trend is to seek external controls from civil and criminal law, and to impose the value systems of nonreligious groups." Jenkins, *Pedophiles and Priests*, 161–162.

151. See, e.g., *Pedophiles and Priests*, 79. On the distinction, see Stephen Rossetti and Leslie M. Lothstein, "Myths of the Child Molester," in Rossetti, *Slayer of the Soul*, 14, and Leslie M. Lothstein, "Psychological Theories of Pedophilia and Ephebophilia," in Rossetti, *Slayer of the Soul*, 20–21.

152. Jenkins, *Pedophiles and Priests*, 79. For a similar apologetic sentiment, see John Baker, Jr., "Prosecuting Dioceses and Bishops," 44 *Boston College Law Review* 1084 (2003).

153. These examples do not exhaust the frames presented in debates over clergy sex abuse. Common frames within the church include reformers' frames of celibacy requirements as a cause of clerical sexual abuse and lack of democracy and transparency in church governance as a cause of the institutional failure of the bishops and conservatives' frame of a breakdown in sexual doctrines and priestly discipline. For the reform view, see Jimmy Breslin, *The Church that Forgot Christ* (New York: Free Press, 2004), and Paul Dokecki, *The Clergy Sexual Abuse Crisis* (Washington, D.C.: Georgetown University Press, 2004); for the conservative view, see Paul Thigpen, ed., *Shaken by Scandals: Catholics Speak Out about Priests' Sexual Abuse* (Ann Arbor, Mich.: Servant Publications, 2002).

154. See Kitzinger, *Framing Abuse,* 54–78.
155. Pope, interview.
156. See Berry, *Lead Us Not,* 237; "Not on Trial!"

5. Placing Clergy Sexual Abuse on Policy Agendas

1. The investigative staff of the *Boston Globe, Betrayal: The Crisis in the Catholic Church* (2002; reprint, Boston: Back Bay-Little, Brown and Company, 2003), 210.
2. David France, *Our Fathers: The Secret Life of the Catholic Church in an Age of Scandal* (New York: Broadway Books-Random House, 2004), 463–465; Michael J. Bemi, interview by the author, June 15, 2006.
3. Paul Thigpen, ed., *Shaken by Scandals: Catholics Speak Out about Priests' Sexual Abuse* (Ann Arbor, Mich.: Servant Publications, 2002), 229.
4. Roger Cobb and Charles Elder, *Participation in American Politics: The Dynamics of Agenda Building,* 2nd ed. (Baltimore: Johns Hopkins University Press, 1983), 85–86. See also John Kingdon, *Agendas, Alternatives, and Public Policies,* 2nd ed. (New York: Longman, 2003), 3–4.
5. Cobb and Elder, *Participation,* 160.
6. Elaine Sharp, "Paradoxes of National Antidrug Policymaking," in David Rochefort and Roger Cobb, eds., *The Politics of Problem Definition: Shaping the Policy Agenda* (Lawrence: University Press of Kansas, 1994), 103–106.
7. Ellen Frankel Paul, "Sexual Harassment: A Defining Moment and Its Repercussions," in Rochefort and Cobb, *Problem Definition,* 94. See also, Thomas Birkland, *After Disaster: Agenda Setting, Public Policy, and Focusing Events* (Washington, D.C.: Georgetown University Press, 1997); Kingdon, *Agendas,* 94–100.
8. Frank Baumgartner and Bryan Jones, "Attention, Boundary Effects, and Large-Scale Policy Change in Air Transportation Policy," in Rochefort and Cobb, *Problem Definition,* 50–53.
9. John Bohte, Roy B. Flemming, and B. Dan Wood, "One Voice Among Many: The Supreme Court's Influence on Attentiveness to Issues in the United States, 1947–1992," in David Schultz, ed., *Leveraging the Law* (New York: Peter Lang, 1998), 23–25. See also Shanto Iyengar and Donald Kinder, *News That Matters: Television and American Opinion* (Chicago: University of Chicago Press, 1987), 16.
10. Gary Langer, "Not Doing Enough Poll: Many Americans Concerned About Sex Abuse by Priests," www.abcnews.go.com (accessed 12/20/06); "Post/ABC/Beliefnet Poll: The Catholic Church, Thursday, April 4, 2002," www.washingtonpost.com (accessed 12/20/06).
11. "Post/ABC/Beliefnet Poll: The Catholic Church, Thursday, April 4, 2002."
12. "ABC News/Washington Post Poll: Church Scandal, February 26, 2004," www.abcnews.go.com (accessed 12/20/06), question #2; "Washington Post Poll: The Catholic Church, Tuesday, June 18, 2002," www.washingtonpost.com (accessed 12/20/06).

13. "New York Times/CBS News Poll, Apr. 28–May 1, 2002" (on file with author).

14. Paul Dokecki, *The Clergy Sexual Abuse Crisis* (Washington, D.C.: Georgetown University Press, 2004), 1.

15. Iyengar and Kinder, *News,* 16–33.

16. Bohte, Flemming, and Wood, "One Voice Among Many," 23.

17. Frank Bruni and Elinor Burkett, *A Gospel of Shame: Children, Sexual Abuse, and the Catholic Church* (1993; reprint, New York: Perennial-HarperCollins, 2002), 15.

18. Philip Jenkins, *Pedophiles and Priests: Anatomy of a Contemporary Crisis* (Oxford: Oxford University Press, 1996), 74.

19. Bruni and Burkett, *Gospel of Shame,* xii. See Peter Steinfels, *A People Adrift: The Crisis of the Roman Catholic Church in America* (New York: Simon & Schuster, 2003), 40 (estimating 12,000 articles in major newspapers, television networks, cable outlets, wire services, and newsmagazines).

20. For an explanation of methodology, see Appendix 1.

21. For an explanation of methodology, see Appendix 2.

22. Birkland, *After Disaster,* 22–27. See also Kingdon, *Agendas,* 94–100.

23. Bruni and Burkett estimate Porter's victims at 200 in *Gospel of Shame,* 24. The investigative staff of the *Boston Globe* estimate Geoghan's victims between 200 and 800 in *Betrayal,* 6. *Boston Globe* reporter Michael Rezendes recounts how the Geoghan case sparked the *Globe*'s coverage. Michael Rezendes, "Scandal: The *Boston Globe* and Sexual Abuse in the Catholic Church," in Thomas G. Plante, ed., *Sin Against the Innocents: Sexual Abuse by Priests and the Role of the Catholic Church* (Westport, Conn.: Praeger-Greenwood Publishing Group, 2004), 4.

24. Heightened media coverage in 1992–1993 and 2002 also coincides with my speculation in chapter 2 that the volume of litigation increased during those years. As anecdotal evidence in chapter 1 suggests, these increases may themselves be attributable to the Gauthe, Porter, and Geoghan cases which served as catalysts to subsequent litigation. Of course, the capacity of these landmark cases to produce more litigation—by encouraging victims to come forward and file lawsuits—is partly attributable to media coverage of them. This suggests a feedback effect—while landmark cases served as focusing events that increased media coverage, media coverage in turn facilitated increases in litigation. I shall take up the issue of feedback effects in chapter 8.

25. Mark E. Chopko, interview by the author, March 22, 2006.

26. James Franklin, "Mass. Catholics Fault Church on Handling of Sex Charges," *Boston Globe,* July 26, 1992, 1.

27. Jim Davidson, "Generational Differences among Catholics Emerge," *National Catholic Reporter,* October 8, 1993, 29.

28. *Emerging Trends,* 15 (October 1993): 5.

29. "Post/ABC/Beliefnet Poll: The Catholic Church, Apr. 4, 2002." Data from the February *ABC News* poll are reported here and compared to subsequent survey responses.

30. Ibid.
31. Michael Paulson, "Most Catholics in Poll Fault Law's Performance," April 17, 2002, www.boston.com (accessed 12/20/06). To obtain poll results, click "Complete List of Poll Questions and Results (Plain text file)."
32. "USA Today/CNN/Gallup Poll, May 28–9, 2002," www.usatoday.com/news/nation/2002/06/03/catholic-poll-results.htm (accessed 12/20/06).
33. "Washington Post Poll: The Catholic Church, Tuesday, June 18, 2002."
34. "ABC News/Washington Post Poll: Church Scandal, February 26, 2004."
35. "Globe Poll Results," May 4–6, 2003, www.boston.com/globe/spotlight/abuse/poll/Q5.htm (accessed 12/20/06).
36. "April 14, 2005—New Pope Must Do More To Curb Abuse By Priests, U.S. Catholics Say 8–1 In Quinnipiac University Poll; Most Catholics Say Pope John Paul Should Be A Saint." www. quinnipiac.edu (accessed 12/20/06).
37. See Mark M. Gray and Paul M. Perl, "Catholic Reactions to the News of Sexual Abuse Cases Involving Catholic Clergy" (Working Paper 8, Center for Applied Research in the Apostolate [CARA], Georgetown University, April 2006).
38. See Jenkins, *Pedophiles and Priests,* 103, 106, 116, 151 (commenting on coverage by the paper in the years from the Gauthe to Porter cases).
39. I conducted this search on August 5, 2005, requesting documents including all of the terms "clergy," "sex," and "abuse" from the online index at http:www.picosearch.com/cgi-bin/ts.pl (August 5, 2005) (printout of first page of results on file with author).
40. I conducted this search on August 5, 2005, requesting documents including all of the terms "clergy," "sexual," and "abuse" from the online index at http:search.atomz.com/search/?sp-i=1&sp-q=clergy+sexual+abuse&sp-a=sp 1001892c&sp-s=1&sp-f=iso-8859-1 (August 5, 2005) (printout of first page of results on file with author).
41. For an explanation of methodology and raw data, see Appendix 3.
42. Search conducted August 5, 2005 (printout of first page of search results on file with author).
43. Search conducted August 5, 2005 (printout of first page of search results on file with author).
44. Michael W. McCann, *Rights at Work: Pay Equity Reform and the Politics of Legal Mobilization* (Chicago: University of Chicago Press, 1994), 279; Lynn Mather, "Theorizing About Trial Courts: Lawyers, Policymaking, and Tobacco Litigation," 23 *Law and Social Inquiry* 923 (1998).
45. Bruni and Burkett, *Gospel of Shame,* 235–249. Jennifer Balboni, in her study of clergy sexual abuse victims in Boston, found that overcoming barriers to legal claims—such as statutes of limitation and charitable damage caps—became a focal point for legislative activism among victims. Jennifer M. Balboni, "'It's Not about the Money': Truth, Consequences, and the Real Meaning of Litigation for Clergy Sexual Abuse Survivors" (Ph.D. diss., Northeastern University, 2006), 235.
46. David Clohessy, interview by the author, March 13, 2006; France, *Our Fathers,* 375.

47. "The Voice of the Faithful Story," www.votf.org (accessed 12/20/06).

48. Frank Fitzpatrick, *Where It All Began: Bringing Father Porter to Justice* (unpublished manuscript, 2004), chap. 15, 5.

49. All information about the NCCB and the USCCB in this paragraph is from "About Us," www.usccb.org (accessed 12/20/06).

50. This paragraph relies on detailed accounts in Jason Berry, *Lead Us Not Into Temptation: Catholic Priests and the Sexual Abuse of Children* (1992; reprint, Urbana: University of Illinois Press, 2000), 96–102, 110–12; Bruni and Burkett, *Gospel of Shame*, 164, 173; investigative staff of the *Boston Globe, Betrayal*, 39; France, *Our Fathers*, 230; Jason Berry and Gerald Renner, *Vows of Silence: The Abuse of Power in the Papacy of John Paul II* (New York: Free Press, 2004), 48; Mark E. Chopko, "USCCB Efforts to Combat Clergy Sexual Abuse Against Minors: A Chronology 1982–2006," www.usccb.org (accessed 12/12/06); Mark E. Chopko, interview by the author, March 2, 2006.

51. Bruni and Burkett, *Gospel of Shame*, 173–174.

52. Steinfels, *A People Adrift*, 48; Harry Flynn, "Keynote: Dallas and Beyond—Perspectives of a Bishop and Pastor," in Marie M. Fortune and W. Merle Longwood, eds., *Sexual Abuse in the Catholic Church* (Binghamton, N.Y.: Haworth Press, 2003), 15.

53. Mark E. Chopko, "USCCB Efforts to Combat Clergy Sexual Abuse Against Minors," www.usccb.org (accessed 12/12/06).

54. France, *Our Fathers*, 230–31; Steinfels, *People Adrift*, 48; Flynn, "Keynote," 15; "NCCB Establishes Committee on Sexual Abuse," 23 *Origins* 104 (1993).

55. See Flynn, "Keynote," 15–17; Steinfels, *People Adrift*, 50–59.

56. France, *Our Fathers*, 362.

57. Raymond O'Brien, "Clergy, Sex and the American Way," 31 *Pepperdine Law Review* 423–428 (2004).

58. *Associated Press*, "State-By-State Summary of the Major Developments since January in the Clergy Sex Abuse Scandal," April 27, 2002. See, e.g., "Diocese of Manchester: Diocesan Task Force on Sexual Misconduct Policy, Report to the Bishop of Manchester," www.bishopaccountability.org (accessed 12/20/06).

59. See chap. 1. For further details and a copy of the report, see Thomas P. Doyle, A. W. R. Sipe, and Patrick J. Wall, *Sex, Priests, and Secret Codes* (Los Angeles: Volt, 2006), chaps. 3–4.

60. Stephen J. Rossetti, *Tragic Grace: The Catholic Church and Child Sexual Abuse* (Collegeville, Minn.: Liturgical Press, 1996), 14.

61. Kingdon, *Agendas*, 168.

62. Ibid., 169.

63. Ibid., 201.

64. Alan Cooperman, "Debate Continues Over Pope's Reaction to Sex-Abuse Scandal," *Washington Post*, April 2, 2005, A36.

65. France, *Our Fathers*, 357; investigative staff of the *Boston Globe, Betrayal*, 169.

66. Investigative staff of the *Boston Globe, Betrayal,* 100, 200; France, *Our Fathers,* 420.
67. Investigative staff of the *Boston Globe, Betrayal,* 212–213.
68. Larry B. Stammer, "Conservative Trend Found in Younger Priests," *Los Angeles Times,* February 21, 1994, A1.
69. "L.A. Times Poll, A Survey of Roman Catholic Priests in the United States and Puerto Rico," www.bishopaccountability.org (accessed 12/20/06).
70. "October 28, 2003—Fall Convocation of Priests," www.nfpc.org (accessed 12/20/06).
71. "Statement of the NFPC—February 27, 2004," www.nfpc.org (accessed 12/20/06).
72. "Fr. Bob Silva's Address to NFPC Portland Convention, April 12, 2005," www.nfpc.org (accessed 12/20/06).
73. "Priest Councils/USCCB Reps from Across the US Gather in Fraternal Call for Unity," www.nfpc.org (accessed 12/20/06).
74. Berry, *Lead Us Not,* 25.
75. J. Minos Simon and David Leon Chandler, *Law in the Cajun Nation* (Lafayette, La.: Prescott Press, 1993), 137, 141. Berry paints a different picture. He credits plaintiffs' attorney Hebert with first bringing the matter to Stansbury's attention and providing him with key witnesses, and he portrays Stansbury as pursuing a prompt and vigorous prosecution based on his own desire to see Gauthe punished for his crimes. Berry, *Lead Us Not,* 20, 25, 49–50, 116–125.
76. Jenkins, *Priests and Pedophiles,* 14, 36, 48, 49.
77. This paragraph relies on France, *Our Fathers,* 207–210, and Bruni and Burkett, *Gospel of Shame,* 12–17.
78. Bruni and Burkett, *Gospel of Shame,* 197–198.
79. "Report of the April 'E' 2002 Westchester County Grand Jury Concerning Complaints of Sexual Abuse and Misconduct against Minors by Members of the Clergy," 1–2 (2002), www.bishopaccountability.org (accessed 12/20/06); "Suffolk County Supreme Court Special Grand Jury, May 6, 2002 Term ID, Grand Jury Report CPL §190.85(1)(C), 175–180," www.bishopaccountability.org (accessed 12/20/06).
80. "The State of New Hampshire Hillsborough, SS Superior Court Northern District, In Re Grand Jury Proceedings, No. 02-S-1154 Agreement," www.bishopaccountability.org (accessed 12/20/06).
81. "In Re: County Investigating Grand Jury, Court of Common Pleas, First Judicial District of Pennsylvania, Criminal Trial Division, Misc. No. 03-00-239," www.bishopaccountability.org (accessed 12/20/06), 4.
82. "Office of the Attorney General, The Sexual Abuse of Children in the Roman Catholic Archdiocese of Boston," www.bishopaccountability.org (accessed 12/20/06), cover letter, 2.
83. "Office of the Attorney General," cover letter, 2, and i–ii.
84. Ibid., 74–76.
85. Ibid., cover letter 2–3.
86. "Office of the Attorney General, On the Allegations of Sexual Abuse of

Children by Priests and Other Clergy Members Associated with the Roman Catholic Church in Maine," www.bishopaccountability.org (accessed 12/20/06).

87. Thomas P. Doyle and Stephen C. Rubino, "Catholic Clergy Sexual Abuse Meets the Civil Law," 31 *Fordham Urban Law Journal* 550–51 (2004).

88. Karen Terry et al., *The Nature and Scope of Sexual Abuse of Minors by Catholic Priests and Deacons in the United States 1950–2002* (Washington, D.C.: United States Conference of Catholic Bishops, 2004), 61.

89. This count is based on news stories posted on the SNAP website at "Legislation," www.snapnetwork.org/legislation/legisindex.htm (accessed 12/20/06) and 2005 Bill Tracking, H.B. 2226 79th Leg. (W. Va. 2005) (LEXIS).

90. "Legislation"; Jesse Belcher-Timme, "Note: Unholy Acts: The Clergy Sex Scandal in Massachusetts and the Legislative Response," 30 *New England Journal on Criminal and Civil Confinement,* 243 (2004); Stephen C. Rubino, "Statute of Limitations in Child Sex Abuse Cases," *Trial Lawyer,* March 1994, 25; Chrissta Forslund to Professor Leslie Griffin, memorandum, July 25, 2004, in *Child Abuse Reporting Statutes and Clergy* (on file with author).

91. Roger W. Cobb and Mark Howard Ross, *Strategies of Agenda Denial: Avoidance, Attack, and Redefinition* (Lawrence: University Press of Kansas, 1997), 25–43.

92. Michael Paulson, "In His First Meeting with Voice of Faithful, Law Seeks Answers," *Boston Globe,* November 27, 2002, B1. (Italics added for emphasis.)

93. See, e.g., *Nightline,* ABC, February 21, 2002. Former Boston mayor and U.S. ambassador to the Vatican Ray Flynn suggested that press attention to clergy sexual abuse in the Boston archdiocese is disproportionate, saying, "Let's not just try to bring down the Catholic church here because of a handful of bad apples in the barrel." For an earlier example, see Berry, *Lead Us Not,* 119. (Italics added for emphasis.)

94. See, e.g., John S. Baker, Jr., "Prosecuting Dioceses and Bishops," 44 *Boston College Law Review* 1061 (2003); Norman Abrams, "Addressing the Tension between the Clergy-Communicant Privilege and the Duty to Report Child Abuse in State Statutes," 44 *Boston College Law Review* 1127 (2003).

95. See, e.g., Patrick J. Schiltz, "The Impact of Clergy Sexual Misconduct Litigation on Religious Liberty," 44 *Boston College Law Review* 949 (2003).

96. See Erving Goffman, *Frame Analysis: An Essay on the Organization of Experience* (1974; reprint, Boston: Northeastern University Press, 1986), 82. I rely here on Goffman's discussion of frame "keying" and "layering."

97. Cobb and Ross, *Strategies of Agenda Denial,* 42–43.

6. Uncovering Concealed Information

1. Michael Paulson and Thomas Farragher, "Crisis in the Church: The Bishops Conference; Bishops Move to Bar Abusers But Removal From Priesthood Not Mandated," *Boston Globe,* June 15, 2002, A1.

2. Sacha Pfeiffer, "Crisis in the Church: The Bishops Conference; Lay Leader Vows Justice," *Boston Globe*, June 16, 2002, A1.

3. Michael Paulson, "Keating's Test of Faith; Oklahoman Talks Tough as He Seeks to Reform Church," *Boston Globe*, September 29, 2002, A1.

4. Michael Rezendes, "Bid to Shield Priest Data Faulted," *Boston Globe*, March 14, 2003, A17.

5. Larry B. Stammer, "Mahony Resisted Abuse Inquiry, Panelist Says," *Los Angeles Times*, June 12, 2003, 1.

6. "Governor Keating Resigns from National Review Board," www.nccbuscc .org (accessed 12/20/06).

7. Quoted in Stephen J. Rossetti, *Tragic Grace: The Catholic Church and Child Sexual Abuse* (Collegeville, Minn.: Liturgical Press, 1996), 38.

8. J. Michael Hennigan, interview by the author, March 29, 2006.

9. See, e.g., Wendy Wagner, "When All Else Fails: Regulating Risky Products through Litigation," 95 *Georgetown Law Journal* 693 (2007); Lynn Mather, "Theorizing About Trial Courts: Lawyers, Policymaking, and To-bacco Litigation," 23 *Law and Social Inquiry* 897, 914–919 (1998); Peter Jacobson and Kenneth Warner, "Litigation and Public Health Policy Making: The Case of Tobacco Control," 24 *Journal of Health Politics, Policy, and Law* 769 (1999); Robert L. Rabin and Stephen D. Sugarman, eds., *Regulating Tobacco* (Oxford: Oxford University Press, 2001); Wendy Wagner, "Stubborn Information Problems & the Regulatory Benefits of Gun Litigation," in Timothy D. Lytton, ed., *Suing the Gun Industry: A Battle at the Crossroads of Gun Control and Mass Torts* (Ann Arbor: University of Michigan Press, 2005), 271.

10. Wagner, "Stubborn Information," 274.

11. Wagner, "Stubborn Information," 274. See also, Wagner, "When All Else Fails," 697–701.

12. See Wendy Wagner and David Michaels, "Equal Treatment for Regulatory Science: Extending the Controls Governing the Quality of Public Research to Private Research," 30 *American Journal of Law & Medicine* 119 (2004). See also, Wendy Wagner, "When All Else Fails," 707.

13. Wagner, "Stubborn Information," 274–276; Wagner, "When All Else Fails," 708.

14. Patrick Schiltz, "Too Much Law, Too Little Justice: How Lawyers Helped to Turn a Clergy Sexual Abuse Problem into a Clergy Sexual Abuse Crisis" (speech, University of Dayton Law School, Dayton, Ohio, January 10, 2005), 4, 6 (on file with author). See also, Rossetti, *Tragic Grace*, 51.

15. *A Report on the Crisis in the Catholic Church in the United States*, (Washington, D.C.: United States Conference of Catholic Bishops, 2004), 37 n. 20.

16. John C. Gonsiorek, "Barriers to Responding to the Clergy Sexual Abuse Crisis Within the Roman Catholic Church," Thomas G. Plante, ed., *Sin Against the Innocents: Sexual Abuse by Priests and the Role of the Catholic Church* (Westport, Conn.: Praeger-Greenwood Publishing Group, 2004), 146–151.

17. Michael Paulson, "Abuse Crisis Tests the Church Doctrine on Scandal," *Boston Globe,* August 25, 2002; Thomas P. Doyle, A. W. R. Sipe, and Patrick J. Wall, *Sex, Priests, and Secret Codes* (Los Angeles: Volt, 2006), 205–206; *Report on the Crisis in the Catholic Church,* 107.

18. Frank Bruni and Elinor Burkett, *A Gospel of Shame: Children, Sexual Abuse, and the Catholic Church* (1993; reprint, New York: Perennial-HarperCollins, 2002), 170.

19. Wilton D. Gregory, "A Catholic Response to Sexual Abuse: Confession, Contrition, Resolve," in Paul Thigpen, ed., *Shaken by Scandals: Catholics Speak Out about Priests' Sexual Abuse* (Ann Arbor, Mich.: Servant Publications, 2002), 222–223.

20. Doyle et al., *Sex, Priests,* 206.

21. Peter Steinfels, *A People Adrift: The Crisis of the Roman Catholic Church in America* (New York: Simon & Schuster, 2003), 46, 61. See also, Rossetti, *Tragic Grace,* 116.

22. John S. Baker, Jr., "Prosecuting Dioceses and Bishops,"44 *Boston College Law Review* 1087 (2003).

23. Bruni and Burkett, *Gospel of Shame,* 169.

24. John Allen, Jr., "Clergy Sexual Abuse in the American Catholic Church: The View from the Vatican," in Plante, *Sin Against the Innocents,* 16–17.

25. David France, *Our Fathers: The Secret Life of the Catholic Church in an Age of Scandal* (New York: Broadway Books-Random House, 2004), 129.

26. Bruni and Burkett, *Gospel of Shame,* 176.

27. Philip Jenkins, *Pedophiles and Priests: Anatomy of a Contemporary Crisis* (Oxford: Oxford University Press, 1996), 45. See also, David B. Caruso, "Victims: Police Hid Priest Cases," *Associated Press,* May 1, 2002; Michael Rezendes, "Diocese Records Show More Coverups," *Boston Globe,* September 13, 2002, B1; Jeanne M. Miller, "The Moral Bankruptcy of Institutionalized Religion," in Anson Shupe, ed., *Wolves Within the Fold: Religious Leadership and Abuses of Power* (New Brunswick, N.J.: Rutgers University Press, 1998), 157; Mary Gail Frawley-O'Dea, *Perversion of Power: Sexual Abuse in the Catholic Church* (Nashville: Vanderbilt University Press, 2007), 197. The John Jay study provides aggregate data on the number of priests reported to the police and the results of those reports. Karen Terry et al., *The Nature and Scope of Sexual Abuse of Minors by Catholic Priests and Deacons in the United States 1950–2002* (Washington, D.C.: United States Conference of Catholic Bishops, 2004), 59–65.

28. See, e.g., Joe Feuerherd, "Maryland Senate Considers Bill to Aid Child Sex Abuse Victims," www.ncronline.org (accessed 12/21/06); the investigative staff of the *Boston Globe, Betrayal: The Crisis in the Catholic Church* (2002; reprint, Boston: Back Bay-Little, Brown and Company, 2003), 134–135; "Limits on Church Suits May Be Altered," *National Law Journal,* February 27, 2006, 4; T. R. Reid, "Catholic Leaders Fight Legislation on Suits; States Consider Easing Statutes of Limitation," *Washington Post,* April 1, 2006, A10.

29. John Dart, "Churches Laud Requiring Clergy to Report Child Abuse," *Los*

Angeles Times, January 11, 1997, B10; Richard Roesler, "Bill Would Make Clergy Report Abuse of Children; Sex Abuse by Priests Behind Effort to Close Loophole in Washington Law," *Spokane Spokesman-Review,* January 29, 2004, A1. Cited in Chrissta Forslund to Professor Leslie Griffin, memorandum, July 25, 2004, in *Child Abuse Reporting Statutes and Clergy* (on file with author). See also Frawley-O'Dea, *Perversion of Power,* 137.

30. Jason Berry, email message to author, July 6, 2005; Jason Berry, *Lead Us Not Into Temptation: Catholic Priests and the Sexual Abuse of Children* (1992; reprint, Urbana: University of Illinois Press, 2000), 109.

31. France, *Our Fathers,* 233–235.

32. Jenkins, *Pedophiles and Priests,* 60–61, 63, quoting Paul Wilkes, "Unholy Acts," *New Yorker,* June 7, 1993, 68.

33. See, e.g., Berry, *Lead Us Not,* 9–24; investigative staff, *Betrayal,* 47–49, 100, 109; France, *Our Fathers,* 151, 204, 212, 288.

34. Jeffrey R. Anderson, interview by the author, March 10, 2006.

35. Carl Eck, "Discovery of Church Records," 35 *Catholic Lawyer* 229, 231 (1994).

36. "In Re: County Investigating Grand Jury, Court of Common Pleas, First Judicial District of Pennsylvania, Criminal Trial Division, Misc. No. 03-00-239," www.bishopaccountability.org (accessed 12/20/06), 42–43.

37. Gustavo Arellano, "Shreddin'!: Other Catholic Diocese [sic] Have Destroyed Incriminating Priest Personnel Files. Why Not Orange?," ocweekly.com (accessed 12/21/06); Robert Patrick, "Center Destroyed Priest Sex Case Records," *Post Dispatch,* October 16, 2005, www.bishopaccountability.org (accessed 1/3/07); Kathyrn Marchocki, "Monsignor: N.H. Priest Files Destroyed to Conceal Abuse Evidence," *Union Leader,* January 8, 2003, www.bishopaccountability.org (accessed 1/3/07); bishop of Manchester, letter to Reverend Peter Lechner, May 3, 1989. The letter, regarding destruction of psychological reports, is available at www.bishopaccountability.org/NH- Manchester/archives/MacRae-11.pdf (accessed 12/21/06).

38. "NCCB Guidelines and Other Considerations in Pedophilia Cases," www.bishopaccountability.org (accessed 12/21/06).

39. Stephen C. Rubino, interview by the author, April 5, 2006.

40. Roderick MacLeish, "Discovery," *CLE Materials, First National Conference on Clergy Abuse* (Benjamin N. Cardozo School of Law, New York, NY, April 10, 2003) (on file with author).

41. John Spano, "Catholic Doctrine is Cited in Priest Sex Cases; In Questioning Clergy," *Los Angeles Times,* March 26, 2007, B4.

42. MacLeish, "Discovery."

43. Sylvia Demarest, interview by the author, April 25, 2006.

44. Raymond Boucher, interview by the author, September 14, 2006.

45. Eck, "Discovery of Church Records," 229, 241.

46. Jean Guccione and William Lobdell, "Details on 11 Priests Missing in '04 Report; Mahony's Disclosure on Sex Abuse Claims Left Out Information

on Clerics Who Stayed in Ministry," *Los Angeles Times,* April 20, 2006, A1. The L.A. archdiocese has also resisted grand jury subpoenas. Jean Guccione and Sandy Banks, "Records Release is Criticized; Critics Dismiss as a PR Ploy the Disclosure by the L.A. Archdiocese of Documents on Priests," *Los Angeles Times,* October 13, 2005, A13.

47. France, *Our Fathers,* 571.
48. Anderson, interview.
49. John Manly, interview by the author, September 5, 2006.
50. Demarest, interview.
51. Rubino, interview.
52. Interview with anonymous attorney.
53. Stephen C. Rubino, telephone conversation with author, June 15, 2006.
54. Interview with anonymous attorney involved in the Boston litigation.
55. See Jennifer M. Balboni, "'It's Not about the Money:' Truth, Consequences, and the Real Meaning of Litigation for Clergy Sexual Abuse Survivors," (Ph.D. diss., Northeastern University, 2006).
56. France, *Our Fathers,* 207; Bill Hewitt, Lauren Comander, and Maureen Harrington, "Serving Rome; Lawyer Jeffrey Anderson Takes His Case to the Top, Suing Vatican for Not Removing Predator Priests," *People,* April 22, 2002, 63.
57. Rubino, interview.
58. Manly, interview.
59. Demarest, interview.
60. "Report to the People of God: Clergy Sexual Abuse, Archdiocese of Los Angeles 1930–2003" and "Addendum to the Report to the People of God," www.la-archdiocese.org (accessed 12/29/06). See also, e.g., "February 26, 2004—Statement of Archbishop Sean P. O'Malley, Regarding Clergy Sexual Abuse in the Archdiocese of Boston from 1950–2003," www.rcab.org (accessed 12/21/06); "Ten Year Report on Clerical Sexual Abuse of Minors in the Archdiocese of Chicago, January 1, 1993–January 16, 2003," www .archdiocese-chgo.org (accessed 12/21/06).
61. "Suffolk County Supreme Court Special Grand Jury, May 6, 2002 Term ID, Grand Jury Report CPL §190.85(1)(C), 175–180," www.bishop accountability.org (accessed 12/20/06), 2, 5.
62. "Suffolk County Supreme Court Special Grand Jury," 106.
63. Ibid., 155–157.
64. "In Re: County Investigating Grand Jury," 29–58.
65. "Office of the Attorney General, "The Sexual Abuse of Children in the Roman Catholic Archdiocese of Boston," www.bishopaccountability.org (accessed 12/20/06), cover letter p. 3.
66. "Office of the Attorney General," Appendix 1-1.
67. Ibid., ii.
68. See bishopaccountability.com; www.snapnetwork.org; www.votf.org; www.members.cox.net/survivorconnections.
69. Berry, *Lead Us Not,* 81.

70. France, *Our Fathers*. See also, Doyle et al., *Sex, Priests*.
71. Nick Madigan, "California Diocese's Documents Show Abuse Cover-up," *New York Times*, May 19, 2005, 18.
72. "A Settlement in Los Angeles," *New York Times*, July 17, 2007, A20; Randal Archibold, "San Diego Settles Lawsuit for $200 Million," *New York Times*, September 8, 2007, A8; William McCall, "Secret Files to be Released as Part of Archdiocese Settlement," www.katu.com (accessed 4/23/07).
73. David Clohessy, interview by the author, March 13, 2006.
74. Howard Hubbard, interview by the author, March 29, 2006.
75. James V. Franco, "The Roman Catholic Diocese of Albany is Spending $35,000 on Radio and Newspaper Advertisements to Urge Victims of Clergy Sex Abuse to Come Forward," *The Record*, May 30, 2003, www.troyrecord.com (accessed 1/3/07).
76. Jean Guccione and Nita Lelyveld, "Archdiocese Says It Didn't Shield Kids from Priests," *Los Angeles Times*, October 12, 2005. See also, Guccione and Banks, "Records Release is Criticized." For similar events in Boston, see Ralph Ranalli, "Plaintiffs Seek Other Problem Priests' Names; Reilly's Records Show 96 More Linked to Abuse," *Boston Globe*, July 31, 2003, B6.
77. Hennigan, interview.
78. Demarest, interview.
79. Doyle et al., *Sex, Priests*, 75. This paragraph relies on ibid., 69–72.
80. Ibid., chap. 1.
81. Boucher, interview.
82. See, e.g., Marci A. Hamilton, *God vs. The Gavel: Religion and the Rule of Law* (Cambridge: Cambridge University Press, 2005), 27–28; Robert Kolker, "On the Rabbi's Knee: Do Orthodox Jews Have a Catholic-Priest Problem?," *New York Magazine*, May 22, 2006, www.nymag.com (accessed 11/7/07).
83. Demarest, interview; Hennigan, interview.
84. Margaret Leland Smith, interview by the author, January 26, 2006.

7. Assessing the Results of Clergy Sexual Abuse Litigation

1. Karen Terry et al., *The Nature and Scope of Sexual Abuse of Minors by Catholic Priests and Deacons in the United States 1950–2002* (Washington, D.C.: United States Conference of Catholic Bishops, 2004), 103–105. These estimates are not in constant dollars.
2. *2006 Annual Report: Findings and Recommendations, Report on the Implementation of the Charter for the Protection of Children and Young People* (Washington, D.C.: United States Conference of Catholic Bishops, 2007), 29.
3. Fox Butterfield, "Church in Boston to Pay $85 Million in Abuse Lawsuits," *New York Times*, September 10, 2003, A1; Joe Mozingo and Joe Spano, "$660-Million Settlement in Priest Abuses," *Los Angeles Times*, July 15, 2007, A1; Tony Perry, "Abuse Claims are Settled for $198 Million," *Los Angeles Times*, September 8, 2007, B1.

4. Terry et al., *The Nature and Scope*, 105; *2006 Annual Report*, 16, 26.
5. Rebecca Trounson and Jay Spano, "Abuse Payout Plan is Taking Shape," *Los Angeles Times*, July 19, 2007, B1; Perry, "Abuse Claims are Settled for $198 Million."
6. Contingent fee arrangements range from 20 to 40 percent depending on the complexity of the case and whether it reaches trial. Jeffrey R. Anderson, email message to author, January 4, 2007.
7. See "Comparative Table of Selected Settlements," www.bishopaccountability.org (accessed 12/28/06)"; Steve Rubino, telephone conversation with the author, November 15, 2007.
8. "Settlements between Dioceses and Victims of Sexual Abuse," www.bishopaccountability.org (accessed 1/3/07); L. Martin Nussbaum, "Changing the Rules: Selective Justice for Catholic Institutions, *America*, May 15, 2006, 13–14; Jessica Garrison, "Why Abuse Settlements Vary Among Victims," *Los Angeles Times*, July 18, 2007, A1.
9. Patrick J. Schiltz, "The Impact of Clergy Sexual Misconduct Litigation on Religious Liberty," 44 *Boston College Law Review* 949, 964 (2003).
10. Ibid., 974.
11. Catholic Charities Network Annual Survey Summaries 1991–2006 (on file with author).
12. Stephanie Ebbert, "Donations to Archdiocese Up; Annual Appeal Nears $12M Goal," *Boston Globe*, January 15, 2006, B1.
13. Interview with anonymous attorney involved in the Boston litigation.
14. Stephanie Ebbert, "Diocese Property Deals Net $90M; Unused Real Estate Being Liquidated," *Boston Globe*, November 6, 2005, A1.
15. Michael Paulson, "Layoffs Completed in Boston Archdiocese," *Boston Globe*, June 20, 2006, B2; "Parish Reconfiguration and Reallocation," www.rcab.org (accessed 11/7/07).
16. Pam Belluck, "Boston Archdiocese Opens Books, Including Abuse Details," *New York Times*, April 20, 2006, A16.
17. Roy Rivenburg, "O.C. Diocese Nears Debt Payoff, Less Than a Year after a $100-million Payout to Alleged Abuse Victims, No Budget Cuts are Foreseen," *Los Angeles Times*, September 20, 2005, B4.
18. The settlement calls for the archdiocese to pay between $250 million and to guarantee payment of an additional $123 million in the event that religious orders not party to the settlement refuse to pay. Trounson, "Abuse Payout Plan is Taking Shape."
19. "FADICA Catholic Donor Survey," www.fadica.org (accessed 12/22/06), 6.
20. We should be careful not to make too much of this data. First of all, not all member agencies submit reports each year, so the data for each year are incomplete. Second, no data are available for 2001 due to serious flaws in the survey instrument that year.
21. Shelley Borysiewicz, email message to author, October 10, 2006, quoting from her own notes for answering press calls in October 2002.
22. "Did you reduce contributions to your diocese's Cardinal's/Archbishop's Appeal because of the scandals?," www.beliefnet.com (accessed 12/21/06).

23. Ebbert, "Donations to Archdiocese Up"; Michael Paulson, "Upswing in Contributions Since Crisis Buoys Diocese," *Boston Globe,* March 2, 2007, B1.

24. "Record Donations in Tucson Diocese," *Chicago Tribune,* July 7, 2006, 10.

25. "Catholic Reactions to the News of Sexual Abuse Cases Involving Catholic Clergy," www.cara.georgetown.edu (accessed 12/22/06), 9.

26. Quoted in David France, *Our Fathers: The Secret Life of the Catholic Church in an Age of Scandal* (New York: Broadway Books-Random House, 2004), 363.

27. David Clohessy, interview by the author, March 13, 2006.

28. Wilton D. Gregory, "A Catholic Response to Sexual Abuse: Confession, Contrition, Resolve," in Paul Thigpen, ed., *Shaken by Scandals: Catholics Speak Out about Priests' Sexual Abuse* (Ann Arbor, Mich.: Servant Publications, 2002), 227.

29. John Manly, interview by the author, September 5, 2006.

30. Office of Media Relations, USCCB, "700 Priests Removed Since January 2002," www.nccbuscc.org (accessed 1/4/07); *2004 Annual Report: Findings and Recommendations, Report on the Implementation of the Charter for the Protection of Children and Young People* (Washington, D.C.: United States Conference of Catholic Bishops, 2005), 19–20; *2005 Annual Report: Findings and Recommendations, Report on the Implementation of the Charter for the Protection of Children and Young People* (Washington, D.C.: United States Conference of Catholic Bishops, 2006), 33, 40; *2006 Annual Report,* 12, 22, 25.

31. *A Report on the Crisis in the Catholic Church in the United States* (Washington, D.C.: United States Conference of Catholic Bishops, 2004), 44–45.

32. See Jason Berry, *Lead Us Not Into Temptation: Catholic Priests and the Sexual Abuse of Children* (1992; reprint, Urbana: University of Illinois Press, 2000), 25; Philip Jenkins, *Pedophiles and Priests: Anatomy of a Contemporary Crisis* (Oxford: Oxford University Press, 1996), 14, 36, 48–49; Frank Bruni and Elinor Burkett, *A Gospel of Shame: Children, Sexual Abuse, and the Catholic Church* (1993; reprint, New York: Perennial-HarperCollins, 2002), 197–198. See also, discussion in chap. 5 of investigations and prosecutions.

33. Clohessy, interview.

34. NCCB/USCCB policies encouraging reporting allegations to public authorities date back to the aftermath of the Gauthe litigation. See chap. 5. The most recent example is the 2002 Dallas Charter which requires that dioceses "report an allegation of sexual abuse of a person who is a minor to the public authorities." "Charter for the Protection of Children and Young People," www.usccb.org (accessed 12/21/06), Dallas Charter Art. 4. Unfortunately, existing data cannot tell us whether these policies had any effect on the rate of bishops reporting allegations to the police or on the rate of criminal prosecutions.

35. Andy Newman, "A Choice for Priests in Sex Abuse Cases: Be Monitored or Resign," *New York Times,* August 31, 2006, B1.

36. Michael J. Bemi, email message to author, October 18, 2006. See also, "VIRTUS Programs and Services" and "Touching Safety Program" at www.virtus.org (accessed 1/10/07).
37. *2005 Annual Report*, 17–19.
38. Clohessy, interview.
39. Mark E. Chopko, email message to author, January 4, 2007.
40. Jerry Filteau, "New, Stricter Priestly Formation Program Issued for U.S. Catholic Seminaries," www.catholic.org (accessed 12/21/06). Later that year, the Vatican promulgated a policy forbidding admission to seminaries to "those who practice homosexuality, present deep-seated homosexual tendencies or support the so-called 'gay culture,'" all of which the Vatican considers risk factors for child sexual abuse. The assertion that homosexuality is a risk factor for child sexual abuse is controversial both within and outside of the Church. For assertions that toleration of homosexuality within the Church is a cause of clergy sexual abuse, see chap. 4.
41. A. W. R. Sipe, telephone conversation with the author, October 5, 2006.
42. Jean O. Pasco and William Lobdell, "Church Settles Suit, Toughens Policies; Court: Man who says O.C. priest abused him gets $5.2 million; dioceses will create program for victims," *Los Angeles Times*, August 21, 2001, 1.
43. J. Michael Hennigan, interview by the author, March 29, 2006. For an extended analysis of parallels between the clergy sexual abuse and the congressional page scandal, see Marci Hamilton, "Congressman Mark Foley's Disgrace and Resignation: What Congress Should Have Learned—And Didn't—From the Catholic Church Clergy Abuse Scandal," www.writ.news .findlaw.com (accessed 12/22/06). For another example of this spillover effect, see Ralph Blumenthal, "Texas, Addressing Sexual Abuse Scandal, May Free Thousands of Its Jailed Youths," *New York Times*, March 24, 2007, A8.
44. Sipe, telephone conversation.
45. Jeffrey R. Anderson, interview by the author, March 10, 2006.
46. Stephen J. Rossetti, *Tragic Grace: The Catholic Church and Child Sexual Abuse* (Collegeville, Minn.: Liturgical Press, 1996), 87.
47. Jennifer M. Balboni, "'It's Not about the Money': Truth, Consequences, and the Real Meaning of Litigation for Clergy Sexual Abuse Survivors," (Ph.D. diss., Northeastern University, 2006), 216–221.
48. Clohessy, interview.
49. Balboni, "'It's Not about the Money,'" 162, 212.
50. Manly, interview. See also, Rebecca Trounson, Tami Abdollah, and John Spano, "Abuse Victims Turned to Mahony in Anger, Pain," *Los Angeles Times*, July 30, 2007, A1.
51. Sarah Kershaw, "Rare Kind of Scandal Accord in Spokane Diocese," *New York Times*, February 2, 2006, A15.
52. Raymond Boucher, interview by the author, September 14, 2006.
53. Leslie Lothstein, interview by the author, November 30, 2006.
54. Donna J. Markham and Samuel F. Mikail, "Perpetrators of Clergy Sexual Abuse of Minors: Insights from Attachment Theory," in Thomas G. Plante,

ed., *Sin Against the Innocents: Sexual Abuse by Priests and the Role of the Catholic Church* (Westport, Conn.: Praeger-Greenwood Publishing Group, 2004), chap. 10.

55. Fred Berlin, interview by the author, January 2, 2007; Lothstein interview.

56. Mark E. Chopko, interview by the author, March 22, 2006.

57. Rossetti, *Tragic Grace,* 32, 40–41.

58. Rossetti, *Tragic Grace,* 47.

59. Peter Steinfels, *A People Adrift: The Crisis of the Roman Catholic Church in America* (New York: Simon & Schuster, 2003), 374; The investigative staff of the *Boston Globe, Betrayal: The Crisis in the Catholic Church* (2002; reprint, Boston: Back Bay-Little, Brown and Company, 2003), 213.

60. *Restoring Trust: A Pastoral Response to Sexual Abuse,* vol. 3 (Washington, D.C.: United States Conference of Catholic Bishops, 1996), 5, 20.

61. Rossetti, *Tragic Grace,* 32–33.

62. "US Priests' Morale High, Conference President Says," www.cwnews.com (accessed 12/22/06) (see subscriber comments at end of article).

63. Quoted in Stephen J. Rossetti, "Post-Crisis Morale Among Priests," *America,* 191 (September 13, 2004), 8.

64. Daniel Wakin, "Priests Organize, Focusing on Rights Within Church," *New York Times,* September 29, 2002, 44; Paul Wilkes, "Boston's Cry is Heard," *New York Times,* December 15, 2002; Chuck Colbert, "Calls for Cardinal Law's Resignation Grow Louder: 'The priests and people of Boston have lost confidence in you as their spiritual leader,' Says Letter from 58 Pastors," *National Catholic Reporter,* December 20, 2002, 9; Mary Gail Frawley-O'Dea, *Perversion of Power: Sexual Abuse in the Catholic Church* (Nashville: Vanderbilt University Press, 2007), 142–144, 208–209.

65. "L.A. Times Poll, A Survey of Roman Catholic Priests in the United States and Puerto Rico," www.bishopaccountability.org (accessed 12/20/06), 18–19.

66. Rossetti, "Post-Crisis Morale," 9.

67. Jerry Filteau, "Priests' Morale Reported High Despite Hurt, Anger at Abuse Crisis," *Catholic News Service,* April 28, 2006.

68. Rossetti, "Post-Crisis Morale," 10.

69. Laurie Goodstein, "As Scandal Keeps Growing, Church and Its Faithful Reel," *New York Times,* March 17, 2002, A1.

70. Rossetti, *Tragic Grace,* 33.

71. Howard Hubbard, interview by the author, March 29, 2006.

72. Laurie Goodstein, "War on Iraq Not Yet Justified, Bishop Says," *New York Times,* November 14, 2002, A31; Don Lattin, "Scandal Affecting Church's Credibility; Sex Abuse Detracts from Other Issues," *San Francisco Chronicle,* June 16, 2002, A1. For another example, see Michael Levenson, "Church Facing Uphill Fight on Casino," *Boston Globe,* August 12, 2007, B1.

73. Hubbard, interview.

74. "Catholic Reactions," 17–19, 25. Trends based on poll data concerning confidence in the leadership of the U.S. bishops and respondents' local bishop are not as clear since data begins only in 2002, after the scandal.

75. Mark E. Chopko, "Shaping the Church: Overcoming the Twin Challenges of Secularization and Scandal," 53 *Catholic University Law Review* 125 (2003).

76. National Catholic Reporter staff, "Boston Cardinal Offers Apology to Sex Abuse Victims," *National Catholic Reporter,* January 18, 2002, 5.

77. "Report to the People of God: Clergy Sexual Abuse, Archdiocese of Los Angeles 1930–2003," and "Addendum to the Report to the People of God," www.la-archdiocese.org (accessed 12/21/06).

78. Gregory, "A Catholic Response," 223.

79. See, e.g., Settlement Agreement at 7, *DiMaria v. Roman Catholic Bishop of Orange,* No. 786901 (Super. Ct., Orange County, Cal., August 1, 2001). Transcript of court proceedings on file with the author; Michael Burnett, interview by the author, October 25, 2006.

80. "Sins of the Fathers: A National Accounting," *Nightline,* ABC, June 11, 2002.

81. Investigative staff, *Betrayal,* 99–100.

82. Katie Zezima, "In Boston, Church Leaders Offer Atonement for Abuse," *New York Times,* May 30, 2006, A14. For another example, see Pam Louwagie, Paul McEnroe, and Warren Wolfe, "Abbey Promises Change, St. John's Apologized and Said an Outside Board and Other Measures will Help Prevent More Sexual Abuse," *Star Tribune,* October 2, 2002, www.bishopaccountability.org (accessed 1/4/07).

83. Burnett, interview.

84. Bruni and Burkett, *Gospel of Shame,* 160. See also, Balboni, " 'It's Not about the Money,' " 225.

85. Balboni, " 'It's Not about the Money,' " 229.

86. Thomas P. Doyle, interview by the author, March 8, 2006.

87. Burnett, interview.

88. David Clohessy, telephone conversation with the author, October 25, 2006 ("almost never"); Mark E. Chopko, email message to author, October 26, 2006 ("rare"). See also, Balboni, " 'It's Not about the Money,' " 228.

89. Patrick Schiltz compares this process to that of truth commissions. See Patrick Schiltz, "Too Much Law, Too Little Justice: How Lawyers Helped to Turn a Clergy Sexual Abuse Problem into a Clergy Sexual Abuse Crisis" (speech, University of Dayton Law School, Dayton, Ohio, January 10, 2005), 4 (on file with author).

90. Chopko, interview. See also, Steinfels, *People Adrift,* 44–45; Schiltz, "Too Much Law."

91. Compare Schiltz, "Too Much Law."

92. Manya A. Brachear, "24 Victims of Priests Settle, 5 Alleged Abusers Identified for 1st Time," *Chicago Tribune,* October 28, 2005, C1; Jean Guccione and William Lobdell, "Details on 11 Priests Missing in '04 Report; Mahony's disclosure on Sex Abuse Claims Left Out Information on Clerics Who Stayed in Ministry," *Los Angeles Times,* April 20, 2006, A1. Previously undisclosed names of priests with substantiated allegations of sexual abuse in the Archdiocese of Chicago were revealed as late as 2006. Manya A. Brachear and

Margaret Ramirez, "Audit Says Archdiocese Botched Abuse Inquiry; Outside Study Says Monitoring of Priests Was Deeply Flawed," *Chicago Tribune*, March 21, 2006, C1.

93. Christine Hanley, "'97 Abuse Claim Named O. C. Bishop," *Los Angeles Times*, September 14, 2007, B1. Notwithstanding a 2004 "Covenant with the Faithful," pledging to deal with clergy sexual abuse in an "open, honest and forthright" manner, the diocese fought unsuccessfully to have the deposition testimony sealed. Christine Hanley, "Diocese Moves to Seal Testimony," *Los Angeles Times*, September 12, 2007, B1; "The Covenant with the Faithful," www.rcbo.org (accessed 11/14/07).

94. Marci Hamilton, "Bringing the Fight for Clergy Child Abuse Victims to an International Arena: Cases Show that California/Mexico Priest Shuffling Also Occurred," www.writ.news.findlaw.com (accessed 12/22/06); Christopher Zehnder, "Priest with a Dangerous Past: Cardinals Mahony and Rivera Said to Have Aided Fugitive Molester Cleric," www.losangelesmission.com (accessed 1/10/07).

95. See, e.g., Brachear and Ramirez, "Audit Says Archdiocese Botched Abuse Inquiry"; Hubbard, interview.

96. Some have accused the bishops of trying to undermine the independence of these audits. See John Chase and Robert Becker, "Priest Abuse Probe, Baby T Case Shape Burke's Image," *Chicago Tribune*, April 6, 2006, C9.

97. See Peter H. Schuck, "Why Regulating Guns Through Litigation Won't Work," in Timothy D. Lytton, ed., *Suing the Gun Industry: A Battle at the Crossroads of Gun Control and Mass Torts* (Ann Arbor: University of Michigan Press, 2005), 241.

98. Michael Paulson, "Gaps Alleged in Church Plan to Prevent Scandal Abuse," *Boston Globe*, February 28, 2006, A1.

99. Compare Steinfels, *People Adrift*, 40–67.

100. Balboni, "'It's Not about the Money,'" 222–227.

101. Schiltz, "Too Much Law"; Michael P. Scharf, "The Case for a Permanent International Truth Commission," 7 *Duke Journal of Comparative and International Law* 375 (1997).

8. The Complementary Policymaking Role of Tort Litigation

1. See Barbara J. Nelson, *Making an Issue of Child Abuse: Political Agenda Setting for Social Problems* (Chicago: University of Chicago Press, 1984); Helen Goode, Hannah McGee, and Ciaran O'Boyle, *Time to Listen: Confronting Child Sexual Abuse by Catholic Clergy in Ireland* (Dublin: Lifffey Press, 2003), 31–35.

2. See Debbie Nathan and Michael Snedeker, *Satan's Silence: Ritual Abuse and the Making of a Modern American Witch Hunt* (1995; reprint, San Jose, Calif.: Authors Choice Press, 2001); Dorothy Rabinowitz, *No Crueler Tyrannies: Accusation, False Witness, and Other Terrors of Our Times* (New York: Free Press, 2003).

3. See Anson Shupe, "Economic Fraud and Christian Leaders in the United

States," in Anson Shupe, ed., *Wolves Within the Fold: Religious Leadership and Abuses of Power* (New Brunswick, N.J.: Rutgers University Press, 1998), 58–59.

4. See Philip Jenkins, *Pedophiles and Priests: Anatomy of a Contemporary Crisis* (Oxford: Oxford University Press, 1996).

5. For an excellent analysis of the cultural and institutional factors that influenced the revelation of clergy sexual abuse within the Church, see Mary Gail Frawley-O'Dea, *Perversion of Power: Sexual Abuse in the Catholic Church* (Nashville: Vanderbilt University Press, 2007), 191–216.

6. This account of the Smyth affair relies on Goode et al., *Time to Listen*, 6–7 and A. W. Richard Sipe, "Clergy Abuse in Ireland," in Shupe, *Wolves Within the Fold*, 133–135.

7. Andy Pollack, "Church Must Face the Unpalatable Truth As List of Offenses Grows," *Irish Times*, September 30, 1995, 6; James MacGuill, email message to author, December 5, 2006.

8. Goode et al., *Time to Listen*, 6–11; Sipe, "Clergy Abuse in Ireland," 133–141.

9. Goode et al., *Time to Listen*, 11–15, 129–131; "Press Release, 19 December 2005, New child protection policy for the Catholic Church in Ireland: *Our Children, Our Church*, is published by the Irish Episcopal Conference, the Conference of Religious of Ireland and the Irish Missionary Union," www.catholiccommunications.ie (accessed 12/26/06).

10. Nuala Haughey, "Compensation for Child Abuse Could Cost State (Pounds) 100m," *Irish Times*, October 5, 2000, 6; Colm O'Gorman, "State Has Put the Interest of the Church Ahead of Victims' Needs," *Irish Times*, February 8, 2003; "Annual Report of The Residential Institutions Redress Board 2005," www.rirb.ie (accessed 12/26/06); "Residential Institutions Redress Board Updates, Newsletter July 2007," www.rirb.ie (accessed 11/13/07); James MacGuill, telephone conversation, December 7, 2006; James MacGuill, email message to author, December 1, 2006.

11. Patsy McGarry, "Public Hearings on Abuse Unlikely," *Irish Times*, August 31, 2006.

12. Andy Pollack, interview by the author, November 28, 2006.

13. See, e.g., Mary Raftery and Eoin O'Sullivan, *Suffer the Little Children: The Inside Story of Ireland's Industrial Schools* (1999; reprint, New York: Continuum, 2001), 3, 402–412; James MacGuill, email message to author, December 1, 2006.

14. Quoted in Sipe, "Clergy Abuse in Ireland," 138–139.

15. "The Ferns Report," www.bishopaccountability.org (accessed 12/26/06), 16; Goode et al., *Time to Listen*, 60.

16. "Ferns Report," 15.

17. Frank McNally, "Committee to Advise Church on How to Deal with Child Abuse," *Irish Times*, October 15, 1994, 3.

18. Deirdre Fitzpatrick, interview by the author, November 22, 2006.

19. See, e.g., Arthur Beesley and Liam Reid, "EUR 370,000 Award May See Abuse Victims Bypass Redress Scheme," *Irish Times*, March 2, 2005, 1.

20. Glenn Frankel, "Ireland Still Coming to Terms with Legacy of Schools'

Abuse: Elderly Victims Grew Up in Church-Run Facilities," *Washington Post*, March 26, 2004, A1.

21. Dearbhail McDonald, "Abuse Probe Grinds to Halt: No Charges to be Brought by Gardai Against Senior Church Figures," *Irish Independent*, September 18, 2006, www.oneinfour.org (accessed 12/26/06).

22. Brian Lavery, "Irish Report on Sexual Abuse by Priests Stokes Outrage," *New York Times*, November 13, 2005, A3.

23. See, e.g., Beesley and Reid, "EUR 370,000 Award."

24. This account of the Mt. Cashel affair and subsequent events relies on Jason Berry, *Lead Us Not Into Temptation: Catholic Priests and the Sexual Abuse of Children* (1992; reprint, Urbana: University of Illinois Press, 2000), 301–322; Raftery and O'Sullivan, *Suffer the Little Children*, 6–8; Paul Ledroit, interview by the author, November 28, 2006; Ronda Bessner, *Institutional Child Abuse in Canada* (Ottawa: Law Commission of Canada, 1988).

25. *From Pain to Hope: Report from the CCCB Ad Hoc Committee on Child Sexual Abuse*, www.cccb.ca (accessed 12/26/06).

26. "Report of the Special Task Force for the Review of *From Pain to Hope*," www.cccb.ca (accessed 12/26/06); "2006 CCCB Plenary Assembly: Bishops of Canada Discuss Question of Sexual Abuse," www.cccb.ca (accessed 12/26/06); "2006 Plenary Assembly President's Report," www.cccb.ca (accessed 12/26/06).

27. Bessner, *Institutional Child Abuse in Canada*.

28. Goldie M. Shea, *Institutional Child Abuse in Canada, Civil Cases* (Ottawa: Law Commission of Canada, 1999), §3.

29. Goldie M. Shea, *Institutional Child Abuse in Canada, Criminal Cases* (Ottawa: Law Commission of Canada, 1999).

30. Ledroit, interview.

31. *From Pain to Hope*, 21.

32. Ibid., 7.

33. Frank R. Baumgartner and Bryan D. Jones, *Agendas and Instability in American Politics* (Chicago: University of Chicago Press, 1993), 1–55.

34. Baumgartner and Jones, *Agendas*, 31.

35. Ibid., 246–248.

36. See, e.g., Richard A. Nagareda, "Litigation in the Mass Tort Context," in Timothy D. Lytton, ed., *Suing the Gun Industry: A Battle at the Crossroads of Gun Control and Mass Tort* (Ann Arbor: University of Michigan Press, 2005), 176; Deborah Hensler, "The New Social Policy Torts: Litigation as a Legislative Strategy—Preliminary Thoughts on a New Research Project," 51 *DePaul Law Review* 498 (2001).

37. Lynn Mather, "Theorizing About Trial Courts: Lawyers, Policymaking, and Tobacco Litigation," 23 *Law & Social Inquiry* 897 (1998); Peter Jacobson and Kenneth Warner, "Litigation and Public Health Policy Making: The Case of Tobacco Control," 24 *Journal of Health Politics, Policy & Law* 769 (1999); Wendy Wagner, "Rough Justice and the Attorney General Litigation," 33 *University of Georgia Law Review* 935 (1999).

38. Lytton, *Suing the Gun Industry*.

39. Stephen D. Sugarman, "Comparing Tobacco & Gun Litigation," in Lytton, *Suing the Gun Industry*, chap. 8; Robert L. Rabin, "The Third Wave of Tobacco Tort Litigation," in Robert L. Rabin and Stephen D. Sugarman, eds., *Regulating Tobacco* (Oxford: Oxford University Press, 2001), chap. 7; Allen Rostron, "Lawyers, Guns, & Money: The Rise and Fall of Tort Litigation Against the Firearms Industry, 46 *Santa Clara Law Review* 481 (2006).

40. Peter H. Schuck, "Why Regulating Guns Through Litigation Won't Work," in Lytton, *Suing the Gun Industry*, chap. 9. See also, W. Kip Viscusi, "Overview," in W. Kip Viscusi, ed., *Regulation through Litigation* (Washington, D.C.: AEI-Brookings Joint Center for Regulatory Studies, 2002), chap. 1; Susan Rose-Ackerman, "Tort Law in the Regulatory State," in Peter H. Schuck, ed., *Tort Law and the Public Interest: Competition, Innovation, and Consumer Welfare* (New York: Norton, 1991), chap. 3; Donald L. Horowitz, *The Courts and Social Policy* (Washington, D.C.: Bookings Institution Press, 1977).

41. See Sugarman, "Comparing Tobacco & Gun Litigation," in Lytton, *Suing the Gun Industry*, chap. 8 and Timothy Lytton, "Introduction: An Overview of Lawsuits against the Gun Industry," in Lytton, *Suing the Gun Industry*, intro.

42. Peter H. Schuck, *Limits of Law* (Boulder, Colo.: Westview Press, 2000), 350 (discussing "lawyerizing" risk).

43. Mather, "Theorizing About Trial Courts"; Jacobson and Warner, "Litigation and Public Health Policy Making."

44. Wendy Wagner, "When All Else Fails: Regulating Risky Products through Litigation," 95 *Georgetown Law Journal* 693 (2007); Robert L. Rabin, "Keynote Paper: Reassessing Regulatory Compliance," 88 *Georgetown Law Journal* 2049 (2000).

45. Gerald Rosenberg, *The Hollow Hope: Can Courts Bring About Social Change?* (Chicago: University of Chicago Press, 1991), 338–342.

46. Peter Huber, *Liability: The Legal Revolution and Its Consequences* (New York: Basic Books, 1988); Walter Olson, *The Rule of Lawyers: How the New Litigation Elite Threatens America's Rule of Law* (New York: St. Martin's Press, 2003).

47. See, e.g., Olson, *Rule of Lawyers*; Catherine Crier, *The Case Against Lawyers* (New York: Broadway Books, 2002); Peter Schuck, "The New Judicial Ideology of Tort Law," in *New Directions in Liability Law*, Walter Olson, ed. (Montpelier: Capital City Press, 1988), 4–17.

48. My use of clergy sexual abuse litigation as a counterexample to litigation skeptics builds on over a decade of scholarship critiquing skepticism about the efficacy of litigation as a reform strategy. See, e.g., Mather, "Theorizing About Trial Courts"; Michael W. McCann, "Reform Litigation on Trial," 17 *Law and Social Inquiry* 715 (1993); Michael W. McCann, "Causal versus Constitutive Explanations (or, On the Difficulty of Being so Positive . . .)," 21 *Law and Social Inquiry* 457 (1996); David A. Schultz, ed.,

Leveraging the Law: Using the Courts to Achieve Social Change (New York: Peter Lang, 1988).

49. Rosenberg, *The Hollow Hope,* 12.
50. Ibid., 338.
51. Ibid.
52. Ibid.
53. For an earlier criticism of Rosenberg for overlooking the influence of litigants and litigation and litigation frames in assessing the policy impact of litigation, see Michael McCann, "Reform Litigation on Trial," 17 *Law & Social Inquiry* 71 (1992), 730–735.
54. See, e.g., Huber, *Liability;* Olson, *The Rule of Lawyers;* Crier, *The Case Against Lawyers;* Philip K. Howard, *The Collapse of the Common Good: How America's Lawsuit Culture Undermines Our Freedom* (New York: Ballantine Books, 2001).
55. For a more systematic, careful, and balanced analysis of the costs and benefits of using tort litigation as a regulatory tool, see Robert A. Kagan, *Adversarial Legalism* (Cambridge, Mass.: Harvard University Press, 2001).
56. See, e.g., Olson, *Rule of Lawyers;* Catherine Crier, *The Case Against Lawyers* (New York: Broadway Books, 2002); Peter Schuck, "The New Judicial Ideology of Tort Law."
57. Peter H. Schuck, *Limits of Law,* 432.
58. Timothy D. Lytton, "Using Litigation to Make Public Health Policy: Theoretical and Empirical Challenges in Assessing Product Liability, Tobacco, and Gun Litigation," 32 *Journal of Law, Medicine & Ethics* 556 (2004).
59. See *Cox Broadcasting Corp. v. Cohn,* 420 U.S. 469, 495–496 (1975).
60. "Pedophile Ex-priest Goes Free," *Associate Press,* February 3, 2000.
61. Catalina J. Sugayan, *Coverage and Liability Issues in Sexual Misconduct Claims* (Princeton, N.J.: American Re-Insurance Co., 2005), ii.

Acknowledgments

This book was made possible by the encouragement of my faculty colleagues at Albany Law School and by the generous support of Dean Tom Guernsey who funded all of my research and granted me two semesters of sabbatical leave. Under Dean Guernsey's leadership, the law school has become an extraordinarily supportive environment in which to pursue scholarship. Associate Deans Dale Moore and Connie Mayer allowed me to teach courses related to my research and scheduled my classes in such a way as to permit me time every day for research and writing. Associate Dean Bob Begg and his library staff spared no effort in responding to research requests. Bob Emery, Mary Wood, and Nancy Lenahan often went to extraordinary lengths to track down obscure materials. It has been a great privilege to work with such talented professionals. Theresa Colbert, Kelly Egan, Ryan Keleher, Kelcie McLaughlin, Theresa Monroe, Luke Nikas, Josh Olsen, Rayleen Schmidt, J. Quentin Simon, Mark Skanes, and Seth Zoracki all provided essential research assistance.

Many individuals read parts of the manuscript and offered helpful advice: Richard Abel, Mitchel Abolafia, Tom Baker, Jen Balboni, Anita Bernstein, Jason Berry, Roger Cobb, Dom Colafati, Stephen Daniels, Tom Doyle, Deirdre Fitzpatrick, Don Gifford, Tony Green, Leslie Griffin, Jim Jacobs, James MacGuill, Greg Mandel, Lynn Mather, Dan Moriarty, Richard Nagareda, Larry Rosenthal, Margo Schlanger, Tony Sebok, Margaret Tullai, Wendy Wagner, and Steve Wasby. Frank Baumgartner read the entire manuscript, and his thoughtful suggestions greatly enhanced my analysis of feedback effects. I received helpful comments also from presentations at NYU, Michigan, and Brooklyn law schools.

Nancy Rapoport and Lynn LoPucki kindly tutored me in bankruptcy law. Maggie Smith patiently helped me understand what statistics can (and can't) teach us about clergy sexual abuse, and she saved me from many elementary mistakes. I apologize to her for any remaining errors. Many people shared their extensive knowledge of clergy sexual abuse with me, generously granted me interviews, provided me with documents and data, and responded to follow-up calls for additional information: Jeff Anderson, Michael Bemi, Fred Berlin, Jason Berry, Shelly Borysiewicz, Ray Boucher, Michael Burnett, David Clohessy, Sylvia Demarest, Tom Doyle, Deirdre Fitzpatrick, Jean Guccione, J. Michael Hennigan, Bishop Howard Hubbard, Paul LeDroit, Leslie Lothstein, James MacGuill, Terry McKiernan, John Manly, Roger Nebergall, Andy Pollack, Peter Persuitti, Steve Rubino, Richard Sipe, Bob Wright, and Barry Yeoman. A number of additional individuals who spoke to me off the record also granted me interviews, provided documents, and answered questions, for all of which I am most grateful.

I owe a special debt of gratitude to Mark Chopko who, while serving as general counsel to the U.S. Conference of Catholic Bishops, granted me a lengthy interview, answered a steady barrage of follow-up questions over the course of a year and a half, provided me with documents and data, read large portions of the manuscript, offered detailed comments, endured many long phone conversations about clergy sexual abuse litigation, and consistently pressed his objections to my thesis with extraordinary grace and clarity. I urge readers to look at his thoughtful critique of an earlier version of chapters 4 and 5. The critique can be found in the Connecticut Law Review, vol. 39, 2007, pp. 897–912. (There is also an excellent critique in the same issue by Steve Rubino, pp. 913–921.)

Austin Sarat and Jim Reische coached me through the process of writing a book proposal and tutored me in how to organize diffuse ideas about the topic of clergy sexual abuse into a coherent whole. Austin's cautions about making causal claims helped me to refine my conclusions. Jim provided steady encouragement throughout the process of writing from conception to final product. Both offered helpful comments on the entire manuscript. I am most fortunate to have benefited from the wise counsel of Michael Aronson, my editor at Harvard, who helped me write a book that would attract a wider audience beyond academic specialists. Tonnya Norwood carefully copyedited and proofed the manuscript.

My understanding of law and regulatory policymaking has been profoundly shaped by the scholarship of Steve Sugarman and Bob Rabin. Both of them took time to mentor me in different aspects of policy analysis. Throughout the project, I found myself returning to them for advice and to their work for insights into the relationship between litigation and regulation. Their extensive comments on the manuscript greatly improved the final product.

Peter Schuck has mentored me since I was a law student in the late 1980s. He has taught me that true understanding of a subject requires appreciating its ambiguities and embracing its complexities. He has consistently impressed upon me the importance of being fair to opposing views and being honest about the limits of one's own analysis. Over the years he has also graced me with his friendship.

My father, Bernard Lytton, and my sister, Jennifer Lytton, have been a constant source of encouragement. My mother, Norma Lytton, died in August 2007. Words cannot express all that I owe her nor the absence that she left behind. My children, Medad, Margalit, and Asher, did absolutely nothing to advance this project. Indeed, it would have been done years earlier had it not been for them. Nevertheless, they are a constant source of joy. My wife, Rachel Anisfeld, sustained me throughout the project. Our ten years together have been extraordinarily happy and productive, as she has helped me improve my writing, develop my scholarship, and learn to enjoy the perpetual chaos of trying to hold down a job while living with three small children.

Index